THE BRIGADE

Dr. H. O. Wagg
367 Hurontario St
Collingwood, ON L9Y 2M5

D1227402

0 11557 03422 6

Other titles in the Stackpole Military History Series

THE BRIGADE

The Fifth Canadian Infantry Brigade
in World War II

Terry Copp

STACKPOLE
BOOKS

Published in paperback in 2007 by
STACKPOLE BOOKS
5067 Ritter Road
Mechanicsburg, PA 17055
www.stackpolebooks.com

Cover design by Tracy Patterson

Photos courtesy of Canadian Forces Joint Imagery Centre (CFJIC), Laurier Centre for Military, Strategic, and Disarmament Studies (LCMSDS), and Library and Archives Canada (LAC).

Printed in the United States of America

10 9 8 7 6 5 4 3 2 1

Library of Congress Cataloging-in-Publication Data

Copp, J. T.
    The brigade : the Fifth Canadian Infantry Brigade in World War II / Terry Copp.
        p. cm. — (Stackpole military history series)
    Rev. ed. of: The brigade : the Fifth Canadian Infantry Brigade, 1939–1945. c1992.
    Includes bibliographical references and index.
    ISBN-13: 978-0-8117-3422-6
    ISBN-10: 0-8117-3422-6
    1. Canada. Canadian Army. Canadian Infantry Brigade, 5th—History. 2. World War, 1939–1945—Regimental histories—Canada. 3. World War, 1939–1945—Campaigns—Western Front. I. Title.

    D768.15.C67 2007
    940.54'1271—dc22

                                        2007022688

Table of Contents

Maps

Air Photographs

Preface

The idea for this book developed during the research for the *Maple Leaf Route* series co-authored with Robert Vogel. We were writing an overview of the Canadian campaign in Northwest Europe in the context of German and Allied strategy, and there was little space for a detailed investigation of combat at the battalion level. I was determined to tackle such a project and initially decided to write a history of the Calgary Highlanders, largely because their War Diary provided the most detailed account of the planning and execution of operations.

The two officers who wrote most of the War Diary, Stuart Moore and Ed Ford, agreed to be interviewed. Both have continued to assist in the work over a five-year period. D. G. MacLaughlan and Dalt Heyland, two of the three men who commanded the unit in action, were also helpful, as were Mark Tennant and Gordon Sellar. Other Calgary veterans sent valuable information and responded to my queries.

Concentration on one battalion provided new insights into what actually went on in combat, but it became clear that the kinds of questions I was asking could be better addressed if the research were extended to the brigade in which the Calgaries served. Fortunately, the commander of the brigade throughout the combat period, Major-General W. J. Megill, agreed to a series of interviews which provided a unique perspective.

Parallel investigations of the Calgary's sister battalions, the Black Watch and Régiment de Maisonneuve, were also begun. A graduate student, Alistair Hain, analyzed the personnel records of those Calgary Highlanders killed in action, and he shared the material with me. Thanks to a research grant from Wilfrid Laurier University, it was possible to employ a brilliant and indefatigable graduate student, Christine Hamelin, to conduct a similar analysis of the Maisonneuve and Black Watch honour roles. Ms. Hamelin also met with Jacques Ostiguy, a wartime company commander in the Maisonneuves, who soon became my highly valued research assistant. Colonel Ostiguy contacted a number of his fellow officers who provided further information on their service with the regiment.

The Black Watch were a more difficult problem. Of the wartime commanders, only Colonel S. W. Thomson, who had taken over the battalion in April 1945, was still alive. None of the company commanders could be contacted. Joe Nixon, who as a young reinforcement lieutenant joined the Black Watch in August 1944, was very helpful, but the key to understanding the history of the battalion was to be found in the Black Watch archives which house a unique body of correspondence between officers serving overseas and regimental headquarters in Montreal.

The book before you could not have been written without the interviews and Black Watch correspondence, but it is not based on this material. In my experience the memories of veterans are frequently unreliable on specifics. What comes across best in interviews are impressions, attitudes, stories of friendship, of admiration, of regret. These recollections provide information and insight which, if carefully used in conjunction with the written record, can prove invaluable.

The written record which forms the core of the evidence used here may be listed in order of importance. The war diaries of the three battalions were all written up shortly after the events. The diarists based the entries on the "message logs" which record all signals sent and received by the unit as well as other signals heard on the wireless set. In the case of the Calgaries, the war diary also contains an extensive summary of events as they were reported to the diarist. Lieut.-Colonel D. G. MacLaughlan insisted on the preparation of such a detailed account, and the practice continued after his departure. The brigade and divisional message logs are also of great importance, and I have checked the account of every operation against these sources.

The Weekly Field Returns provide detailed information on the strength of the battalions and list the officers by name and seniority with their dates of joining and quitting the battalion. I have used the Casualty Returns, prepared at the end of the hostilities, for all statements on casualties.

The Canadian army was exceptionally well served by historical officers attached to each division. In the immediate aftermath of most battles, interviews were conducted with officers and NCOs, and these accounts offer valuable firsthand information. Other primary material listed in the bibliography is also important, but these basic sources are indispensable in studying the conduct of military operations.

What follows is a narrative history of the Fifth Canadian Infantry Brigade. Narrative history, which had long been out of fashion among professional historians, is today enjoying a new respectability as the relationship between its form and its content have become better understood. *The Brigade* is a narrative in the sense that I have taken a wide variety of source material and fashioned a "story" about a group of Canadian soldiers. The "story" also offers an analysis of the meaning of these events, addressing a set of questions which arise both from the story itself and from its relation to a much wider body of writing about the Second World War.

Questions about the recruitment, training, and leadership of Canadian and other Allied infantry units have usually stemmed from a belief that on the battlefield Allied soldiers performed poorly in comparison to their German counterparts. This study of one infantry brigade presents the reader with evidence of both success and failure. The training period is particularly difficult to evaluate, but the evidence does show that, in the year before D-Day, this brigade was trained intensively in most aspects of the kind of warfare that soldiers would meet on the European continent.

The record also demonstrates that the Anglo-Canadian armies developed a clear and coherent battle doctrine before the invasion of Northwest Europe. This artillery-based doctrine, which was similar to the one used by American forces, has been widely criticized by historians for its rigidity. Divisional, brigade, and battalion commanders were handed detailed operational orders, based on an artillery fire plan with precise trimmings and locations, well before the battle commenced. The experience of 5th Brigade certainly reinforces this view of a highly centralized system, but it also suggests that the doctrine evolved out of the unique situation confronting the Allies in 1943–44: the necessity of attacking strong defensive positions with inferior armour and infantry weapons.

German defensive doctrine, with its emphasis on an immediate counterattack against any Allied advance, is also very much a part of this story. Critics of Allied tactics have rarely commented on the weaknesses of German practices, but the history of 5th Brigade suggests that the Allies quickly learned to take advantage of the patterned behaviour of their enemies. Immediate counterattacks are not always a good idea if your opponent is expecting them and is ready with a defensive fireplan.

The reader may be struck by the relative lack of attention paid to the relationship between the tactical air force and the brigade. The British decision to emphasize "direct support" attacks on pre-arranged targets in the battlefield area instead of "close support," coordinated strikes against objectives under attack by ground troops, left little opportunity for British or Canadian brigades to become involved in the uses of air power.

The impact of Allied strategy is another important theme. On a number of occasions, the choices made by Montgomery required the forces on the left flank of the Allied advance to fight with limited resources of both men and material. During the battles on the roads to Falaise, in the battle of the

Scheldt in October 1944, and again in "Blockbuster" in February–March 1945, the Canadians were required to pay a high price for decisions over which they had no control.

Canadian casualties, especially infantry casualties, occurred at a much higher rate than in comparable British formations largely because Canadian troops were committed to action more often and in more adverse circumstances than their British (though not their American) counterparts were. This was not entirely the consequence of broader strategic decisions. Senior Canadian officers appear to have functioned in the shadow of the great reputation won by their predecessors who commanded the Canadian Corps in the First World War. Generals Crerar and Simonds sought to win great battles like those at St. Julien or Vimy Ridge, and to mastermind offensives on the scale of Canada's "Hundred Days" in 1918. Whereas Montgomery and other British commanders husbanded their manpower resources, Canadian generals showed no such reluctance to incur losses. Second Division was particularly unfortunate in this regard as Major-General Charles Foulkes seemed especially willing to persist in costly attacks of limited value. The officer commanding 5th Brigade, Brigadier W. J. Megill, sometimes questioned divisional orders, but he never failed to carry them out. The Calgary Highlanders, who suffered the highest number of casualties of any infantry battalion in 21st Army Group, and the Black Watch, who had the second highest number, paid a very high price for these attempts to emulate the old Canadian Corps.

The division fared very differently under the leadership of Major-General Bruce Matthews. A militia officer who never attended staff college, Matthews learned his trade first as a divisional and then as a corps artillery commander. He listened to brigade and battalion officers before formulating a plan. Matthews understood both the power and the limitations of the barrages which were key to Allied advances. Under his leadership 5th Brigade improved its effectiveness and greatly reduced casualties.

A great deal of attention is paid to other individuals in this story. Colonel C. P. Stacey, the doyen of Canadian military history, once reminded an audience of the old adage, "There are no bad regiments, only bad officers." Fifth Brigade did not suffer from a high proportion of bad officers, but what a difference the really good ones made. Lieutenant colonels such as Stuart Cantlie, Ross Ellis, or Julien Bibeau were priceless assets to the officers and men. Below these exalted figures, it was a war of company and platoon commanders, sergeants, and, above all, the junior NCOs who led troops into battle. Many of these were unlikely heroes, for the infantry rarely attracted the biggest, the best, and the brightest. The very ordinary young Canadians, the "long, the short and the tall," who fought the battles to liberate Northwest Europe turned out to be quite extraordinary. Bless them all!

Introduction

This study of a Canadian infantry brigade was first published in 1992. Since then, a great deal of new research on the campaign in Northwest Europe has been completed, including my own two-volume study of the Canadian army, *Fields of Fire* (2003) and *Cinderella Army* (2006). Despite the wealth of new information, it has not proven necessary to revise a manuscript that focuses on battalion-level actions.

Non-Canadian readers may appreciate a brief summary of the context within which the 5th Canadian Infantry Brigade operated. Canada, a self-governing nation within the British Commonwealth, had a population of eleven million in 1939. Roughly two-thirds spoke English as their first language while 30 percent, the descendants of the original French settlers of North America, spoke French. During the First World War, these two linguistic groups were deeply divided over the introduction of conscription for overseas service so that when Canada declared war on Hitler's Germany on September 10, 1939, all political parties agreed that military service would be voluntary. By war's end, almost one million men and women had volunteered, but a shortage of trained infantry in the fall of 1944 forced the government to send conscripts to Europe.

The overall contribution to the Allied war effort included a large commitment to RAF Bomber Command; roughly 25 percent of aircrews were Canadian, and half the squadrons of 83rd Group, Second Tactical Air Force, were Canadian. The Canadian-based British Commonwealth Air Training Plan was the major Commonwealth training facility for aircrews. The Royal Canadian Navy played a major role in the Battle of the Atlantic, utilizing corvettes, frigates, and destroyers.

The 5th Brigade, one of the twelve Canadian infantry brigades (each equivalent to an American Second World War regiment) that fought in Italy and Northwest Europe, was trained and equipped to serve alongside British formations. The doctrine outlined by Lieut-General Guy Simonds in February 1944 (chapter 3) was closely based on British as well as Canadian experience in North Africa and Italy. American doctrine was broadly similar though much of the terminology was different. The smallest infantry unit was a section rather than a squad, and each section included a Bren light automatic machine gun. The riflemen carried the bolt-action Lee Enfield rifle, but in an experienced hand, it could fire as rapidly as a semi-automatic. Three sections plus headquarters made up a platoon, and three platoons plus a headquarters made up a company. A battalion of four rifle companies (129 officers and men each) also included a large support company (250 all ranks) composed of a mortar platoon with 3-inch mortars, equivalent to the 81mm, an anti-tank platoon with 6-pounder guns (57mm), a carrier platoon with four lightly armoured and tracked Bren gun carriers, and a pioneer platoon for light engineering tasks, especially mine laying and detecting. The 2-inch mortar (60mm) was deployed at the company and platoon level as was the British "bazooka" known as a PIAT (Projector, Infantry, Anti-Tank). Battalions in combat invariably drew upon the divisional machine-gun and mortar unit, which in the case of 5th Brigade was the 1st Battalion Toronto Scottish Regiment (MG), equipped with the venerable Vickers medium machine gun and the 4.2-inch heavy mortar. Elements of the 2nd Anti-Tank Regiment, Royal Canadian Artillery—equipped with the M10 "Tank Destroyer" with a 3-inch high-velocity gun as well as towed and self-propelled 17-pounder anti-tank guns—could be under battalion or brigade control.

The Canadian armoured regiments relied on the standard Sherman IV tank, but every troop of four tanks included a Sherman V, known as a "Firefly," mounting the powerful 17-pounder anti-tank gun. Normally, a squadron of sixteen tanks worked with an infantry battalion. The divisional artillery consisted of three field regiments with 25-pounder guns similar to the 105mm howitzers in the U.S. forces. Regiments of three batteries of eight guns were committed to individual brigades though centralized control of the artillery through the divisional CRA (Commander Royal Artillery) was common. Infantry battalions relied on the artillery forward observation officer (FOO) to provided timely concentrations of fire from regimental, divisional, and corps artillery, especially DF (defensive fire) tasks to deal with German counterattacks. This centralized system permitted a FOO to request a regimental, or "Mike," concentration on a single target or an "Uncle," an entire divisional artillery target. Brigadier Cunningham did not recall any occasion when 5th Brigade requested a "Victor," an entire corps artillery target.

Canada's current armed forces include the 5th Mechanized Infantry Brigade Group, which maintains a connection with the men who fought from Normandy to the Baltic.

CHAPTER 1

Mobilization

News of the German invasion of Poland reached Canada in the early hours of September 1, 1939, in time for the morning papers and the early radio programs. There was little surprise. Canadians had been following events in Europe with growing certainty that war was inevitable. If the British and French governments finally gathered the courage to act, English-speaking Canadians would insist that Prime Minister Mackenzie King declare war. A broad consensus about the need to stop Hitler was evident in all parts of English Canada, though not everyone shared the majority view that the nation had to be actively involved.

The majority view certainly seemed to be evident in Calgary that Friday morning. Recruiting for active service began immediately with calls for volunteers. One infantry battalion, two artillery field regiments, an engineer company, signal and service corps units, and the 8th Field Ambulance were authorized to take enlistments.[1] Southern Alberta had a remarkably rich military inheritance from the First World War. The Lord Strathcona Horse, one of the permanent force regiments, and the 15th Alberta Light Horse perpetuated the cavalry tradition. The Calgary Regiment (Tank), the South Alberta Regiment, and the Calgary Highlanders competed with the more glamorous horsemen for recruits. Initially, the army had selected the Edmonton Regiment (later the Loyal Edmonton Regiment) and the 15th Alberta Light Horse as the two area battalions to be mobilized if war came, but in the summer of 1939, cavalry were reluctantly abandoned. The Calgary Highlanders, an infantry regiment, was selected to form the core of the southern Alberta contingent.[2]

The Highlanders had been created in 1921 to perpetuate the traditions of one of the most famous Canadian infantry battalions of the First World War. The 10th Battalion had been raised in Calgary and Winnipeg in September 1914. Eight months later, it led the Canadian counterattack at St. Julien, the action which helped to stop the German chlorine gas attack of April 1915. The Calgary Highlanders adopted the battle honours of the 10th and became a kilted regiment, one of the many new "Highland" units created for Canada's Non-Permanent Active Militia.

1

First Battalion, Calgary Highlanders, 1935.

The government's initial interest in organizing Canada's militia units for peacetime soon evaporated. Throughout the twenties and thirties, the Calgary Highlanders, like its counterparts across the country, struggled to maintain a semblance of military coherence. The nominal strength of the regiment did not exceed two hundred men until 1939, and many, if not most, of these were boys of high-school age.[3] The cadre of officers and NCOs from the 10th Battalion gradually retired, to be replaced by volunteers whose experience was acquired at the annual ten-day summer camp. When war came, the regiment provided a framework for mobilization but not much more.

The commander of the 13th Military District, Brigadier George R. Pearkes, V.C., was well aware of the weaknesses in the local militia. If the Calgary Highlanders were to succeed, they would have to draw upon the best men available from the whole area. Pearkes recommended that the CO of the 15th Alberta Light Horse take command of the Highlanders and told him to seek officers and NCOs from all local militia regiments. Lieut.-Colonel J. Fred Scott, who was to lead the Highlanders for three years and shape them into a regimental family, was by all accounts a remarkable man. Calgary veterans interviewed in the 1980s recall Fred Scott with warm affection, insisting that he was the "Father of the Regiment," the man who created and nurtured a strong sense of camaraderie which survived long after his return to Canada.[4]

Scott was born in Meaford, Ontario, in 1892 and arrived in the west in 1911 to join his brother on a homestead. Four years later, he moved to Calgary to begin an apprenticeship in law. Scott joined the Canadian Expeditionary Force in 1915 and was soon seconded to the Royal Flying Corps as an observer. Wounded, he returned to Canada and served with a remount unit organized to round up wild horses in the Alberta foothills. After the war Scott studied law at Osgoode Hall in Toronto. He returned to Alberta in 1922.[5]

Scott became a successful lawyer and prominent militia officer, but he was best known as a superb polo player and point-to-point rider. Appointed CO of the 15th Canadian Light Horse in 1935, he was subsequently offered command of the 15th Alberta Light Horse, a new amalgamated regiment. Southern Alberta was a place where horsemanship and skill at games counted for a great deal. Scott knew most of the keen, young militia officers who rode, and when he took command of the Calgaries, he was determined to recruit as many of them as he could.

For his second-in-command, Scott chose Fred Johnston, a Dublin-born veteran of the British army who had won a battlefield commission and a Military Cross while serving with the Black Watch in the First World War. Johnston had emigrated to Calgary in 1920 and was a captain in the Calgary Tank Regiment before transferring to the Highlanders. Johnston, nicknamed "Black Douglas," was a formidable presence in the regiment until he was declared

Lieutenant-Colonel J. Fred Scott. LCMSDS

medically unfit in August 1941. As the only man in the regiment who had served as an infantry officer in the Great War, Johnston played a vital role in the early training of the unit.[6] He was assisted in this task by a fellow Calgary Tank officer and Great War veteran, E. V. Stanley, who resigned his commission to become Regimental Sergeant-Major of the Highlanders.[7]

The company commanders included one veteran of the Western Front, Major R. Denny Bryan. He had served with the Canadian Light Horse and was twice wounded in France. Bryan was one of Scott's horsemen who joined the regiment in September 1939. The other three company commanders were all Calgary Highlander militia officers who had served in the unit since the 1920s. One of these, D. G. MacLaughlan, was to command the battalion throughout the summer of 1944. In 1939 MacLaughlan was an eighteen-year militia veteran and "one of the province's outstanding rifle shots."[8] The other officers included two from the Calgary Tank Regiment, three from the Alberta Light Horse, and three from the South Alberta Regiment. Before their departure for England, other officers from the prewar militia joined the unit and a number enlisted as private soldiers to avoid being left behind.[9]

The Department of National Defence had allowed twenty-one days to bring units up to war strength, and Scott and his officers went about the task systematically. The notion that the first units of the army were recruited from among unemployed drifters is a curious piece of Canadian folklore. First, it suggests that being unemployed in 1939 was a personal failing rather than a result of the Depression, and second, it greatly underestimates the competition that existed for places in the expeditionary force. The Calgaries certainly enlisted a number of men who had no regular jobs,[10] but most recruits were from rural and small-town Alberta, where employment for young men in the late 1930s often meant a season's work in ranching, harvesting, or labor on the family farm.

A sample of twenty-three men who enlisted in September 1939 indicates that seventy percent were from small centres, the balance from Calgary. Five were farmers, eight tradesmen, five labourers, three clerks, and two students. Two men reported they had no formal education, but among the others only three had not completed primary school. The median was grade nine. Seventeen were born in Canada, six in the United Kingdom, and one in Poland. The median age for the group was twenty-four. Only one man was recorded as having been on relief immediately before enlisting.[11] These statistics are suggestive, not conclusive, but they cohere with the picture drawn by the War Diary which suggests careful recruiting and rapid discharge of men who proved unsuitable, medically unfit, or underage.[12]

The circumstances of Canadian army life in 1939 certainly challenged the physical and mental fitness of recruits. National Defence had determined that if war broke out in the fall troops would not be concentrated at any bases until the following spring. It was up to each military district to find local accommodation for the mobilized units. For the Calgaries this initially meant a camp on the Sarcee Indian Reserve, the site of summer training exercises. By the end of September, the cold forced a move into the Mewata armouries in the heart of Calgary. Elementary training at the section and platoon level was conducted at Hillhurst Park, but shortages of weapons, uniforms, and transport limited what could be accomplished.[13] For Lieut.-Colonel Scott the fall of 1939 was a nightmare spent in search of hats, boots, mittens, and coats. The regimental history notes:

> As the winter drew on and the weather became colder, the supply of suitable headgear and footwear for the men became of increasing and vital importance. Ordnance authorities at Military District headquarters were apparently powerless to help. They could and did supply material from which khaki glengarries were improvised at the unit's expense. During this period the Calgary Highlanders spent two hundred and seventy dollars on the manufacture of khaki glengarries and one hundred and twenty-five dollars on the purchase of woollen mittens for each man in the unit. Calgary ladies came to the rescue with hand-knit gloves and sweaters. [14]

These stop-gap measures were of some help, but by December, when the cold really set in, clothing shortages meant the men frequently could not leave their huts.

Weapons training was limited largely to practice at the ranges with the Lee-Enfield .303 rifle. In mid-October a Bren gun arrived in Calgary, and thirty Highlanders were given a chance to fire it before it was shipped on to Vancouver for the same purpose.[15] A week later a Boyes anti-tank rifle, touted as "effective protection against tanks,"[16] was available and eighteen men were introduced to its mysteries.[17]

The battalion War Diary for the fall–winter of 1939 records a long list of other problems, chief of which were influenza of almost epidemic proportions and scarlet fever. In February 1940 the long-promised battle dress finally arrived, and the men could parade without raucous comments about the varieties of uniform.[18]

The best work done in the winter of 1939–40 may well have been on the skating rink and in the gymnasium. Team sports were not just ways of keeping the men busy. Organized on a platoon or company basis, they provided an essential foundation for the kind of teamwork and spirit essential in military organizations.

Lieutenant-Colonel D. G. MacLaughlan (left). LAC

As the time approached for the move to Shilo, Manitoba, the battalion went through another recruiting drive to bring it up to the new war establishment. The War Diary comments that "great care has been exercised in selecting these more recent recruits from the large number of applicants presenting themselves for enlistment."[19] Twelve men from the Calgary Highlander's sample were recruited in this period. Median age was twenty-two and education grade ten. Seven were from southern Alberta and three from Calgary. Five were born in western Canada, five in the United Kingdom, one in Norway, and one in Newfoundland. Most listed farmer as their occupation, with laborer next in frequency. All were exceptionally fit.[20]

Scott and his officers were well pleased with the battalion when the order came to move to Camp Shilo. The unit was far from being a trained, equipped military force,[21] but it was full of fit, enthusiastic young men who were eager to learn. Preparations for the move took place in the fateful month of May 1940, when all the certainties of Allied war strategy were shattered by the rapid defeat of the French army. In that dark period no opportunity was lost to put the Canadian army on display. The trains were loaded at Mewata, then moved to the main Calgary station. Soldiers and civilians lined the tracks from the armouries to East Calgary. From Calgary to the Saskatchewan border, groups large and small gathered at railway stops to cheer and wave. When the first train reached Medicine Hat, it was met by most of the people of the city. Since there were many local boys in the regiment it was decided to stage a march through the town. The pipe band led the men along the streets, then back to the train. The Calgary Highlanders would not return to Alberta for five long years.

Camp Shilo in Manitoba is a large military reserve near the city of Brandon. The Calgaries moved into long lines of tents set down in a flat, endless prairie that stretched beyond any point the eye could see. They were now part of 2nd Canadian Infantry Division assigned to 6th Canadian Infantry Brigade, a western Canadian formation which included the Queen's Own Cameron Highlanders of Canada from Winnipeg and the South Saskatchewan Regiment.

The Calgaries' regimental history describes the period at Shilo as one of the "happiest" in memory of the battalion. The summer weather was pleasant, there were weekend passes to Brandon, and the training seemed to be more realistic than it had been before. Sports continued to play a central role in the life of the battalion. Baseball, softball, and volleyball replaced winter games as companies vied with each other and with teams from other battalions. Regimental baseball and soccer teams carried the colours to nearby towns and to the final Brigade Sports Competition.

Those activities helped to build morale and unit pride, but after eleven months of mobilization, equipment shortages were still severe. On August 6 Lieut.-Colonel Scott noted that "although there were sufficient rifles for a full issue to each man, the unit had on its charge only four Bren guns, two anti-tank rifles and twenty-five Lewis guns,"[22] not to mention the absence of mortars, grenades, mines, radios, Bren gun carriers, and a host of other items of importance to a unit preparing for war.[23]

The days of prairie sunshine were abruptly ended by British Prime Minister Winston Churchill, who had been informed that 2nd Canadian Division, or part of it, was slated for garrison duty in Iceland. Churchill dispatched one of his famous "action this day" minutes. "It would surely be a great mistake," he wrote, "to allow these fine troops to be employed in so distant a theatre. . . . We require two Canadian divisions to work as a Corps as soon as possible . . ."[24] Despite Churchill's decision, most of August was spent dealing with a spate of orders and counter-orders which added up to "wait and see." Then, on August 22, the Calgaries boarded two troop trains which took them directly to Halifax and the French luxury liner *Pasteur*. On September 4 the *Pasteur* docked in Scotland and the regiment immediately entrained for the south of England. They arrived in Cove, Sussex, two days before the British Chiefs of Staff issued the code word "Cromwell," meaning "invasion imminent," which placed all troops on stand by. On September 11 Churchill issued a public warning:

[W]e must regard the next week or so as a very important period in our history. It ranks with days when the Spanish Armada was approaching the Channel and Drake was finishing his game of bowls; or when Nelson stood between us and Napoleon's Grand Army at Boulogne. We have all read about this in history books; but what is happening now is on a far greater scale and of far more consequence to the life and future of the world and its civilization than these brave old days of the past.

He concluded, "Every man and woman will therefore prepare himself to do his duty whatever it may be with specific pride and care . . ."[25]

For the Calgaries, September in Sussex was a period of intense excitement. Air raids were a daily occurrence; gas equipment and steel helmets were issued, and along with these came Bren guns and ammunition on a scale never before seen.[26] The invasion crisis passed before the men really understood what was happening. Everything was new and much was surprising, including the news that they were now part of 5th Canadian Infantry Brigade.

The Calgary Highlanders leave for Camp Shilo. LCMSDS

The decision to transfer the Calgary Highlanders to a Quebec brigade arose from the failure of a long, complicated attempt to establish a French-language brigade. Originally, the Royal 22nd Regiment [R22R], the Fusiliers Mont Royal, and the Maisonneuves were to be combined in 5th Brigade, but it was then decided that a French-Canadian unit was needed in 1st Division. So the Black Watch, an English-speaking unit from Montreal, replaced the R22R in 5th Brigade. Since there was not to be a French-language brigade, there was no point in concentrating the two remaining French-language battalions, so the Fusiliers Mont Royal went to 6th Brigade while the Calgary Highlanders joined the Maisonneuves and the Black Watch in 5th Brigade.[27]

The Calgaries' new sister units came from quite different worlds. English-speaking Quebecers were subject to the same influences that shaped the response of southern Albertans to the war. The series of international crises which accompanied Hitler's aggressive activities in the 1930s evoked a growing fear that a second German war could not be avoided indefinitely. In September 1938, when it appeared that even Neville Chamberlain would be unable to swallow Hitler's demands on Czechoslovakia, Montrealers prepared to enlist. The last-minute Munich agreement was greeted with relief and rejoicing, but within a month the shocking example of Nazi terror known as *Kristallnacht*, "The Night of Broken Glass," put an end to optimism about future relations with Germany.[28]

Militia units in Montreal traced their lineage well back into the nineteenth century. The Black Watch (Royal Highland Regiment) of Canada was the oldest Highland regiment in the Dominions. Founded in 1862 at the time of the American Civil War, it became part of the fabric of Montreal society. The armoury on Bleury Street near the centre of the city had been built in 1905. When war broke out in 1914, the Black Watch recruited thousands of men, and Black Watch officers played a major role in the leadership of the Canadian Corps.[29]

During the interwar years the regiment had continued its central role in the Quebec militia. With Sir H. M. Allan as Honorary Colonel and a good number of the sons of Montreal's most influential families among its officers, the Black Watch could afford to maintain activities that kept it up to "good strength" and in an "excellent state of efficiency."[30] When the crisis over Germany's demands on Poland came in the last days of August 1939, the Dominion government ordered the Black Watch to mobilize a battalion to guard the Soulanges Canal, one of the main links in the St. Lawrence–Great Lakes waterway. More than four hundred men responded to the order, and guard posts "stretching 15 miles on either bank"[31] were mounted by August 27. This battalion, designated 2 RHC, was quickly overshadowed by the order to mobilize 1 RHC to full war establishment for inclusion in the expeditionary force.

There was no difficulty in obtaining men for active service. Many of 2 RHC wanted immediate transfers and others flocked to the armoury in the week before Canada's official declaration of war. Montreal was not the home of any permanent-force regiment, and there were no barracks to move into. The Black Watch obtained the use of an office building across from the armoury and marched up to the McGill University campus each morning to "train" in full view of admiring crowds.[32]

Command of the active battalion was given to Colonel K. G. Blackader, who reverted to the rank of lieutenant colonel and gave up his post as Commander of the Internal Security Force for Military District No. 4 (Montreal). Blackader was a Great War veteran with a Distinguished Service Order (D.S.O.) and a Military Cross (M.C.)[33] His second-in-command, Major I. L. Ibbotson, also dropped a rank to serve with 1 RHC.[34]

The Black Watch was able to draw upon a number of Royal Military College graduates as company commanders. Two of these, F. W. Mitchell and B. R. Ritchie, were to command the regiment in battle during 1944. Mitchell was thirty-one in 1939; he had graduated from RMC in 1930 and obtained a degree in architecture at McGill. Ritchie had gone to Ashbury College in Ottawa, then to RMC, class of 1934, and finally to McGill Law School. In 1939, at age twenty-seven, he was employed in the Law Claims Department of Sun Life Insurance.[35]

Most of the other original officers were from similar backgrounds. The regimental personnel records list a remarkable number of officers with private school educations and university degrees, including several who answered the "present occupation" question with the words "private means."[36] The regiment intended to keep its officer corps in such hands. All prospective subalterns had to be vetted by a regimental committee and approved by the existing officer cadre.[37]

When it came to the selection of NCOs and other ranks for the 1st Battalion, the regiment looked for military experience and physical fitness. As in Calgary there was no shortage of volunteers. Recruiting began officially on September 7 with scores of regimental veterans of the Great War, most of whom had to be rejected as "over age." A limit was placed on the number of French Canadians enrolled, in "fairness to the French units in the city." Within two weeks the policy of enlisting only single men of "good bearing and education" was being reconsidered as married men of "good physique and undoubted ability" were available in large numbers and were being taken on by other units.[38] The youngsters in the ranks quartered at the Caron Building and the Drummond Street YMCA were also said to be boisterous and somewhat undisciplined, adding to the argument for enrolling older men.[39]

The Black Watch on parade on Sherbrooke Street in Montreal. LCMSDS

Neither the wealth and influence of the regiment's officers nor the careful selection of subalterns and other ranks made much difference when it came to training. There was simply no equipment beyond rifles and bayonets available. There were not enough boots to permit arduous route marches, and when the weather turned cold in October, trips to the firing range presented new difficulties, as no gloves or mittens had been issued. Two quotations from the War Diary illustrate the frustrations of the period:

19 October 1939. An example of the difficulty experienced by the Q.M. in obtaining stores and equipment is furnished by the reply to an order for two hundred dummy hand grenades stating that only one hundred and sixty-five had been allowed for the whole district.

22 November 1939. All attempts at camouflage on the defence lines at Longeuil were destroyed today by local enthusiasts who set fire to the grass and bush. Possibly these pyromaniacs consisted of children whose skating rink was drained as a necessary measure to clear the trenches.

The Ladies' Auxiliary soon dealt with the question of mittens and warm sweaters, but the lack of barracks, bus trips to makeshift training grounds, and the absence of modern equipment were taking their toll on morale. Three days after Christmas, the men were marched to Windsor Station to entrain for Toronto, where part of the Canadian National Exhibition complex, vacated by 48th Highlanders of First Division, was available. Other ranks, all 843 of them, were assigned to the Horse Palace with four men to a stall, yet it was warm and dry and everyone was together. The officers quartered in the "cold and draughty Women's Building" were somewhat less enthusiastic.[40]

The move to Toronto provided the battalion with its first taste of barracks life, but there was no improvement in equipment or training. Much of January was spent providing guards for soldiers entraining for Quebec and Halifax, giving rise to the quip, "when Britain calls for men the Black Watch will see them off."[41] Strep throat raged through the battalion like wildfire; at one time more than four hundred men were confined to hospital.

In February either things improved remarkably or the War Diarist was reprimanded for his pessimism. An entry for February 15 set the tone for a series of positive reports about training: "contrary to rumours the men are happy, well fed and well disciplined." A number of Bren guns were borrowed from the Royal Canadian Dragoons, allowing the men temporarily to supplement their stock of twenty-five aging Lewis guns.[42] By late March sufficient battle dress had arrived to equip the battalion, and the kilt was no more. An account of the first occasion on which battle dress was worn in an exercise noted that because of the pouring rain, it was "extremely useful" and no one cared that "battle bloomers" were soaked, whereas kilt and tunic in such conditions would have required much repair.[43]

On May 26 the Black Watch moved to Valcartier, Quebec, the camp created by Sir Sam Hughes as the base for the Canadian Expeditionary Force in 1914. The War Diary's record of this period is refreshingly honest about the difficulties the battalion continued to face. Route marches overland were a big improvement over city streets, but June is a dreadful month in the Quebec wilderness; "black flies, mosquitos, deer flies, hornets—havoc"[44] was the diarist's description. There followed also a constant shuffling off to courses and a steady drain of the well-educated to staff positions. It was inevitable that the Black Watch, with its elite officer corps, would supply a disproportionate number of officers to the expanding army bureaucracy, but the result was tough on the battalion.

The equipment problem was still serious and training suffered. The performance of the battalion at the Valcartier rifle range led the War Diarist to lament that "all companies had to begin firing practice from the beginning as battalion is not good. . . . This does not intend to convey that our average is below that of other units, the contrary exists, but the standard arrived at after nine months training is not desirable and reflects strongly on the lack of equipment which has hampered training since mobilization."[45]

The stay at Valcartier was mercifully short, but the next destination was the Bay of Exploits on the Newfoundland coast. This did nothing to improve morale or fitness for war. The Black Watch had been sent to Newfoundland to build defensive lines and to guard Gander airport. The men were split up into isolated groups to follow a military routine that consisted of trench duty, drill, and kit inspections. Fortunately, as we have seen, Churchill intervened and Lieut.-Colonel Blackader was informed on June 27 that the unit would proceed overseas in August. The War Diary records their departure:

> 11 August 40. *Duchess of Richmond* left Botwood at 12:30 hrs . . . all ranks showed no regrets at leaving Newfoundland and the barren, unpleasant conditions under which they served for seven weeks.

On September 5 they arrived at Aldershot and were immediately caught up in the drama of an air raid. Within a week "equipment of every description" was issued and morale soared. Blackader and his officers met the brigadier and their counterparts in their sister battalions. A brigade exercise involving movement by mechanical transport introduced everyone to the complexities of the new role of "mobile offensive forces"[46] to counter the expected invasion. The Black Watch thus began four long years of training in England.

The third battalion assigned to the 5th Canadian Infantry Brigade was the Régiment de Maisonneuve. The name had been selected in 1920 to designate a new militia unit which would perpetuate the honours and traditions of the 85th Regiment. The 85th had begun in 1880 as a rural unit made up of six scattered companies. Eventually the Regiment's headquarters were established at the Craig Street Armoury in old Montreal, and the 85th increasingly recruited its soldiers from among French Canadian workers in the east end of the city. When war came in 1914, existing militia units were ignored by the government and, like its sister regiments, the 85th had to be content with sending its members to newly created battalions. The regiment recruited 1,286 men, of whom 524 served in France and 122 in Great Britain. Of those who served, 102 were killed and 198 wounded.[47]

The regiment's new name was selected to honour the founder of Montreal rather than the industrial suburb of Maisonneuve.[48] The cadre of officers who served with the regiment in the interwar years were drawn from the French-Canadian aristocracy and bourgeoisie of Outremont and the upper city, not the east end. A strong military tradition persisted in a number of French-Canadian families and the Maisonneuve enlistment rolls contain numerous cases of sons and grandsons following fathers into the regiment. For example, the first commandant of the 85th Battalion was Lieut.-Colonel Julien Brosseau, who died in 1912. One son, Charles-Auguste, commanded the regiment from 1930 to 1934, and a second son, Paul, was to lead the battalion during its first two years in England.[49]

Family traditions could keep the regiment alive, but in the twenties and thirties, the Maisonneuves did not even possess an armoury of their own. This *vacabondage* might have threatened the existence of the regiment were it not for organized sports. The Maisonneuves were keen participants in militia leagues, especially softball. The officers' team had won the district championship eight times since 1921. The team for NCOs and other ranks was always competitive, winning the league championship in 1938–39. When war broke out in 1939, the regiment was one of the first in Canada to fill its ranks.

Historians have no ready explanation for the large-scale enlistment of French-Canadian volunteers in 1939. Most have either pretended it did not happen or suggested that the volunteers were all, like Florentine's father in *The Tin Flute*[50] (*Bonheur d'Occasion*), made desperate by unemployment.

Canada's entry into the war, we have been told, was opposed by French Canadians, and only the promise of no conscription for overseas service prevented a major disruption.[51]

This traditional view of the events of 1939 commits the cardinal error of treating French Canada as a monolith rather than as a normally complex society. The Maisonneuves, like the city's other French and English militia regiments, found that there was no shortage of officer or other rank volunteers. Nationalist opposition to Canadian participation in the war was strongly expressed in the pages of *Le Devoir, L'Action Catholique,* and a few other journals, but the mass-circulation newspapers *La Presse, La Patrie,* and *Le Canada* had kept French-speaking Montrealers abreast of events in Europe and had endorsed Canada's declaration of war. Ernest Lapointe, federal minister of justice and the leading French-Canadian political figure of his generation, insisted that Canadian neutrality was inconceivable and proclaimed the justice of the Allied cause. He and like-minded colleagues campaigned energetically to defeat the anti-participation provincial government of Premier Maurice Duplessis, and in October 1939 the Liberals swept Duplessis from office. This is not to argue that the majority of French Canadians fully supported Canadian participation or were anxious to enlist personally, but rather that the tens of thousands who did enlist in 1939–40 did so without isolating themselves from French-Canadian society.

When the Maisonneuves were ordered to mobilize on September 1, Lieut.-Colonel Robert Bourassa, a Great War veteran, was commanding the regiment. Bourassa was a Crown Attorney, prominent in Montreal legal circles, the third generation of his family to serve in the regiment.[52] Bourassa was not an easy man for the Canadian army to deal with. He was taking a refresher course for field officers when word came that war was imminent. Reaching Montreal on August 25, he quickly became involved in a bitter dispute over the command of guards posted in the city. The men were from the Maisonneuves, but the officers were English-speaking and artillery to boot. Bourassa would not accept this injustice both to his regiment and to French Canadians, and a long battle of words ensued.[53]

This quarrel did not interfere with recruitment. According to the War Diary, more than two thousand men presented themselves to be enlisted in the first week of September, before Canada was officially at war. Many of these were rejected because they were overage, married, or of poor physique, but a steady stream passed the medical exam and joined the ranks during September. Almost all the militia officers volunteered for active service, although most of them were too old to be employed overseas when the time came. One exception was Lieutenant Julien Bibeau, a thirty-one-year-old sales manager for Maple Leaf Milling Company. Bibeau was commissioned through the

The Black Watch training on Mount Royal, Montreal, 1939. LCMSDS

Canadian Officers Training Corps at the University of Montreal and had joined the Maisonneuves in 1937.[54] A natural leader and instinctive soldier, Bibeau became one of the outstanding battalion commanders in the Canadian army. The Maisonneuves had no First World War veterans to draw upon for training and no one from the regular army. A young graduate of the Royal Military College, Lieutenant Jacques Ostiguy, was attached to the regiment in November. Ostiguy, who became a respected company commander in Northwest Europe in 1944, turned his infectious enthusiasm to the task of organizing the Sports Committee of the regiment.

The Maisonneuves trained in even worse circumstances than the Calgaries and the Black Watch. They shared the Craig Street Armoury with an artillery unit and were forced to billet many recruits in their own homes. It was not until January 1940 that a large factory building in St. Henri was obtained as a temporary barracks. In the meantime trips to the Mount Bruno firing range and endless drill and bayonet practice were all that could be managed—except for sports. In the winter of 1939–40, boxing, gymnastics, and, above all, hockey played a crucial role in the life of the regiment.[55]

It was not easy to maintain morale that winter. Lieut.-Colonel Bourassa might have felt better if he had known that in Calgary the same problems persisted, but in Montreal the Maisonneuves appeared to be particularly hard done by. *Le Devoir* kept its readers aware of the continuing struggle over the use of the Craig Street Armoury, reporting in early January that the regiment was being denied space for offices and training by "un regiment de langue anglaise."[56]

The Maisonneuves were also having difficulties with some of their recruits. Initially the Canadian army had enlisted men without the aid of X-rays, urinalysis, or other modern medical techniques. In November all recruits had to be re-examined, and a large number of Maisonneuves failed their second test. Bourassa was unhappy with this procedure, and on January 25, 1940, he put his views in writing:

1. Practically every day we receive orders to send some of our men for medical examinations and so forth.
2. Amongst those to be ordered to be re-examined, there are men who are very good and whom we desire to keep.
3. Since mobilization, we have been operating under the most unhealthy conditions.
4. While we were at Craig Street, the men had no boots and they had to be in the open, whatever the weather was. When they could not be on Champ de Mars, they had to be in the Drill Shed, where there was no heat. Now that we are in Rose de Lima

Barracks we have to suffer the dust from cement floors which according to our Medical Officer and the Hygiene Officer is very unhealthy, endangering the men's health.

5. When the weather is unfavourable, the men are in the cellar of the building, exposed to the cement dust all day long and to the humidity of the cellar, which is not heated. As a matter of fact, the Hygiene Officer condemned the place while he was here.

6. Under the circumstances, I think it is most unfair for men to be called to a Reboard, when they have been living under such circumstances and such unfavourable conditions.

7. I think that before my men are called to Reboard, they should be allowed a period of rest under favourable conditions as it would bring them back to normal and allow them to be on the same stand as the others when they arrive for their Board.[57]

Conditions did not improve significantly, and on May 30 the regiment travelled to Valcartier to join the Black Watch—and the black flies. The Maisonneuves were not sent to Newfoundland; instead they spent the summer of 1940 at Valcartier in training exercises and guard duty for German prisoners of war arriving in Quebec. On August 24 the battalion sailed for England. The voyage was marked by extensive fog and warnings of the presence of enemy submarines. The sound of depth charges could be heard on the troopship, and life-boat drill seemed far from routine. But on September 4 they reached Scotland, and the next day the trains moved off to Aldershot. That evening Lieut.-Colonel Bourassa was rushed to hospital with what turned out to be a brain tumour; he would never see his regiment again. Major Paul Brosseau, the second-in-command, took over the next day.[58]

The convoy that had brought the Maisonneuves to England had also carried other elements of the brigade, including the 5th Field Regiment, Royal Canadian Artillery. The gunners, like the infantry, had yet to see modern weapons, but they too were assigned to an immediate role in the defence of Great Britain. The Canadian government had done little to prepare its young men for the tasks that now faced them. Fortunately, there was time to make up for years of neglect.

CHAPTER 2

Preparation

On September 6, 1940, Major-General V. W. Odlum issued an order-of-the-day declaring that the 2nd Canadian Infantry Division was "concentrated" under his command. He tried to link the formation "with the Second Division of the last war . . . which helped to smash the armed might of the Kaiser. In the Divisional Sign on our transport and in the distinguishing blue patches we will wear on our shoulders," he declared, "the spirit of the old division will spring to life again . . ."[1] Odlum's attempt to establish a sense of common membership in the new division fell on deaf ears. The Anglo-Canadian armies were committed to their regimental traditions, and the creation of divisional or brigade loyalties was difficult to achieve.

Fifth Brigade was perhaps an extreme example of the impact of regimental exclusivity, but the situation was similar throughout the army. The Black Watch, the senior battalion in 5th Brigade, was determined to select and train its own officers and men from recruits presenting themselves to the regiment in Montreal. A "Provisional Officer's Training Scheme" (POTS) was created to ensure that reinforcement officers were "thoroughly inculcated with Black Watch tradition," and a Black Watch company at the holding unit in England received other rank reinforcements already wearing RHC shoulder flashes.[2]

Neither the Calgary Highlanders nor the Maisonneuves possessed such an elaborate regimental structure but they were equally determined to maintain their separateness, employ their own officers, and promote from within their own ranks. This system no doubt strengthened a sense of belonging and encouraged regimental pride, which veterans insist was a vital ingredient in sustaining battlefield morale, but there were costs. The army was desperately in need of battle training. Little had been accomplished in Canada, and the commitment to the defence of southern England, necessary as it was, meant that a great deal of time was spent constructing fortifications and patrolling sections of the coast. The training that was carried out in 1940 and 1941 was largely at platoon and company level and was too often conducted by officers and NCOs who knew little more than the men they were instructing. Individuals could be sent off to take courses, but no system was put in place to ensure that good instructors were available in each unit or that a common doctrine was effectively taught.[3]

Equipment shortages continued to bedevil the efforts of the most determined commanders. In the winter of 1940, 5th Brigade still had no mortars, anti-tank guns or grenades.[4] The 5th Field Regiment, normally associated with the brigade was committed to a separate static coastal defence role.[5] All the battalions were short of officers and NCOs, many of whom were off at training courses or on assignment in staff positions. The Canadian army overseas was building up rapidly, and as the administrative tail of the army grew, there was enormous demand for officers and NCOs in ancillary units.

When Brigadier A. V. Whitehead took command in April 1941, he found that the troops were in good spirits. They were enjoying England and their coastal defence role. Individual training had improved and tough route marches contributed to physical conditioning, but the first attempts to manoeuvre as a brigade, Exercise "Dog," bogged down in a three-mile-long traffic jam.[6] Another anti-invasion exercise, "Benito," went much better because the men moved to contact on foot with frequent pauses,[7] but a brigade withdrawal scheme in late April revealed that traffic control and communications were still major problems.[8]

Whitehead worked to improve the situation before Exercise "Waterloo," scheduled for June 14, began. This was the largest manoeuvre yet to be held in England. First Canadian Corps, with the two infantry divisions and 8th British Armoured Division, was briefed to counterattack a large enemy force of paratroops supported by coastal landings. The umpires decided that the invaders had been thrown back into the sea, but through much of the exercise, no one seemed to know exactly what was happening.[9] Major-General Odlum, who had commanded a battalion and then a brigade on the Western Front in the First World War, conducted a post-mortem noting that "the confusion in 'Waterloo' was typical of the confusion to be expected in war."[10] This insight might have been used to improve the realism of training schemes, but there was no immediate follow-up; the summer of 1941 was spent back in static coastal positions, and training reverted to company and platoon activities.

The brigade returned to the exercise field in late September for "Bumper," which General Alan Brooke, then Commander-in-Chief, Home Forces, organized to "give commanders including army commanders the opportunity of handling large forces."[11] In an overall evaluation of the experience, Brooke noted the improvement in traffic control and motorized movement. He declared that "the exercise once again clearly demonstrated the influence of armoured formations on any battle. So long as they remain in being, and retain their power of manoeuvre, they will dominate the battlefield."[12] Brooke's solution was to create more armoured divisions and improve army-air cooperation. The infantry, which had yet to receive even the obsolete 2-pounder anti-tank gun,[13] was not mentioned. Brooke still had a great deal to learn.

Lieut.-General Bernard Montgomery, who acted as Chief Umpire, was critical of 2nd Division for missing opportunities,[14] but division and brigade officers were too pleased with the improvements in traffic control and communications to let this bother them.[15] At the battalion level it seemed evident that the men were chiefly present to provide staff officers with practice in organizing large-scale movement. Certainly, no one could imagine that those who would be at the sharp end had learned much about attacking a well-organized enemy.

The brigade now returned to Sussex to take up its coastal defence role for a second winter. Life quickly reverted to the familiar routine of the parade square, company training, and route marches, spiced by frequent weekend leaves. Inevitably, the rate of absence without leave and other minor military crimes increased, though considering the age distribution of this male population, crime rates of every kind were extraordinarily low.[16] A great deal of effort went into keeping them that way. The prospect of another winter spent bivouacked in the south of England spurred commanders to redouble efforts to maintain morale. Officers and NCOs had opportunities to go "on course" but, for the other ranks, training was repetitive and boring. Much energy was directed to hockey games, craft shows, broadcasts home, Saturday night dances, and a multitude of other morale-building activities related only distantly to preparation for battle.[17]

Salvation came not from Generals Brooke, Montgomery, McNaughton, or Crerar, but from a man described as the "best platoon commander in the British Army." Major-General J. E. Utterson-Kelso had been promoted to command the 47th (London) Division after serving under Lieutenant General Harold Alexander in the retreat to Dunkirk. Alexander had long been fascinated with small scale tactical problems, and his experience in fighting the Germans in 1940 led him to examine the stormtroop tactics developed by the German army. After Dunkirk, Alexander distributed "1st Corps Tactical Notes" to his units, suggesting that they learn simple rules for conducting themselves on the battlefield much the way athletes practice for team sports.[18]

Utterson-Kelso was not content to leave the introduction of these ideas to battalion commanders, and in the summer of 1941 he authorized the creation of a divisional battle school. A 169-page mimeographed book, *Battle Drill*, was produced to explain the theory.[19] Drills for movement in battle could be taught on a parade square or any open space, but "Battle Drilling Training,"[20] with its emphasis on physical conditioning, fieldcraft, fire, and movement in a variety of settings, required a good training area with an imaginative obstacle course.

Second Division was serving alongside 47th Division during the fall of 1941, and Utterson-Kelso invited Lieut.-Colonel Fred Scott to attend a demonstration. Scott was convinced that this revolutionary system of training could refocus the energy and enthusiasm of his men. Officers and NCOs were put through the 47th Division course while a Calgary battle drill school was created. On October 23 Captain John Campbell led a platoon through the new course at Burnt Wood, Bexhill, before an audience that included Col. J. L. Ralston, the Minister of National Defence, as well as Generals McNaughton, Crerar, and Odlum.[21] In the weeks that followed, battle-drill fever spread "like wildfire" and the whole battalion passed through a two-week course. Visitors from other units came to see what was going on and left clasping a copy of the "Battle Drill Bible," which the Calgaries had borrowed from the 47th Division and "surreptitiously printed in the battalion orderly room."[22]

The use of the word surreptitious does not mean that 47th Division claimed copyright. Resistance came from a number of senior officers in the British and Canadian armies, and in late November the War Office ordered Utterson-Kelso to close his school.[23] The Calgary Highlanders were left to carry on their crusade, offering training courses to other battalions and many 2nd and 3rd Division units sent groups of officers and NCOs to take courses.[24] The Calgary's sister battalions were not among the early converts. Neither the Maisonneuves nor the Black Watch became involved until all 2nd Division units were invited to a demonstration on December 30, 1941.[25]

The corps commander, Harry Crerar, was uncertain about how to react to this grassroots revolt. After a visit to Bexhill he thanked Lieut.-Colonel Scott for providing a "satisfactory number" of officers and NCOs in the corps with the "tactical and psychological advantages" of battle-drill training but noted that, "with the invasion season not many weeks off," schools and courses would have to be closed. Students were to return to their sub-units to "apply their knowledge."[26] Crerar did not, however, order the Calgaries to close their school immediately or to cease training the other battalions. Brigadier J. H. "Ham" Roberts, who assumed command of 2nd Division in early November,[27] had authorized two other demonstration days to which all Canadian units were invited. And the British army announced that Utterson-Kelso was to take charge of the infantry-training directorate while his chief battle drill instructor, Lieut.-Colonel Wigman, took charge of a new GHQ Battle School at Barnard Castle in Yorkshire. The British also authorized the formation of battle schools in each division.[28]

McNaughton and Crerar soon followed the British lead. Lieut.-Colonel Scott had been ordered to return to Canada to run a course for "senior officers" at the Royal Military College,[29] but in May he was placed in charge of The Canadian Battle Drill School in Vernon, British Columbia.[30] In England a Battle Drill Wing was added to the Canadian Training School with Major John Campbell of the Calgaries in command.[31]

Utterson-Kelso and Scott had transformed the training procedures of the British and Canadian armies at the platoon and company level, but what was to be done about preparing for a return to the continent? Practice in small-unit tactics would help men to survive and win in certain phases of a battle but the Anglo-Canadian armies would also need new dimensions of fire support and a well thought-out battle doctrine for divisions and corps if they were to take on the German army. Both of these requirements were utterly lacking in 1942.

In North Africa, where the best-trained and best-equipped divisions were serving, the British and Commonwealth forces operated under a set of assumptions—one would hesitate to use the term "battle doctrine"—that were deeply flawed. Despite a significant inferiority in infantry weapons, tanks, and anti-tank guns, commanders in North Africa employed aggressive tactics that played into the hands of Rommel's Afrika Korps and led to a series of defeats.

Historians who recognize these problems attribute the situation to the low priority given to the army in overall British war planning and to the inadequacies of the generals who failed to develop an appropriate battle doctrine. It is usually suggested that this problem was resolved by 1943 as a consequence of the delivery of new weapons (most noticeably the 6-pounder anti-tank gun and the Sherman tank) and the transformation of battle doctrine under the leadership of Lieut.-General Bernard Montgomery.[32] Perhaps so, but in 1942 the Canadian and British divisions in England frequently lacked even the obsolete weapons available in North Africa. And, as both the training exercises of 1942 and the raid on Dieppe show, Home Forces, including those commanded by Montgomery, operated with an equally flawed set of assumptions about battle.

When Montgomery assumed command of "South Eastern Army" on November 17, 1941, he prepared a "Personal Memorandum" on training which reflected the current wisdom on all-arms brigade groups and the need to imitate the Germans by breaking down the large-scale divisional battle to "continue the fight by means of very hard-hitting smaller pockets." He went on to stress "a very high standard of battle drill and operational discipline."[33] In early 1942 he admonished I Canadian Corps to abandon its defensive

Training for amphibious assault landings. LCMSDS

mentality and its system of linear defence of the coast in favour of widely dispersed defensive localities. "Enemy penetration through these gaps," Montgomery insisted, "is of no great importance so long as the localities can hold out till our counter attacks can be launched . . ."[34] How this was to be accomplished by troops who were armed only with personal weapons was not clear, nor were the enormous communication problems created by inadequate wireless sets mentioned.

For offensive operations, Montgomery emphasized "The Correct Mentality" and offered a series of statements about "stout-hearted soldiers who were mentally alert, skilled in field craft, expert in the use of their weapons and offensive minded."[35] He set out to visit all of the subordinate units in his command in an attempt to instill these principles. Canadian units were examined during the winter and early spring of 1942, and Montgomery's reports have survived in the Crerar Papers at the National Archives.[36]

Montgomery found much to criticize and much to praise, but his views, which were based on the briefest of visits, should be treated with caution. For example, on January 28, 1942, he arrived at 6th Brigade headquarters for a visit that lasted several hours. Brigadier W. W. Southam, who was to command the brigade at Dieppe, made a most favourable impression and was judged to be "first class, will be a divisional commander before this war is over." Lieut.-Colonel A. G. Gostling of the Queen's Own Cameron Highlanders of Winnipeg, and Lieut.-Colonel Sherwood Lett of the South Saskatchewan Regiment were also rated excellent, while the CO of the Fusiliers Mont Royal and most of his officers were said to be "very poor."

Eighth Brigade was next. Kenneth Blackader, who had just left the Black Watch to take command, was also praised as a "future divisional commander, and all three battalion COs were said to be "good chaps." The brigade was described as in "a very backward state." This was not exactly a revelation to Crerar. Third Division had only arrived in England in the last half of 1941. On February 2 Montgomery went to see 1st Infantry Brigade. Brigadier Rod Keller "was away sick" so we will never know if Monty's magic eye would have spotted the weaknesses he would find in Keller during the battle of Normandy.[37] Lieut.-Colonel T. E. Snow of the Royal Canadian Regiment greatly impressed the visitor, who described Snow as "the best CO I have met." Similar praise was directed at Lieut.-Colonel Graham of the Hastings and Prince Edward Regiment, but the commanding officer of the 48th Highlanders really offended the general and was described as "the worst and most ignorant CO I have met in my service in the army." Montgomery's anger was not extended to the officers or men, who were said to be "very intelligent."

The inspections were interrupted by other events, but on February 25, 9th Brigade had its day. Brigadier E. W. Haldenby was rated impressive, as were the three battalion commanders. The next day 4th Brigade was under scrutiny. The officer commanding was hard of hearing and though "an extremely nice person . . . a very poor Brigadier." Montgomery was greatly impressed with the Royal Regiment of Canada. The company officers were "a first class lot" and Lieut.-Colonel Basher, the CO, despite giving "the impression of being over 50," was a "very good" commander. The Essex Scottish also won high marks as "a good battalion; it is well commanded and has good officers." Montgomery was not pleased with the Royal Hamilton Light Infantry. R. R. Labatt, the CO, was "adequate" and "teachable," but the company commanders were "not up to the standards of the other two battalions."

The inspections continued in the same vein. When reporting on 2nd Brigade, Monty's "General Notes" began:

> This is an interesting Brigade
> Seaforths have the best officers
> PPCLI have the best NCOs
> Edmontons have the best men

This did not mean they were ready to see action as they had not yet been taught the "art of war."

Fifth Brigade's turn came on March 3. The brigade and battalion War Diaries indicate that Montgomery's visit was both unexpected and brief. He did not like what he saw. Whitehead was judged to have "a good brain" and to "inspire confidence," but he had "no great training ability." The Black Watch, a "fine battalion" had good officers but "patchy NCOs" and the new CO, Lieut.-Colonel S. D. Cantlie, knew "nothing whatsoever about how to command and train a battalion." The Calgary Highlanders included "a very decent lot of company commanders without being outstanding. They have never been taught how to train their companies." The men were "quite first class," but Lieut.-Colonel Donald MacLaughlan, a Calgary veteran who had replaced Scott the previous month, was described as "completely out of his depth as a battalion commander . . ." The Maisonneuves were seen while doing an exercise in the field so Montgomery had "no opportunity of talking at length with the CO or anyone else. This didn't prevent him deciding that Lieut.-Colonel Roche, while "very alert and very keen" knew "very little about how to train a battalion." The company commanders were introduced but did not impress. "From what I saw of the battalion," Montgomery commented, I would say it is an amateur show."[38]

The "General Notes" on 5th Brigade maintained that the "art of training is not understood in this brigade." Montgomery was particularly critical of the Calgary Highlanders. "It does not seem to be understood," he wrote, "that Battle Drill is really a procedure, applicable to unit and sub-unit action. The company still has to be taught how to carry out the various operations of war." He referred Crerar to a paragraph in his "General Notes" on 2nd Brigade which "applies similarly to the Calgary Highlanders." That paragraph contained the gist of Montgomery's criticism of Canadian and British training and is quoted in full:

> The Coy Training period is now nearly over. But so far no company has done more than about two days really proper coy training i.e. complete company exercises, as a company. A good deal of battle drill training has been done; but this is not Company training; it is practicing a procedure. The Coy has got to be taught the art of war:
>
> > How to fight the contact battle.
> > Offensive action in fluid conditions.
> > The set-piece attack.
> > Re-organization, and holding the ground gained.
> > The counter attack.
> > The night attack.
> > The dusk attack.
> > Forcing the passage of obstacles.
> > etc.
> > etc.
> > These things have not been done.

What are we to make of all of this? Historians familiar with the subsequent history of the battalions, and of the officers singled out for comment, will be at a loss to do much with these snap judgements. Montgomery's positive appraisal of 4th and 6th Brigades and his criticism of 5th Brigade were crucial factors in deciding which units would be designated for the Dieppe Raid. This was one competition 5th Brigade was fortunate to have lost. But was Montgomery right in this or in his other recommendations? Brigadier Southam led 6th Brigade during the Dieppe raid and was the only officer of his headquarters to go ashore. Wounded, he continued to direct the withdrawal and returned to England. His subsequent service was in staff appointments.[39] Lieut.-Colonel Sherwood Lett was promoted to command 4th Brigade after Montgomery's visit. He too was wounded at Dieppe but returned to command 4th Brigade until wounded a second time in the first days of combat in Normandy. Senior Canadian officers had a very high opinion of Lett, and he was offered command of 3rd Division in August 1944. Lett was "not enthusiastic" but agreed to serve. Crerar decided that "Lett had done enough" and looked elsewhere."[40]

Lieut.-Colonel Gostling, an officer of exceptional bravery, was killed while leading the landing at Pourville, and Lieut.-Colonel Labatt was taken prisoner on the main beach at Dieppe. Lieut.-Colonel Basher of the Royals was judged too old for a combat assignment. The second-in-command, D. E. Catto, who was away during Montgomery's inspection, led a party of men up the cliff at Puys but was taken prisoner, as was Lieut.-Colonel Jasperson of the Essex Scottish. The Fusiliers Mont Royal and its officers had been found wanting by Montgomery, but they were still used at Dieppe. Lieut.-Colonel D. Menard, appointed to replace Lieut.-Colonel Grenier, was one of eight FMR officers wounded after the tragic decision to land the reserve battalion at the main beach was made.[41]

Montgomery's optimistic assessment of most of the officers and men of 4th and 6th Brigades was coupled with a very favourable appraisal of the divisional commander, Major-General Ham Roberts, and his senior staff officer Brigadier Churchill Mann. He had "watched 2nd Division carefully" during Exercise "Beaver III" in April of 1942 and come to the conclusion that "Roberts was the best divisional commander in the Corps" and Churchill Mann "first class." The division itself had emerged from the exercise with "high morale." This was high praise indeed especially because the same report described 1st Division as "badly handled" and condemned Major-General George Pearkes, VC as a "gallant soldier" with "no brains." Two of his three brigadiers were dismissed as "too old, and too set and rigid in their ways."[42]

So the "Montgomery Measurement" meant that when it was decided to use Canadian troops for a projected raid on the coast of France, two brigades of 2nd Division were selected for the task.[43] The Dieppe raid was an important test of the quality of leadership and training in the Anglo-Canadian forces in 1942. But it was above all a test of current concepts of how to wage a modern war. The British army and its leaders, including Montgomery, failed this test abysmally.

The assault in Dieppe was to be carried out by infantry battalions imbued with offensive spirit after two months of intensive assault training. Commando-like skills, high morale, and surprise were to overcome an entrenched enemy. No support artillery was available, and even the light anti-aircraft gunners had to leave their 40mm guns at home. The Royal Canadian Artillery personnel who embarked were trained to operate captured German weapons. The air battle, which was one of the objects of the raid, was conducted as a separate operation and the navy limited its support to the landing craft flotillas and six small destroyers.[44]

The Boyes anti-tank rifle, 1941. LCMSDS

How could professional soldiers have allowed such a plan to go forward? The simple truth is that in the spring of 1942 the British army did not have a realistic idea of the kind of fire support that would be required in offensive operations against the German army. As C. P. Stacey pointed out, all of the plans for large- and small-scale raids on the European coast, including the "emergency" invasion of the Cherbourg peninsula (Operation "Sledgehammer"), were based on surprise, speed, and air cover. No allowance for enhanced artillery firepower was made.[45] The artillery-based battle doctrine which emerged in North Africa and which came to dominate British military thinking for the rest of war was quite foreign to the generals in Britain in 1942.[46] Brooke, Paget, and Montgomery were still planning exercises in which armoured and infantry brigades, without continuous artillery support, moved over great distances rehearsing the "encounter battle."[47] It was not until August 1942 that 5th Canadian Infantry Brigade conducted the first scheme in which battalions, supported by squadrons of tanks, advanced with the suppressing fire of three field artillery regiments.[48] No wonder Montgomery could write of the Dieppe plan that it "has a good chance of success, given—a) favourable weather b) average luck c) that the Navy put us ashore roughly in the right place, and at the right time."[49] He had not yet learned how real battles would have to be fought.

The 2nd Canadian Infantry Division lost 214 officers and 3,153 men at Dieppe. Fourth and 6th Brigades had to be completely rebuilt, reequipped, and retrained.[50] Little attention was paid to 5th Brigade, which spent the next six months in further company and battalion training. The first full divisional scheme after Dieppe, Exercise "Elm," was held on February 21. It was not a success, but one week later, 2nd Division was declared ready to take its place in "Spartan," the largest exercise of the war.

"Spartan" was yet another scheme to practice large-scale movement in open warfare. The specific task given to First Canadian Army was to attack across the river Thames and capture the capital of "Eastland" which was defended by "German Sixth Army" made up of II British Corps.[51] This was the first exercise for Lieut.-General Andrew McNaughton and First Canadian Army Headquarters' staff. McNaughton's performance in "Spartan" was not impressive. His insistence on using the newly created (January 1943) headquarters of II Canadian Corps to control the armoured divisions led to serious traffic-control problems, and throughout the exercise he appeared uncertain and indecisive. It had become obvious to all who saw McNaughton in action that he was not cut out for operational command.[52]

"Spartan" also revealed that 2nd Canadian Division was not yet properly trained. By 1943 the lessons of the North African campaign had reached Home Forces in England and there was a new emphasis upon the coordination of infantry and artillery. General Crerar sharply criticized 2nd Division for failing to achieve such coordination and for not digging in after the attack. These problems were serious enough to cost Major-General Roberts his command.[53] The 5th Brigade War Diary reports a very different view of "Spartan." Brigadier Whitehead thought that it had been an "excellent" exercise in which 5th Brigade had "done well." The battalion war diarists were equally enthusiastic, but the narrative of events suggests that the critics were partly right. For example, the Calgary Highlanders excelled at cross-country movement and were successful in an attempt to force a crossing of the Thames but, before "Spartan" was over, umpires declared most of the battalion had been destroyed. Lack of preparation for enemy counterattacks and failure to dig in quickly on captured ground were said to be the principal causes of the "losses."[54] This prophetic view of the problems of combat in Europe suggests that senior officers were beginning to gain a clearer picture of what the war would actually be like.

Through the balance of 1943, the brigade operated from familiar territory in Sussex. The traditional coastal defence role was by no means abandoned even at this late stage of the war,[55] but most of the exercises were concerned with methods of attacking and then holding ground. Brigade exercise "Outburst" held in June called for an advance to high ground to establish a defensive position and then a staged withdrawal. The battalions had to cross a river in assault boats while the engineers constructed a Kapok raft for the Bren carriers.[56] The growing emphasis on infantry-tank cooperation, which was considered a fundamental lesson of the North African campaign, was evident in schemes such as "Hammer," in which each battalion practiced with an armoured squadron for several days.[57]

The more sophisticated and realistic training of the last half of 1943 was paralleled by improvements in the weapons available to the infantry. There was much excitement when each battalion received eight of the new PIATs (Projector, Infantry, Anti-Tank) in April. This British version of the "bazooka" provided the infantry with a portable launcher which in certain circumstances could serve as an effective anti-tank weapon. By late summer battalion anti-tank platoons traded in their 2-pounders for the battle-tested 6-pounder gun. The new "stepped-up" 3-inch mortar gave the battalion a weapon as fully effective as the German 81mm mortar.[58]

New weapons were not the only change. In May 1943 a fundamental revision of the structure of Anglo-Canadian infantry battalions was authorized. The new order of battle provided for 38 officers and 812 other ranks (with six Pipers for Highland Regiments). Battalion headquarters included six officers and fifty-four men, separate from a headquarters company of five officers and ninety-four other ranks to handle signals, administration, and

supply. A new support company was created with an establishment of 7 officers and 184 men. The support company was intended to give the battalion
greater mobility, firepower, and flexibility. The 3-inch mortar platoon could
be concentrated or used in sections. The anti-tank platoon, with its own universal carriers to tow the 6-pounders, gave the battalion its own reliable anti-
tank unit, able to destroy enemy tanks at ranges of five hundred to one
thousand yards. The carrier platoon could fill a variety of roles from supply
and casualty clearing to reconnaissance and pursuit. The pioneer platoon
dealt with the many engineering tasks, especially mine-clearing. This left
four rifle companies of 5 officers and 120 men each. Rifle companies were
divided into a company headquarters and three platoons; the platoon in
turn operated with a headquarters and three sections each, with a corporal,
lance corporal, and eight men. The sections usually fought with a two- or
three-man Bren-gun group and a rifle team. The 2-inch mortars and PIATs
were controlled by company headquarters.[59] The new order of battle greatly
increased the striking power of an infantry battalion.

Much of August was spent in learning the procedures for passing troops
through a concentration area for the invasion. This exercise, code-named
"Harlequin," was also part of an elaborate, but unsuccessful, scheme to draw
the Germans into an air battle in response to an amphibious feint in the
English Channel.[60] The pace picked up considerably in October when all
2nd Division units went through the intense assault training course on the
west coast of Scotland. Most of the men thoroughly enjoyed the challenge of
"cliff-scaling, of crossing deep ravines on a slender bridge made of toggle
ropes, traversing fiendishly devised obstacle courses, and of navigating by
compass in the mountains on a dark night."[61]

After Scotland it was back to Sussex for night training and schemes such
as "Always," a rehearsal of the kind of attack against defended high ground
that the brigade would repeatedly undertake in Normandy.[62] During 1943
the Canadians, like the other Allied troops in the United Kingdom, were
gradually developing the artillery-based battle doctrine which built on the
strengths rather than the weaknesses of the Allied armies. This doctrine was
summed up for the Canadians in a memorandum written by the new commander of II Canadian Corps, Lieut.-General Guy Granville Simonds (see
chapter 3), but brigades had been practicing elements of the doctrine for
some time.

The new year, 1944, brought a number of changes in command. On January 10 Major-General Charles Foulkes, a Permanent Force infantry officer
who had served in staff positions and in command of 3rd Infantry Brigade,
became GOC 2nd Division. The selection of Foulkes as the man to lead the
division into battle was indicative of a serious flaw in the structure of the

Canadian army. Charles Foulkes was a man of intelligence and ability, but he had no experience of combat, no reputation as a trainer of troops,[63] and no personality characteristics which were likely to attract the loyalty of the men who served under him. Foulkes appears to have received the job because he was a senior infantry officer in an army dominated by gunners. Crerar, who had succeeded McNaughton as army commander, was sensitive to complaints that preference went to artillery officers and he was determined to alter this situation.[64]

The arrival of Foulkes heralded other changes. On February 27 all three infantry brigadiers were replaced by younger officers.[65] Whitehead, who was forty-five years old, had left 5th Brigade in January and was replaced by a veteran of the Italian campaign, Brigadier J. C. Jefferson, but in February Jefferson was transferred to 10th Brigade, and the CO of the Algonquin Regiment, Lieut.-Colonel W. J. Megill, was promoted to command 5th Brigade, a position he held for the rest of the war.

W. J. "Bill" Megill was an unusual Permanent Force officer. He had enlisted in the signal corps at the age of sixteen and served in the ranks as a wireless operator and instructor from 1923 to 1928. He left to study engineering at Queen's University, but in 1930 returned to the army, accepting a commission with a leave of absence to complete his degree. Megill held a variety of posts in the signal corps during the 1930s and then attended the Militia Staff College Preparatory Course at Royal Military College. Despite having forgotten much of his math, Megill had no trouble winning a place at an imperial staff college and decided to take the course at Quetta in India rather than Camberley in England.

Megill's year at Quetta, 1938–39, was spent in the shadow of the crisis in Europe, and the course focused on preparation for war on the western front. Megill received "above average marks." One of his instructors, Oliver Leese, who was to succeed Montgomery in command of Eighth Army in Italy, praised his tactical and administrative abilities and noted "a marked aptitude to adapt his mind to the modernized formations on which we have based the course." On reaching Canada, Megill was posted to a series of staff positions in the rapidly expanding army. He was promoted to lieutenant colonel in 1942, serving as GSO I in 3rd Division. The next summer, he was made an acting brigadier and served as Crerar's senior staff officer (BGS) in I Canadian Corps. Megill was not a success in this posting. Crerar praised his professional abilities but reported that "Brig. Megill is the type of man who needs to experience in order to know. He is not what I would call imaginative . . . his lack of field experience definitely handicaps him . . ."[66]

Megill requested the opportunity to escape from staff duties to command an infantry battalion. In October 1943 he reverted to the rank of lieu-

The PIAT (Projector, Infantry, Anti-Tank). LAC

tenant colonel and took charge of the Algonquin Regiment. He was enthusiastic about his first command, and the Algonquins benefited from his considerable professional knowledge.[67] The order to leave the battalion and take
over 5th Brigade was a considerable shock. Megill was a career soldier, and
he certainly sought promotion; he hoped it would come after he had
obtained battle experience with his battalion.[68] But the Canadian army desperately lacked experienced officers, and within that context Megill was an
obvious choice for promotion.

Brigade officers had regretted the loss of Whitehead and were just getting used to Jefferson when Megill arrived to find the brigade busy preparing
for a round of inspections. Montgomery's pep talk, with the men gathered
round his jeep, was followed by a visit from King George VI and the Queen.
It was late March before serious training began again, but Exercises "Allez,"
"Vicci," and "Step" were highly realistic brigade schemes[69] which gave Megill
a good opportunity to learn the strengths and weaknesses of his new command.

It was immediately apparent that the brigade was very well served by
Lieut.-Colonel E. D. Nighswander and his gunners. The 5th Field Regiment
had been created in 1939 when two Quebec and two New Brunswick batteries had been mobilized. In the years that followed the regiment had been
quartered alongside the brigade in Sussex and had supported it in several
schemes.[70] Nighswander, a prewar militia officer from Toronto, took over the
regiment in 1942,[71] and he and his battery commanders worked hard to
train themselves and their men to the highest possible standard. Megill was
to use Nighswander as his deputy commander throughout the campaign in
Northwest Europe, leaving the artillery officer in charge of brigade headquarters while he operated from a tactical headquarters close to the battle.[72]
Nighswander had complete faith in his battery commanders. He concentrated on working with the young forward observation officers, FOOs,
who provided the vital link between the infantry companies and the field
regiment.

The infantry battalions presented a more complex picture. There had
been an incredible turnover in both officers and NCOs in 1943, and a shortage of infantry other ranks had forced repeated postponement of the new
four-company system authorized in May. How the Canadian army, which was
now in its fourth year of preparation for war, managed to create so much
confusion is not clear, but schemes such as the attempt to reclassify all soldiers point to the workings of a bureaucracy focused on its own interests
rather than on preparation for war.[73] The consequences at the battalion level
were to exacerbate the wide swings in morale which were inevitable after
four years of waiting.

The last months of 1943 were a particularly difficult time for 5th Brigade. An inspection in October rated both the Calgary Highlanders and Maisonneuves as "below average" units. Rumours that "2nd Division was about to be re-organized" and 5th Brigade "changed about" had to be officially denied by the army commander.[74] Other reports of problems with discipline and lack of enthusiasm in schemes suggest that the entire division was in danger of growing stale. On December 28 Foulkes issued a new training instruction which required all battalions to go back to basics. January 1944 was to be spent in platoon activity with February devoted to company and March to battalion training. At each level special attention was to be paid to identifying "DF," defensive fire, tasks for the artillery.[75]

Megill was naturally most concerned with getting to know the officers of the three battalions and trying to estimate their strengths and weaknesses. He was especially impressed with Lieut.-Colonel S. S. T. Cantlie, the new CO of the Black Watch.[76] Stuart Cantlie, a Royal Military College graduate and Black Watch veteran, had done well in a number of specialized training courses. He had commanded the battalion for a brief period in 1943 before being recalled to a staff appointment.[77] Cantlie's return was a welcome boost to Black Watch morale. Megill was also impressed with the battalion's company commanders, especially Major Eric Modzfeldt who served as a battle adjutant in schemes and in the first battles in Normandy.

Lieut.-Colonel Lefort Bisiallon had taken command of the Maisonneuves in November 1943. Bisiallon was a good administrator and a competent soldier, but it was the battalion 2/iC Major Julien Bibeau who struck Megill as the key officer. The brigadier's reaction to the Calgary Highlanders was similar. The CO, Lieut.-Colonel Donald MacLaughlan, seemed a question mark, but Major Vern Stott, the 2/iC, was a natural leader with an easy manner that inspired confidence. Megill thought about recommending changes in command but decided to reserve judgement until both he and they had been tested in battle.[78]

The business of preparing for war continued throughout the last months before D-Day. Squadrons from 4th Armoured Division worked with each battalion for short periods, but this was no substitute for attaching an armoured brigade to the division. There were also problems in the battalions' own support units. For example a "Report on 3" Mortar Platoons," issued on February 14, 1944, was sharply critical of the performance of the platoons in most 2nd Division units. The major reason for the "lack of improvement" was said to be turnover in officer and NCO personnel. Fifth Brigade came off better than other units, with the Black Watch graded fair. The Calgary Highlanders platoon was the only one in the division to be rated "well trained in every respect."[79]

The most interesting innovation was the chance for officers to practice close air support techniques with squadrons of 84th Group, Second Tactical Air Force. There had been much talk about army-air cooperation before the invasion of Northwest Europe, but little action. Exercise "Lambourn" was the first attempt to work with what the air force called an Air Support Signal Unit (ASSU) at brigade headquarters. The RAF firmly resisted all attempts to have their aircraft committed to the support of specific divisions or corps, never mind brigades. Coordination could only occur at the army level where the senior officers of the tactical air group could deal with their army counterparts as equals. The ASSU "tentacle" at brigade was supposed to overcome the rigidities of this centralized system by providing a method of obtaining emergency close support in battle through a direct link from brigade.[80] In "Lambourn" the system worked well, for the aircraft were on assignment waiting for the ASSU message. In combat, requests for close air support were frequently sent off to army, but few were approved in time to be of use at the battalion level. The tactical air force was too busy with armed reconnaissance, interdiction of enemy supply, and what the air force called direct support, attacks on military targets in the battle area, to consider close support missions a priority.[81]

On April 22 the brigade moved to the banks of the River Trent to begin practicing an assault crossing of a tidal estuary. First Canadian Army was scheduled to take over the left, or coastal flank, of the Normandy bridgehead and would therefore come up against the River Seine as it widened out between Rouen and the sea. Montgomery's forecast of operations envisaged an Allied breakout from Normandy followed by a German retreat to the Seine, so it was assumed that an assault crossing of the river would be one of the major operations undertaken by First Canadian Army. Divisional, corps, and army engineers acquired valuable practical experience during April and May,[82] but the exercise was poor preparation for what the infantry battalions would face in Normandy.

The brigade returned to Sussex in late May. During June the focus was on battle drill, especially applied to street fighting and house clearing. There were the usual route marches, including a grueling twenty-mile trek on a rainy night three days after D-Day. The move to the marshalling area began on July 1, 1944. Everyone was confident that what could be done had been done. The long wait was at last over. It was time to go to war.

CHAPTER 3

Initiation

The 5th Canadian Infantry Brigade arrived in France during the worst days of the battle of Normandy. The Allies had expected heavy losses on the D-Day beaches and then, once through the Atlantic Wall, lighter casualties in a war of rapid movement. The opposite had happened. The coastal defences had been quickly breached, but then there was only slow movement and horrendous casualties. In one month more than forty thousand U.S. troops were killed, wounded, or missing, while almost thirty-eight thousand British and Canadian troops shared the same fate. The Allied air forces enjoyed total air superiority over the battlefield, but in June alone the cost was sixty-two hundred aircrew. Soldiers on both sides were beginning to say that it was 1914–18 all over again—a static battle of attrition—gains measured in yards and thousands of dead.[1]

Generals in their memoirs and historians in their books on Normandy have usually focused attention on controversies over Allied strategy, especially the Montgomery-Eisenhower debate, but the real problem was at the operational, not the strategic level.[2] It is an axiom of military science that the attacker needs a three-to-one margin over the defender to have a reasonable chance of success. If the defence is well dug in, even better margins are required. The Allies had landed in Normandy prepared for a war of mobility in which the tactical air forces and the armoured regiments would dominate the battlefield. Instead they were confronted with a German army able to maintain a continuous perimeter and defence in-depth.

The Allied battle doctrine available for such situations was outlined for the Canadians by corps commander Lieutenant-General Guy Granville Simonds in a memorandum dated February 14, 1944. Simonds was forty-one years old in 1944. Born in Britain, he was raised in Canada and graduated from the Royal Military College in 1925. He was commissioned into the Royal Canadian Horse Artillery, and it was as a gunner that he first went to the United Kingdom to pursue staff training. Simonds was bright and ambitious and very much at home with his British army counterparts. He spent a good deal of the prewar decade in Britain, returning to RMC as the senior instructor in tactics in 1938 with a pronounced English accent.[3] Most of the senior officers in the Canadian army regarded Simonds as the outstanding divisional command prospect, and he was the logical choice to take command of 1st Division when Major-General Salmon died in a plane crash.[4]

In Sicily and Italy Simonds was a solid, reliable divisional commander whom Montgomery came to regard as one of his proteges. Promoted to command II Canadian Corps for Operation "Overlord," Simonds emerged from the battles of 1944–45 with a reputation as a brilliant, innovative commander. To his staff officers, Simonds was the consummate professional soldier. His chief-of-staff, Brigadier Norman Roger, wrote of him,

> Never have I worked for anyone with such a precise, clear and far-seeing mind—he was always working to a plan with a clear-cut objective which he took care to let all of us know in simple and direct terms. . . . He reduced problems in a flash to basic facts and variables, picked out those that mattered, ignored those that were side-issues and made up his mind and got on with it.[5]

Not every soldier who served with, or especially under, Simonds shared Brigadier Roger's enthusiasm, but most would agree with this appraisal. The problem was that the general's cold, detached, analytical mind was accompanied by the appearance of overwhelming self-confidence and a degree of arrogance which did not encourage expressions of dissent. Simonds did not attempt to lead; he sought only to command. His directive on operational policy (or battle doctrine) reveals both of these aspects of his personality. The document is brief, coherent, and all-encompassing. There is no room for discussion; it is an outline of a procedure which is to be followed. Simonds began:

> When the Germans decide to stand and fight a defensive battle, attack without adequate reconnaissance and preparation will not succeed. The attack must be carefully organized and strongly supported by all available artillery. The frontage of attack must be limited to that on which really heavy support may be given. The essence of the German system of defence is the counter attack. His forward defences are not thickly held in terms of men, but are strong in automatic weapons and well supported by mortars, sited up to three or four thousand yards in rear of forward defended localities. These mortars are capable of bringing very heavy fire to bear in front of, or within, the German defensive position. A well planned infantry attack, with ample fire support, will penetrate such a position with comparative ease, but the first penetration will stir up a hornet's

Lieutenant-General Guy Simonds with his mentor, General Bernard Montgomery. LAC

nest. As long as fresh reserves are available the Germans will counter-attack heavily and continuously, supported by self-propelled guns brought up to close range and by any mortars which have not been over-run in the initial assault. The success of the offensive battle hinges on the defeat of the German counterattacks, with sufficient of our own reserves in hand to launch a new phase as soon as the enemy strength has spent itself. The defeat of these counterattacks must form part of the original plan of attack which must include arrangements for artillery support and the forward moves of infantry supporting weapons—including tanks—on the objective. Further, in selecting the objectives, the suitability from the point of view of fighting this "battle of counter-attacks" must receive important consideration. The following points must be considered in the initial planning:

a. The depth of initial objectives. To over-run the German mortar positions requires penetration of his forward defences to a depth of some four thousand yards. Unless these mortars are dislodged, or dealt with by a pre-arranged counter-battery programme (this is often very difficult, owing to the siting of the mortars behind very steep cover) the effect of mortar fire makes mopping up and reorganization on the objective a most difficult task for the infantry. The Germans do not hesitate to engage a position on which their own troops are still holding out.

b. The phase of the attack at which the bulk of the artillery is to be moved forward must receive early consideration. There is bound to be a pause during this phase when the leading troops on the objectives are going to be without the full support of the artillery. This is the period at which the employment of all available air support is most useful to tide over the gap. When the Germans really stand to fight, it is seldom that the full depth of their defences can be penetrated without a forward displacement of the bulk of the artillery.

c. The way in which the Germans support their infantry in the counter-attack must be clearly understood. They move tanks or self-propelled guns to within close range of the objective they are trying to retake. These do not support by neutralizing fire, in the ordinary sense, but with aimed fire shell directed through telescopic sights at a range at which individual infantry-dispositions can be picked out. The moral and material effect on our own troops of this type of fire is considerable.

Any one of the following have proved effective in making the German tanks or self-propelled guns stand off at a range which greatly reduces their effect:

a. Anti tank guns well up with the leading infantry.

b. Tanks following close behind the leading infantry.

c. Medium artillery concentrations directed onto the enemy tanks or self-propelled guns by a forward observation officer with the leading troops.

The initial plan of attack should legislate for at least two of these forms of support being available to leading infantry on arrival on their objective.

For a defensive battle the Germans generally dispose their main position behind an anti-tank obstacle or thick minefields. The initial attack, therefore, must be made by infantry to secure gaps through minefields or a bridgehead across an obstacle.

The infantry division is the "sledge-hammer" in the attack against an organized defensive position, for it is strong in infantry and has the staying power to carry an attack through in depth . . .[6]

In theory there was nothing wrong with Simonds' version of Allied battle experience but in practice the thinly armoured, undergunned Sherman tanks were seldom able to accompany the infantry onto the objective, and almost never able to stay to help meet the counterattacks. The self-propelled anti-tank guns stayed well to the rear, and it usually took some time to get the towed 6-pounder and 17-pounder anti-tank guns into position. All too often the infantry had only the artillery to reply upon, not only to "shoot" them onto the objective but also to break up the counterattacks with well-directed concentrations. More than one infantry company commander has described his role in Northwest Europe as "escorting the artillery Forward Observation Officer across France."

The 2nd Tactical Air Force, based in England for most of June because of the narrowness of the bridgehead, had discovered that while the Luftwaffe was not a significant threat, anti-aircraft guns were. With most missions devoted to armed reconnaissance or bombing of German lines of communication, the air force was helping to weaken German resistance in the long run, but it was providing little in the way of effective direct support in the land battle.[7]

When 5th Brigade arrived in Normandy on July 6, General Montgomery was preparing an attack on Caen and the fortified villages around it that was a typical example of the 1944 set-piece battle. Third Canadian Division took

A Canadian patrol enters Caen, July 1944. LAC

close to one thousand casualties in a period of sixteen hours and while the German defensive line north of Caen was broken, the enemy was able to retreat across the Orne to hold the industrial suburbs of the city. The infantry units engaged in the battle also experienced a rapid rise in the number of battle exhaustion cases with several hundred men evacuated due to the stress of combat. Regimental Medical Officers were learning that neither elaborate selection methods nor extensive training could prevent a considerable number of combat soldiers from breaking down.

The men of 2nd Division knew nothing of the reality of "Charnwood." They arrived in France in broad daylight after an uneventful crossing of the Channel. The Black Watch War Diarist noted that the weather was warm and clear. "We passed," he wrote, "alongside the battleship HMS *Rodney* which was shelling the enemy. This part of the channel," he continued, "was busier than St. Catherine Street on Saturday night." After disembarking and shedding their "Mae Wests," the battalion marched from Courseulles to Vers-sur-Mer, where Major Motzfeld and the advance party had laid out the battalion position.[8] The Calgaries followed the same route, stopping for tea and bully beef. They quickly got rid of their blankets and gas respirators and, since the CO was still safely aboard ship, removed their tunics and fastened them to their backpacks.[9] The Maisonneuves had an equally light-hearted introduction to France, playing softball and visiting a cinema.[10]

On the afternoon of July 11, II Canadian Corps became operational. A very tired 3rd Division, in continuous contact with the enemy since D-Day, was withdrawn for a short rest, and 2nd Division's 4th Brigade was sent forward to take over part of the line. Brigadier Sherwood Lett and his men found that a week of being shelled and mortared produced some casualties and a number of battle exhaustion cases but not much else. Fifth and 6th Brigades remained well behind the lines in relative safety[11] thanks to the achievement of air superiority.

Simonds and Foulkes must have regarded 2nd Division as fully trained, for there was little attempt to provide the battalions with realistic information on the nature of the fighting. Simonds addressed the brigade on its second day in France, but "rain was coming down in torrents and gas capes were ordered worn, leaving bivouacs entirely open to the mercy of the elements." The troops stood waiting in the rain for three-quarters of an hour before Simonds arrived. Simonds was incapable of displaying warmth or emotion. His "pep talk" fell flat, and one condescending comment "was taken in the wrong light by the men and hard feelings resulted."[12]

There was opportunity for some to learn. A Royal Artillery officer gave a lecture on Allied and German tanks to the anti-tank platoons and a squadron commander from the Sherbrooke Fusiliers arrived to discuss infantry-tank cooperation with each CO and the company commanders. Brigadier Megill was attached to 4th Brigade Headquarters as an observer, but since the brigade was concentrating on staying well dug in, there was little to learn.[13] The Maisonneuves had the best time. They mixed easily with the French civilian population, and on July 14, "Bastille Day," they provided a guard of honour for the first local celebration of the national holiday since 1939. The officers then got to drink champagne, "hidden since the occupation," and in return "presented personal subscriptions towards the reconstruction of the parish church" in Rots.[14] On July 18, 5th Brigade moved to an assembly area on the western outskirts of Caen. It was time to go to war.

"Goodwood Meeting," the Anglo-Canadian operation on July 18–21, was the largest single battle fought by Montgomery's 21st Army Group in the Normandy campaign. Lieutenant-General Miles Dempsey, commanding Second British Army, planned to use three armoured divisions, assisted by RAF heavy bombers, to break through the German defensive perimeter south of Caen. Lieutenant-General Richard O'Connor, the architect of the British army's 1941 advance across North Africa, was to command an all-armoured VIII Corps in a "blitzkrieg" attack towards Falaise and the roads to Paris. The armour was to pass through a narrow bridgehead and then fan out with 11th Armoured Division aimed for Verrières Ridge. Infantry divisions would follow along, mopping up on both flanks. On the right, 3rd Canadian Division would capture the Caen suburbs on the south side of the river Orne.[15]

The decision to lead with the armoured divisions was made against all the available evidence about the effectiveness of German anti-tank guns because the British were facing a severe shortage of infantry replacements while "tank reinforcements were pouring into Normandy." As Dempsey put it, ". . . we could well afford, and it was desirable, to plan an operation in which we could utilize that surplus of tanks and economize on infantry."[16]

The 2nd Canadian Infantry Division was part of the Goodwood plan, but its exact role was uncertain. Simonds was told to use the division to exploit southwards after 3rd Division had completed its tasks. As the armoured advance began on the morning of July 18 and 3rd Division moved steadily towards its objectives, Simonds ordered 4th Brigade to capture Louvigny on the west bank of the Orne as a preliminary to crossing the river at that point. The Royal Regiment of Canada was assigned the lead and thus entered its first battle since the fateful attack on Dieppe in 1942. The Royals took heavy casualties and made slight progress against a well-supported enemy. Brigadier Sherwood Lett was wounded during the encounter, and there was a disturbingly large number of battle exhaustion casualties.[17] Simonds decided to abort this operation and use the route through Caen where 5th Brigade was waiting to cross the river.

Lieutenant-Colonel E. D. Nighswander (standing, left) and Brigadier W. J. Megill (standing, right) with other 2nd Division officers. LCMSDS

A Royal Canadian Engineer looks across the Orne River in Caen. LAC

The situation in the Caen suburbs on the afternoon of July 18 was confused. Third Division had become bogged down in the Vaucelles industrial area. Simonds ordered Major-General Rod Keller to put his reserve brigade across the river from the centre of Caen directly into Vaucelles. The 7th Brigade accomplished this task readily enough, but intense mortar and artillery fire prevented the engineers from bridging the Orne.[18]

Caen was packed with troops all under fire. Brigadier Megill had selected the Black Watch to lead the brigade. B Company, with thirty-six men from the support company and one section from the carrier platoon, was to make the crossing using eighteen-man assault boats. The battalion waited on the edge of the Caen race course throughout a long, hot afternoon. Between noon and eight o'clock, Lieut.-Colonel Cantlie called four different Order Groups, three of which were mortared, as the battle on the south bank of the river raged on.[19] Fifth Brigade was supposed to lead the exploitation south and not become involved in 3rd Division's struggle.

During the afternoon Lieutenant Jack Neil and Sergeant Nelson became the battalion's first battle casualties as they attempted a reconnaissance of the south bank of the river. H-Hour was finally set for 10:15 P.M., which, given that the army was operating on double daylight savings time, meant it was still daylight. No artillery support would be provided because the exact location of 3rd Division units was not known.

Fire support for the assault boats was to be provided by D Company, which would take a position "along a ditch and line of trees bordering the river." The men had to cross eight hundred yards of ground open to German observation to reach the river. D Company, supposed to be in position before the assault troops moved, was slow to move forward. Halfway to the river the assault platoons realized that D Company was not yet in position, but as no fire was directed at it, B Company kept moving. When the lead boat was just fifty yards from the river, enemy machine guns and mortars opened up on the right and centre platoons. There were a number of casualties and the survivors went to ground along the riverbank, joining D Company which was now engaging the enemy. The platoon on the left flank reached the river and crossed without meeting any opposition. It was able to install a kapok footbridge, and when night fell, the balance of the battalion crossed the river. The night was spent "patrolling, neutralizing enemy snipers and digging in."[20]

The Black Watch suffered thirty-six casualties in this difficult assault crossing. Major Alan Stevenson, B Company commander, was wounded, and Lieutenant Austin was killed leading his assault platoon. The Black Watch War Diary records a story that one of the boats from the two heavily-hit platoons did cross the river, "though Cpl. Watson and others were killed in so doing." A wireless operator, Private Robert Ernest Stephen, was mentioned in dispatches for swimming to shore, restoring his wireless set, and maintaining communications throughout the battle.[21]

The decision to try to cross the Orne in daylight was based on the hope that the now quiet enemy had been forced to withdraw by 3rd Division and the fear that a night crossing would lead to chaos and delay. Fifth Brigade was supposed to be in position to attack south from Caen early the next day. The Black Watch attack, carried out with considerable courage, accomplished this purpose, though in the event 3rd Division could not complete the clearing of Vaucelles until the next morning. Shortly after noon the Régiment de Maisonneuve crossed into Vaucelles and moved quickly through the Black Watch to its start line at the southern edge of the built-up area.

The Maisonneuves had been briefed for a rapid advance to La Haute, a village five kilometres down Route 162. They were to follow an artillery barrage to the objective with two companies up. A platoon of carrier-mounted medium machine guns of the Toronto Scottish Regiment was to protect the left flank. A squadron of Sherbrooke Fusiliers (27th Armoured Regiment) was to support the advance, and a troop of the Divisional Anti-Tank Regiment, 20th Anti-Tank Battery, was available to assist consolidation.[22] Initially it all went wrong. A and D Companies advanced two or three hundred yards ahead of their start-time, and "when the artillery barrage began the two forward companies became trapped in their own artillery." Major Lucien Brosseau, commanding D Company, was killed, as was Captain A. L. Oriens, the mortar platoon officer. Eleven other men were killed and thirty-seven wounded; another twenty-seven had to be evacuated with battle exhaustion.[23]

Lieut.-Colonel Bisiallon moved swiftly to get things under control. B and C Companies were ordered forward. They found that there was little opposition, and both companies were on their objective by 4:30 P.M. That evening A and D Companies, now reorganized, joined their comrades to establish a firm base for the brigade.

Historians have frequently drawn attention to this incident but at the time it seemed to be just another example of the chaos that enveloped all battlefields. War, when described by generals and historians, takes on an organized, coherent pattern which is not at all evident to the men who are asked to carry out the grand design. Lines marked on a map board at an Orders Group may be difficult to relate to ground which has been bombed and is still under shelling. What was significant on July 19 was the speed with which the Maisonneuves recovered and pressed on to their objectives. The battalion's command structure remained intact, and morale, while shaken, was not shattered.

While the "Maisies" were consolidating at La Haute, the Calgary Highlanders were preparing for the next round. They entered Fleury-sur-Orne

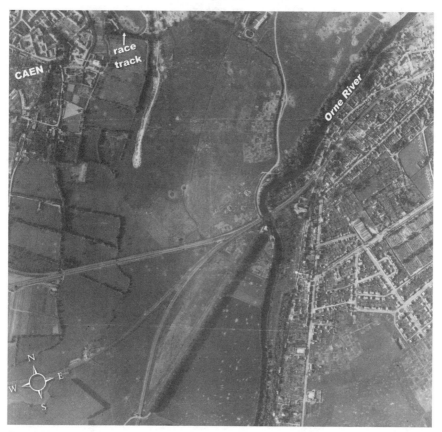

Aerial photo of the edge of Caen and the Orne River. The race track where the Black Watch waited is visible at the top of the photo. They crossed the river to the east of the bridge. Photo taken on July 16, 1944. LCMSDS

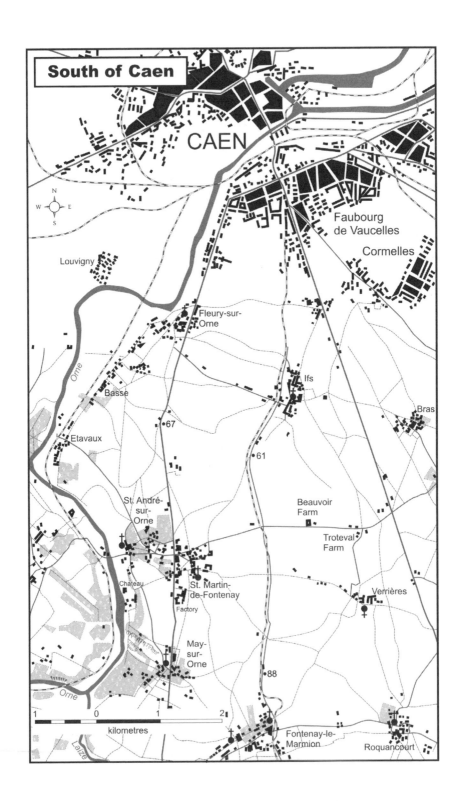

South of Caen

CAEN

Faubourg
de Vaucelles

Cormelles

Louvigny

Fleury-sur-
Orne

Ifs

Basse

Bras

•67

Etavaux

•61

St. André-
sur-
Orne

Beauvoir
Farm

Troteval
Farm

Chateau

St. Martin-
de-Fontenay

Verrières

Factory

May-
sur-
Orne

•88

Orne

Orne

Laize

1   0   1   2

kilometres

Fontenay-le-
Marmion

Roquancourt

without meeting any opposition and prepared to move over the northern spur of Verrières Ridge towards St. Andre-sur-Orne. This was not an inviting prospect. If you stand at the southern edge of Fleury today, you can clearly see the high ground on the west side of the Orne which the Germans still occupied on July 19. Route 162 is overlooked by this high ground all the way to May-sur-Orne. Looking due south, the low ridge marked "Pt 67" on the map seems to be of little consequence, unless you are a foot soldier who has to walk up and capture it in broad daylight. At 5:15 P.M. the pipes began to play, and the Calgaries moved carefully forward, two companies up. They were slowed by terrific mortar fire which was so accurate that the headquarters group turned off its radio set, fearing the enemy was homing in on it.[24]

The Sherbrooke Fusiliers in support of the brigade had sent a troop of tanks forward on each side of the road. They were able to deal with several machine-gun posts and a number of snipers. One enemy strongpoint was not so readily overcome, and a quick plan was made to "shell and co-ax" the position from the flank in support of a platoon frontal attack. B Company decided to make use of the artillery first, putting down ten minutes of fire on the strongpoint. As the tanks manoeuvred into position, two were hit by long-range anti-tank guns though the crews escaped. The others provided enough suppressing fire to get the Calgaries onto the target without casualties.[25] By 6:30 P.M. the Calgaries were digging in under a hail of mortar bombs. C Company, commanded by Major Franco Baker, was positioned on the right at Point 67, and it bore the brunt of a classic German counterattack.

The German defences south of Caen were manned by elements of the 272nd Infantry Division, a unit formed in 1943. The division included large numbers of Russians who had chosen service with the Wehrmacht over near-certain death in prisoner-of-war camps. On D-Day it was located in the south of France at Port Vendes. Ordered north on July 3, the division reached the front eight days later.[26] By July 16 it had relieved units of I SS Panzer Corps in the section west of the Caen-Falaise road. A company-sized battle group of tanks from 1st Panzer Division was provided to stiffen the division's resolve.[27] It was part of this battle group that was advancing down Route 162 to meet the Calgaries.

Major Baker had sent Lieutenant Vern Kilpatrick with a fighting patrol ahead of the company, and some four hundred yards south of Point 67, the panzer group appeared. Kilpatrick and his men were overrun, though not before hitting several German tanks with PIAT bombs. Kilpatrick was recommended for a posthumous mention-in-dispatches for his actions.[28]

The panzer grenadiers surged forward, and just as General Simonds had predicted, they attacked individual infantry positions with close-in, aimed fire from armoured vehicles. Fortunately, the Calgaries were well dug in,

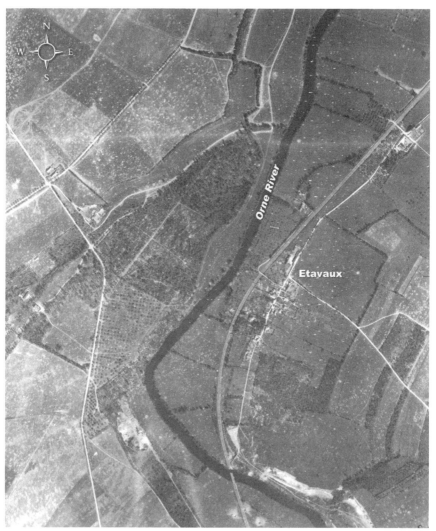

Etavaux and the high ground west of the Orne River were held by elements of the
German 272nd Infantry Division. Photo taken on August 7, 1944. LCMSDS

their speed in getting underground assisted by the sound of the engagement with Kilpatrick's patrol. For the next hour the Calgaries held on; B Company to the left was able to bring supporting fire to bear, and the SS were unable to commit enough infantry to take the battalion position. As darkness fell, two platoons of D Company reinforced C Company's position. The mortaring did not stop, but it was now possible to evacuate the wounded. There were surprisingly few fatal casualties, but ninety-two men, almost all from C Company, were evacuated with wounds, including Major Baker, who was suffering from a chest wound and exhaustion. A number of others were sent to the rear areas as battle exhaustion casualties.[29]

The Calgaries were not left on their own. At 7:00 P.M. the Black Watch, supported by two troops of Sherbrooke tanks, moved forward to secure the left flank occupying the village of Ifs. Probing attacks by small groups of enemy troops looking for a way around the Calgary position were beaten off, and Ifs quickly became a target for German mortars. During the night, mortaring set the regimental aid post on fire. Sergeant W. F. Clements, the senior NCO at the RAP, organized the evacuation of the wounded in a demonstration of tireless resolve under fire. He was awarded the Military Medal (M.M.) for his action that night.[30]

Fifth Brigade's first day in battle had been relatively successful. There had been plenty of mistakes, as is inevitable when "green" troops commanded by equally inexperienced officers are committed to action for the first time. The errors had not led to undue confusion or collapse of unit morale. Infantry-tank cooperation had worked well, and the 5th Field Regiment had demonstrated its professionalism both in the barrage and in rapid and accurate response to requests from the FOOs.

The most disturbing feature of the day's proceedings was the way in which each of the battalions had gone forward in tight box formations, relying on the artillery and a handful of tanks for protection. The battalions moving uphill in open country were terribly vulnerable should a determined counterattack have developed. The Calgaries had even brought their battalion headquarters with them, and Lieut.-Colonel MacLaughlan positioned it in the centre of his four rifle companies. Shortly after arrival a mortar-bomb set the battalion's ammunition reserve on fire, and the fifteen-ton truck "blew up in a grand display of fireworks."[31]

Guy Simonds' plans for the next day called for 6th Canadian Infantry Brigade to pass through 5th Brigade and establish itself on the "Verrières feature" on the southern spur of the ridge. This order conflicted with the one issued to 7th Armoured Division to advance along the ridge from its position at Hubert Folie. The "Desert Rats" began their attack at mid-morning using a company of motorized infantry and a squadron of tanks. Troteval farm was

Major Jacques Ostiguy (third from right) and his headquarters section, Etavaux, July 1944. LCMSDS

their initial objective but "opposition was too strong,"[32] and 7th Armoured was only too happy to agree to leave the battlefield to the Canadians when Simonds suggested that his fresh, reinforced infantry brigade could accomplish the task.

Sixth Brigade's attack turned into a bloody nightmare. Torrential rain which ended air sorties and artillery observations was coupled with a major German counterattack. On the right flank the Camerons were able to secure a hold on part of the village of St. André, but in the open grain fields along the ridge, German tanks roamed at will, machine-gunning the infantry and knocking out the handful of Shermans that had ventured forward. The reserve battalion, the Essex Scottish borrowed from 4th Brigade, was also hit hard, and parts of the battalion broke under pressure.

By evening on the twentieth, some degree of order had been restored, but the next day as the very heavy rain continued, 6th Brigade's finger-hold on the ridge began to slip. The Black Watch was ordered to try to restore the situation. Lieut.-Colonel Cantlie called an Orders Group and quickly assigned tasks. The Sherbrookes provided B Squadron, which was almost at full strength, to go forward with the infantry.[33] At 6:00 P.M. the barrage began and the Black Watch leaned into it, moving up the hill in a "text book operation."[34] The tanks remained at the crossroads until the battalions' anti-tank guns were in position. The Canadians now held a line which stretched along the road from St. André to the Caen-Falaise highway, but they were still on the lower slope and Verrières Ridge loomed ahead. Casualties in Operation "Atlantic" had been horrendous. Second Division had lost 1,149 men, including 254 killed. Battle exhaustion accounted for more than two hundred additional losses. Sixth Brigade and the Essex Scottish of 4th Brigade had suffered most of these casualties.[35] Fifth Brigade was by comparison in good shape; morale, after what appeared to be some success in battle, was high.

Still, there were problems. The Canadian army, like its British and American allies, placed an enormous burden on the junior officers of its rifle companies. They were expected, indeed required, to lead from the front, bringing predictable results. To take one example, during the period July 19 to 24, the Black Watch had three platoon commanders killed and five wounded. The regiment lost two company commanders, including Major George Fraser, who was killed, during the consolidation on July 20.[36] The situation in the other two battalions was similar, and a large number of officer reinforcements had to be brought forward before the first week of battle was over.

Operation "Atlantic" and its parent Operation "Goodwood" came to an end on July 21 when the Black Watch restored the line. But no one told the enemy, so the counterattacks continued. Now it was the Germans who were taking the heavy losses including precious tanks. Second British Army claimed to be pleased with the progress made in three days of fighting. VIII Corps had advanced ten thousand yards, enabling II Canadian Corps to capture Vaucelles and exploit south. Two thousand prisoners were captured and a like number of enemy killed or wounded. The British army had lost a considerable number of tanks, but they could easily be replaced; its human losses had been low in proportion to the troops engaged.[37] Canadian casualties had been heavily concentrated in the last day of fighting when operations were supposed to be winding down.[38]

While Montgomery and Dempsey turned their attention to new schemes for breaking through the German defensive perimeter, II Canadian Corps reorganized. For 2nd Division the major problem was bringing reinforcements forward to rebuild the units shattered in Operation "Atlantic." The battalions still in the line had other work to do. When "Goodwood" was planned, it was assumed that XII British Corps, to the west of the River Orne, would have succeeded in clearing Hill 112 and the high ground overlooking Fleury and St. Andre. Operation "Greenline" began on the night of July 15–16, but it proved impossible to capture the initial objective, Evrecy, and the attack stalled.[39] The village of Maltot in the shadow of Hill 112 remained in enemy hands as did Etavaux, a straggling village on the east bank of the Orne.

Etavaux was the tip of a very large thorn stuck into 2nd Division's flank. The Queen's Own Cameron Highlanders defending the ruins of St. André had to deal repeatedly with troops infiltrated across the river from Maltot on "a wooden bridge slung across the river at night."[40] The Calgaries, at Point 67, had tried to protect their position by masking Etavaux. Major John Campbell's A Company became involved in some long-range fire-fights, but Brigadier Megill refused to allow the Calgaries to become embroiled in a battle for a village that the enemy would have to evacuate as soon as 43rd British Division cleared Maltot.[41]

Unfortunately, the British were having a difficult time breaking the German hold on the west bank. Hill 112 was one of the most notorious killing grounds in Normandy, where the British and German armies had fought each other to a standstill in a number of bloody encounters. On July 22 the 4th Battalion, Wiltshire Regiment, was told to clear Maltot to assist the Canadians, and the Régiment de Maisonneuve was ordered to stage a raid on Etavaux to help out the Wilts.[42]

The Maisonneuves used two companies to attack astride the railway. Lieut.-Colonel Nighswander arranged a fire plan designed to walk them into the village. The Sherbrooke Fusiliers provided a troop of tanks which took up position on high ground overlooking the line of approach.[43] D Company on the left ran into heavy fire, and the company commander, Major Gérard Vallieres, was killed. To the right of the railway, Major Jacques Ostiguy's C

Private P. P. Beauchamp of Le Régiment de Maisonneuve (left) and Dr. Cohier examining captured German mortar, Fleury-sur-Orne, France, July 20, 1944. LAC

Company moved forward hesitantly.[44] The barrage had failed to destroy a large number of machine-gun posts, and the Sherbrookes were unable to provide aimed fire from their perch above the village.

There is an old adage that battles are won by the handful of determined men who instinctively attack while their comrades equally instinctively hit the ground. One such determined fellow was Sergeant Benoit Lacourse, who inspired four of his men to follow him in a mad run at an enemy position which was sweeping the approaches to Etavaux with machine-gun fire. Lacourse destroyed three machine-gun posts.[45] The advance was again brought to a halt by "very heavy machine-gun fire from several cunningly sited posts in a hedge running across rising ground." The company commander, Major Jacques Ostiguy, grabbed some grenades and dashed forward. He used the grenades to destroy four enemy posts and a rifle to finish off a fifth.[46] C Company then advanced into Etavaux, maintaining pressure until the British barrage on Maltot was due to begin and the order to pull out came. Across the river the battle lasted until late that night. When 43rd Division reported that the Maltot show was over, A and B Companies returned to Etavaux and occupied it, gathering close to one hundred prisoners from 272nd Division.[47] Maisonneuve casualties on the twenty-third were ten killed, forty-eight wounded, and fifty evacuated with battle exhaustion.[48] The Maisonneuves had now lost more than two hundred riflemen, and since French-speaking reinforcements were in short supply, the battalion could not be brought back up to strength. In the next operation 5th Brigade was to go into action with just two battalions.

CHAPTER 4

Verrières Ridge

While the battle for control of the St. André-Etavaux-Maltot was fought, the army commander, Lieut.-General Miles Dempsey, met with Guy Simonds to plan a new offensive in the Canadian sector. On July 21 Montgomery had issued a directive which required II Canadian Corps to remain "as active as possible" so that the enemy would believe that "we contemplate a major advance towards Falaise and Argentan." "The Germans must," Montgomery wrote, "be induced to build up strength east of the Orne so our affairs on the western flank can proceed with greater speed."

This directive is often cited as proof that the Canadian assault on Verrières Ridge, code-named "Spring," was planned as a holding action to assist the American breakout, Operation "Cobra," but on July 22 Montgomery changed his plans. He explained a new scheme to Eisenhower in a letter which stated that he was not going to "hold back or wait" for the Americans. Instead, II Canadian Corps, reinforced with two British armoured divisions, was to attack on July 22, capturing Verrières Ridge and advancing south to secure the next high ground at Point 122 near Cranmesnil. Two days later XII British Corps, west of the Orne, would once again try to capture the Hill 112 area. Once this was accomplished, VIII Corps—the armoured divisions restored to it—would thrust down the road to Falaise. All of these operations, described as a series of left-right-left blows, would culminate in a new "Goodwood," using "three or four armoured divisions" to break through to Falaise.[1]

Second Canadian Corps was still operating under Second British Army in July. Simonds discussed the details of the operation "fully" with General Dempsey, and obtained his approval, but "Spring" was Simonds' plan.[2] He designed it as a three-phase battle involving the two Canadian infantry divisions and 2nd Canadian Armoured Brigade, plus Guards and 7th Armoured Divisions. Second Tactical Air Force was to devote its full resources to the battle, and the medium guns of three Army Groups Royal Artillery (AGRAs) were to supplement eight field regiments. In the first phase 3rd Division was to capture Tilly-la-Campagne while 2nd Division seized May-sur-Orne and Verrières village. Phase II required 2nd Division to capture Fontenay-le-Marmion and Rocquancourt while 7th Armoured Division attacked Cran-mesnil and 3rd Division assaulted Garcelles-Secqueville. These moves were to set the stage for the Guards Armoured Division to seize the high ground about Cintheaux and the river crossings at Bretteville-sur-Laize,[3] the same objectives listed for the third phase of Operation "Goodwood."

Allied intelligence on enemy defences in the area was limited by poor weather which prevented photo reconnaissance. Prisoners of war from the 272nd Division brought news of the attempted assassination of Hitler, order of battle information, and stories of their ten-day trek to Normandy from the Spanish border, but nothing was learned about the strength or location of the battle groups of 9th SS and 2nd Panzer Divisions supporting them.[4]

Intelligence officers also failed to appreciate that 272nd Division had committed two of its three regiments to the defence of St. Andre and St. Martin. This was the main line of German resistance on the left flank, and it was held by two battalions and elements of two others. The division's artillery and anti-tank regiments, scores of mortars, and a *Nebelwerfer* regiment were also committed to the defence of the area.[5]

Simonds believed that a repetition of the daylight attack of July 19 had little chance of success, so he decided to undertake Phase I in full darkness, hoping to be past the first line of enemy resistance before daybreak. Since the enemy overlooked the area from the west side of the Orne as well as the ridge, the troops would have to wait until close to midnight before beginning to move to their forming-up places. This meant that H-Hour was delayed to 3:30 A.M., leaving less than three hours of darkness to complete Phase I if Phase II was to begin in darkness.[6]

The Anglo-Canadian forces had very limited experience with night attacks. Second Division had begun to study the problem in 1943 when Major-General E. L. M. Burns was in command. A divisional night-fighting course offered instruction in orientation and controlling troops,[7] but everyone who has been on a night exercise in strange country knows how difficult it is to keep direction even when no one is shooting at you. The British army's operational research group had devised a number of navigational aids for night-fighting, but their focus was on vehicles, not marching troops.[8] Artificial moonlight—searchlights bounced off clouds—was the only practical measure available to assist infantry.

"Spring" was supposed to involve four divisions, but most of the troops were assigned to the later phases. The night attack involved just three battalions, each committing between 300 and 350 men to the assault. This meant that 272nd Division and the panzer battle groups, who were well dug in with

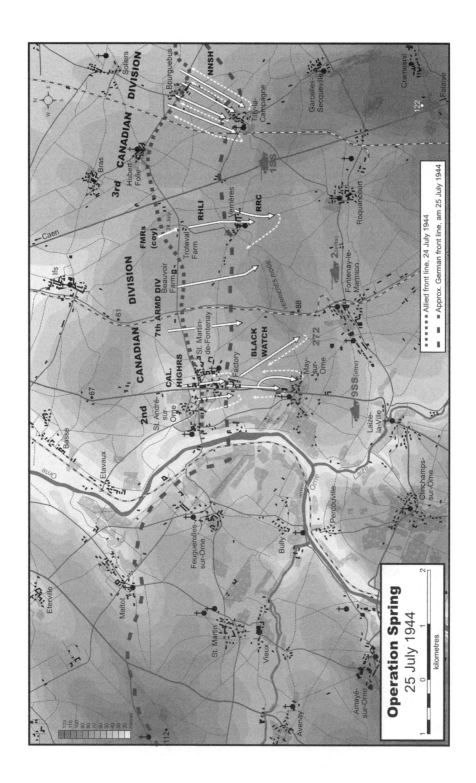

Operation Spring
25 July 1944

············· Allied front line, 24 July 1944

– – – Approx. German front line, am 25 July 1944

NNSH

3rd CANADIAN DIVISION

Soliers

Bourguebus

Garcelles-Secqueville

Cramesnil

Falaise

122

Tilly-la-Campagne

Bras

Hubert-Folie

1SS

Caen

FMRs (coy)

RHLI

Verrières

RRC

Roquancourt

Ifs

24 July

Troteval Farm

CANADIAN DIVISION

Beauvoir Farm

VERRIÈRES RIDGE

Fontenay-le-Marmion

2 (ctre)

61

7th ARMD DIV

88

St. Martin-de-Fontenay

.67

CAL. HIGHRS

BLACK WATCH

272

2nd CANADIAN DIVISION

Factory

May-sur-Orne

St. André-sur-Orne

9SS (ctre)

Laize-la-Ville

Basse

Laize

Clinchamps-sur-Orne

Orne

Etavaux

Orne

Percouville

Feuguerolles-sur-Orne

Bully

Eterville

Maltot

St. Martin

Vieux

Amayé-sur-Orne

Avenay

112•

120
110
100
90
80
70
60
50
40
30
20
metres

kilometres

1   0   1   2

A German Tiger pointing toward Bourguebus, photographed in 1946. CFJIC

carefully prepared interlocking fields of fire, outnumbered the attackers by a considerable margin. The corps commander counted on darkness and the artillery to overcome these odds and get his troops forward.

Simonds' orders left the divisional commanders with little latitude. H-Hour had been determined, and both air strikes and the medium artillery program of harassing fire on known German positions were set. Major-General Foulkes had to determine how best to carry out a divisional attack while two of his nine battalions were out of action recovering from their mauling in "Atlantic."[9] Foulkes faced a difficult situation. In theory his troops held a line from St. André-sur-Orne along the road which ran on the lower slope of Verrières Ridge through Beauvoir farm to the village of Hubert Folie. In practice this was was far from the case, particularly on the right flank where the Camerons had been struggling just to hold on to parts of St. André. When Brigadier Megill was informed that for the first phase of "Spring" the St. André–Beauvoir road would be the start line, he sent his G-3, Captain de Salaberry, and another officer to the village to prepare a tactical headquarters. They arrived without any difficulty, but when they opened the door of a likely house, they heard German voices and withdrew.

Megill decided to go and see the situation for himself. The Camerons had lost a number of officers in the past few days, including their CO, but the acting commander, Major J. Muncie, had a good grasp of the situation. He told Megill that the Camerons did not control most of St. André, never mind the adjacent village of St. Martin-de-Fontenay. The Camerons faced continuous mortar fire, frequent enemy counterattacks, and the constant infiltration of small groups of enemy soldiers. As late as the morning of the twenty-fourth, a patrol of approximately twenty-five Germans appeared in a quarry to the left-rear of battalion headquarters. Fortunately, a section of Toronto Scottish medium machine guns was deployed in the area and the enemy patrol was destroyed.[10]

Megill went immediately to division headquarters to ask to have the Maisonneuves, now in divisional reserve, returned to the brigade so they could clear the start line for the Calgaries. Foulkes refused, insisting that 6th Brigade did hold St. André and could clear St. Martin. After some acrimonious discussion Foulkes agreed to place the Camerons under 5th Brigade to secure the start line.[11] The Camerons began this task on the night of the twenty-fourth, just hours before "Spring" was to begin. "Stiff opposition" was met from the beginning, and it was necessary to keep reinforcing the Camerons' attack force, which lost three officers in the first hour. By midnight the actual start line seemed to be quiet.[12] This did not mean that St. Martin-de-Fontenay had been cleared, nor had anyone attempted to occupy the factory area three hundred yards south of the St. Martin church.

A knocked-out Canadian Sherman tank in Normandy, photographed in 1946. CFJIC

This complex of buildings, with a single prominent tower housing machinery for a mine shaft, was targeted in the divisional artillery plan as part of a rolling barrage which was to lead the Calgary Highlanders from their check line, the St. André–Verrières road where the barrage would begin, to their objective, May-sur-Orne. The Germans occupied the mine workings in strength and maintained well-concealed positions throughout the southeastern fringe of St. Martin.

Foulkes, by retaining the Maisonneuves in divisional reserve and assigning the Black Watch to Phase II, left Megill with a single battalion which had been briefed to advance quickly, two companies up, following the barrage into May.[13] With hindsight it can be argued that Megill should have intervened during the night and ordered the Calgary Highlanders to use at least one company to clear and occupy St. Martin and the factory area, although how this change could have been communicated to the Calgaries is not immediately apparent. Throughout the hours of darkness, the battalion was moving from Point 67 to its forming-up place, and company commanders were fully taxed keeping their men together. A large part of D Company, including company headquarters, did in fact get lost and had to return to Point 67 to re-orient themselves.[14] At the last moment Lieut.-Colonel D. G. MacLaughlan, the Calgary CO, changed the plan, ordering one of his reserve companies to advance with the barrage to protect the right flank of the assault companies. MacLaughlan's concern with the wooded areas along the River Orne was no doubt justified, but this change did not address the problem of St. Martin or the factory and left him with only the small part of D Company which had arrived as a reserve.[15]

What MacLaughlan called his "main effort" force, Major John Campbell's A Company and Major C. C. Nixon's B Company, were lined up east of the St. André–May road. A company on the left "discovered that the area was not clear" and "had to fight to get on the start line." They hit the check line on time and swung farther east to bypass the factory area, but came under small-arms fire from the eastern edge of St. Martin. Major Campbell had to choose quickly between detaching men to deal with this position and pressing on to May with the barrage. He chose to keep his men moving, "leaving enemy behind in slit trenches and dug-outs who later on were to fire on us to our cost."[16]

Campbell's men advanced towards the eastern edge of May and informed battalion headquarters that they had reached their objective.[17] The artillery continued to pound the village with some shells falling short on the men waiting on the sloping field. According to Lieutenant Morgandeen, the company stayed in that position "only about fifteen minutes." He told the historical officer, who interviewed him four days after the battle, that "light was breaking

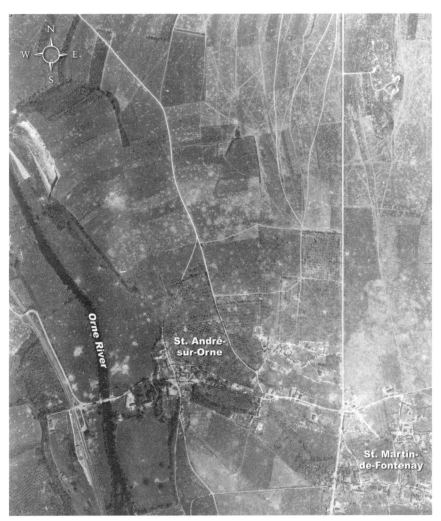

St. André-sur-Orne and St. Martin-de-Fontenay. The road from St. André to Beauvoir Farm (the start line) and the road through St. Martin to Verrières are clearly visible. Note the separation of the two villages. Photograph taken on August 7, 1944. LCMSDS

and our artillery remained on the objective. There was no area between the position we had reached and our final consolidation position where we might have set up a proper defensive area. Hence we came back and took up position to the right [east] of St. Martin."[18]

Campbell's men were immediately pinned down by the enemy force they had bypassed during their advance to May. Heavy mortaring kept the men in their slit trenches, and Campbell, who had lost his wireless link, was not able to get a message through to battalion informing MacLaughlan of their withdrawal from May.[19] MacLaughlan, Megill, Foulkes, and Simonds all believed that A Company was on its objective.

B Company was to advance on A Company's right flank. They met machine-gun fire the moment the start line was crossed. Fire from a German outpost at the checkline, the sunken Verrières road, dispersed the company, and the commanding officer, Major Nixon, was killed. The company continued south "on a magnetic bearing of 197 degrees," but two of the platoons were forced to the ground "after meeting enfilade fire from eight machine-guns in St. Martin." The third platoon, commanded by Lieutenant John Moffat, was on the left flank and continued south, arriving at a "waterhole on the eastern edge of May-sur-Orne." The village was still being shelled by Allied artillery "which came in so low" the men had "to take shelter from it in dead ground."[20] When the barrage stopped, Moffat set off to recce the crossroads in May. While he was gone, it began to get light. Sergeant Wynder told the historical officer that, "as first light came we saw three Tiger tanks and two SP guns. Just along the south side of the road" to Fontenay. "When we were spotted by them the tanks and SPs tore in behind the ramps" of a blockhouse and began firing. Lieutenant Moffat returned from May and decided that "the objective was held by too strong a force for twenty men and one PIAT to contest." They proceeded "slowly and carefully" back towards St. André and met men from A Company "who told us the rest of our company was in the area just east of the factory. We moved to this area and took up a common front in defence with the rest of B Company between 0730 and 0830 hours."[21] All of the officers except Moffat were now casualties, and CSM Ralph Wilson and Sergeant George Brandon were preparing to lead their platoons against the German positions in the factory area. No one contacted battalion headquarters.[22]

C Company, assigned to the area west of the main road, ran into opposition "from both flanks" from the start line on. "Three men of the leading section were killed." Scouts were sent forward to "see if we could clear out this opposition," but it was "too dark and too difficult to clear the enemy out at night." It "was cloudy and smoky and so thick we could not see anything."[23] The company commander decided to wait until morning.

As dawn broke, C Company moved towards May. They "advanced in single file up the ditches on either side of the road to the factory area. There as before were some snipers and also some groups of men who wanted to surrender." The advance continued using the left-hand ditch, which was very deep. The lead platoon, under Lieutenant Mageli, was within two hundred yards of May when Major Sherwin Robinson called an Orders Group. He knew that "men had been in May-sur-Orne without meeting any fire, notably the signals sergeant"[24] who had twice entered the village in an attempt to lay a cable to A Company.[25]

It was now 9:00 A.M., and Robinson ordered his men to clear the buildings on both sides of the road "right up close to the church." They "found no one." At this point snipers to the rear of the church and from the right began to fire on Mageli's platoon. Over on the left 13th Platoon had "worked up in extended order to the houses. There were many snipers in the orchards to the east of the houses and the platoon had a sticky time. About the same time we came under fire of what seemed to be our own artillery."[26] This new hazard was in fact the barrage intended to lead the Black Watch from May to Fontenay. C Company, which knew nothing about this plan, took cover in the ditches along both sides of the road and remained there throughout the Black Watch attack.

The two platoons of the reserve company that did arrive at the forming-up place, improvised a company headquarters, and set off behind B Company. The situation quickly became confused. One platoon became involved in a fire fight with four light machine guns located in an orchard just south of the start line. Lieutenant E. A. Michon, who commanded the other platoon, learned that the acting CO had been wounded and went forward to take command. Michon led the company "straight down the wheat fields to what he thought was the east side of May-sur-Orne. The men took up positions around a church which turned out to be in St. Martin not May."[27]

Michon told the historical officer that "in the confusion of the night and the battle, I lost my sense of time and space . . ." With daybreak Michon, still convinced he was in May, organized his men to clear the eastern part of the village systematically. "We took many prisoners there and on our way through the eastern edges of the factory district. While there I met a 'B' Coy FOO (Artillery Forward Observation Officer) who also thought we were in May-sur-Orne." Michon did not learn where he really was until the Black Watch arrived in the area shortly after 7:00 A.M..[28]

The Calgary attack on May had yielded close to a hundred prisoners and inflicted other casualties, but their objective was still in enemy hands. And the forming-up area for the Black Watch, never mind their intended start line, was still dominated by German mortar and machine-gun fire. This situ-

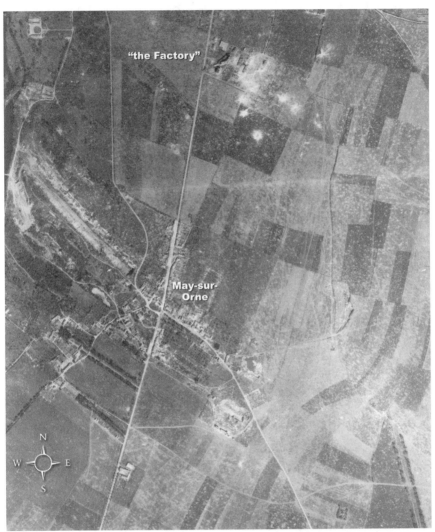

"the Factory"

May-sur-Orne

N
W—E
S

The "factory" south of St. Martin and May-sur-Orne. The crest of Verrières Ridge may be identified by the shape of the fields. The double row of trees in the lower right lead to Fontenay. The Black Watch "start line" was the road just north of the water-filled quarry on the eastern edge of May. Many of the Black Watch casualties were suffered before they reached this line. Photograph taken on August 7, 1944. LCMSDS

ation was the result of divisional headquarters' failure to recognize that St. Martin and its factory area were well organized, strongly held defensive positions. It is clear that the first phase of "Spring" should have been an attack on St. Martin, not May-sur-Orne.

Given the difficulty of their task the Calgaries had shown initiative and determination if not much skill in the art of mounting a night attack. Today, military training manuals emphasize what is called C3—command, control, and communications—as the key to successful operations. Apart from the jargon, the concept appears obvious to veterans of the 5th Brigade. The difficulty is that command and control are not possible without communication, and in 1944 infantry companies frequently lost touch with both their battalion headquarters and each other. Quite apart from casualties to platoon and company signals sections, the back-packed No. 18 set was subject to interference and frequent failure. The Calgaries do not seem to have paid enough attention to providing backup for wireless communication. Foulkes and Megill were left to guess at what had happened to the four Calgary companies. During the three hours of darkness and confusion, the failure to send runners to battalion headquarters was understandable, but between 7:00 and 9:00 A.M., when the Black Watch were preparing their attack, only the reserve company made contact with battalion headquarters, and MacLaughlan did not take steps to remedy the situation.[29]

Phase II of "Spring" was scheduled to begin at first light, with the Royal Regiment of Canada seizing Rocquancourt and the Black Watch advancing from May to capture Fontenay-le-Marmion. These attacks were supposed to take place in conjunction with an advance by 7th Armoured Division attacking between the Canadian brigades to capture the high ground near the village of Cranmesnil.

The Black Watch left the area north of Beauvoir farm at 3:30 A.M. and moved in a long, snaking column along the road to St. André. A few casualties were inflicted by machine-gun fire, but it was not until the lead companies turned south towards their planned assembly area near the church in St. Martin that real resistance was met.[30] St. Martin was far from clear of the enemy. Along the eastern edge of the build-up area, there were "high walls and hedges surrounding orchards. Next to these were three or four knocked-out Panther tanks."[31] The whole area was studded with machine-gun and sniper posts with "weapon slits outside the walls and hedges and dug-outs and scurry holes inside."[32] The artificial moonlight did nothing to

St. Martin-de-Fontenay and the mine, or "factory," area. Photograph taken on August 7, 1944. LCMSDS

help locate these positions, and in the darkness everyone was aware that valuable time was slipping away. Just as some degree of control was established, an undetected enemy post opened fire on the battalion's command group, mortally wounding Lieut.-Colonel Cantlie and injuring Major Modzfeldt, the senior company commander. It was now almost 5:30 A.M., and soon the first faint light of dawn would be visible on the horizon. Most of the battalion was still strung out along the hedgerow leading to St. Martin, instead of at the start line in May-sur-Orne.

Command of the battalion passed to the senior surviving company commander, a tall, slim, twenty-four-year-old, Major Phillip Griffin.[33] He faced a daunting task. His fellow officer Major Edwin Bennett recalled the moment of crisis in an interview recorded just five days after the battle:

Major Griffin's problem was that the battalion was rather extended. The companies were still intact and under good control but the threat of dispersion and of possible confusion was near. Light was breaking and we were under fire from the ridge. We had just made contact with the tanks in St. Andre-sur-Orne. They had moved into the orchard as a harbour and had lost two tanks coming through the town. Furthermore it was getting close to H hour for the attack and the battalion was far from the start line. Soon the artillery fire would begin and would be of no value. Major Griffin had to make time to liaise with the artillery and, if possible, retime their shoot. He had to get the tank commander into the picture and make use of his force in any new plans. Before this could be done, he had to find out the situation in St. André sur Orne from the Camerons of Canada and obtain what reports he could on the Calgaries and the situation at May-sur-Orne.

Major Griffin is a brilliant officer of absolutely outstanding courage and ability. His take-over in this strained and ticklish situation was superb. There was no uncertainty whatever in his actions. He foresaw only a delay, which would at the outside be two hours, while he rearranged timings and obtained essential information. The plan for the attack would be the same as had been previously set. In the meantime the battalion was to move to St. André-sur-Orne and occupy the X rds there on the Verrières rd so that the men would be less obvious targets for the fire from the left flank and so that a firm base for ops would be available. So complete was his control and so well trained the battalion that this was done at once and in incredibly good order. All the companies were in their new positions within 20 minutes of the conclusion of the "O" Group. Up to this time our casualties, aside from the three serious losses in leadership, were slight, amounting to ten or fifteen altogether.[34]

Griffin's actions between 6:00 and 9:30 A.M., when the Black Watch attack began, cannot be fully reconstructed. What is known is that a new artillery fire plan was agreed upon and tank support arranged with Major Walter Harris, the commander of B Squadron of the First Hussars.[35] The artillery plan was simply a repetition of the original scheme to lead the battalion from May to Fontenay, but Griffin decided to move directly to the start line on a compass bearing rather than by the road to May. He now wanted the tanks to protect his right flank rather than the left as in the original plan, hoping that the advance of 7th Armoured Division would fully occupy the enemy to the east. At about 8:30 A.M. Griffin made contact with Lieutenant Michon, commanding D Company of the Calgaries and asked him to "clear out the factory area." Michon "went forward to recce to discover very heavy machine-gun fire coming from the factory area on the right and from the knocked out tanks on the high ground on our left." Michon told Griffin that "this was too strong opposition for one company to clear without artillery support or smoke. He then asked me to go forward to see if the Start Line was secure and to send him word as he had no information concerning our forward companies."[36] The Black Watch start line was a road angling out of May-sur-Orne, and Michon would not agree to recce it for Griffin.

He was unable to contact the other Calgary companies, and when he reported to battalion headquarters, MacLaughlan ordered him to "try and get forward to the objective." Captain Harrison and the missing part of D Company had arrived, but their attempt to "get forward" to May was stopped cold by an intense mortar barrage which caused "very heavy casualties."[37]

Griffin had sent a patrol consisting of his intelligence officer, Lieutenant L. R. Duffield, Sergeant Benson, and one scout to May-sur-Orne. The patrol moved straight down Route 162 "without using the ditches"[38] and walked into the centre of May-sur-Orne without seeing or hearing any Germans or Calgary Highlanders. At the crossroads in the centre of the village, they turned left towards the road which marked the battalion start line. Fifty yards before reaching it they were fired on by a machine gun, and Duffield returned to tell Griffin that the Calgaries were not in May and that the machine gun would be able to fire into the flank of the battalion. Griffin's response was to order Duffield to lead a reinforced patrol of six men back to May to "take out" the machine gun.[39]

Duffield's patrol was not the only force to visit May-sur-Orne that morning. Major Walter Harris, commanding the First Hussars squadron, had listened to divisional and brigade orders "to go ahead" with Phase II and had

Looking south toward Verrières Ridge. The mine shaft south of St. Martin is in the centre of the photograph (taken in 1946). CFJC

sent one of his tank troops forward. This troop "located some of the Calgary Highlanders in a hollow north of May, badly cut up and in need of stretcher-bearers, ammunition, etc." Leaving two tanks to assist the Calgaries, the other two tanks proceeded to feel their way cautiously into the village. At the main crossroads the lead tank was holed by an anti-tank gun, and the remaining tank withdrew to a hull-down position on the north edge of the village.[40]

Meanwhile, Major Griffin was conferring with Brigadier Megill, who had learned through the gunner radio net that a fire plan, timed for 9:30 A.M., had been requested by the Black Watch. Megill recalls that Griffin was on the veranda of a building on the forward edge of St. Martin looking out towards May. There did not seem to be any shelling at that time, and Major Griffin calmly explained his plan. Megill thought it looked like "a dicey proposition" and suggested that the Black Watch secure May-sur-Orne first. According to Megill, Griffin replied that they had "patrols into May" and he doubted that it was held on "a continuous basis." Griffin felt sure that if the Black Watch attack went in, then once it had passed its start line the Calgary Highlanders could "fill in behind, on into May-sur-Orne." Megill accepted this assessment and returned to his headquarters.[41]

The Black Watch had to move quickly if its lead companies were to take full advantage of the timed artillery program. Unfortunately, the Hussars were delayed owing to the narrowness of the sunken approach road, and when the first tanks arrived at the forming-up place, the Black Watch had already begun to move forward. The Hussars could still see the infantry moving in single file with the men close together,[42] and the tanks quickly started across the open ground, aiming for the gap between May and the ridge east of the village. Accurate, large-calibre anti-tank fire struck the lead tanks immediately, and the others sought dead ground. By 10:20 A.M. six tanks had been lost and Major Harris wounded. At least one troop reported reaching the start line but their tanks were then caught in enfilade fire from the eastern edge of May.[43]

The infantry moved in single file, with the men close together, until they emerged from the houses and hedgerows of St. Martin. Lieutenant W. B. Wood, who was wounded by machine-gun fire before the company started up the hill, suggests that the men were well-spaced out as they moved forward through the tall grain.[44] Three hundred men, spread out over a wide area, had little sense of what was happening around them, and the battalion did not falter. Griffin's plan assumed that the Black Watch would be able to reach the start line as the artillery barrage began, but the battalion was subjected to heavy mortar and machine-gun fire as it advanced to its start line. When the survivors reached the crest of the hill, the barrage had passed, and the enemy was able to react quickly.

Looking north toward St. Martin from the edge of May-sur-Orne. The mine shaft and the church in St. Martin can be seen. Point 67 is in the far background. Photograph taken in 1946. CRJC

Captain John Taylor described the advance in a letter to his father dated August 15, 1944:

> To begin with I might say that you never need be ashamed of having belonged to the Black Watch. We started across country at 0900 hours. By then the Jerries were thoroughly awake as to what was going on and from the start we had trouble from very heavy machine-gunning from the flanks, mortars and artillery fire. The troops were steady as a rock and we kept going. I was the left forward company and on my right was B company, then commanded by Sergeant Foam, all the officers having been knocked out. We overran two strong points, then I got hit so I can't be accurate as to the rest of the story but I understand they got to the objective.[45]

Taylor was wounded before Griffin and approximately sixty men crossed the crest of the ridge. One survivor, Private Montreuil, reported that Captain John Kemp, commanding D Company, urged Major Griffin to call off the attack but Griffin replied "that the orders were to attack and that the battalion would therefore carry on."[46] On top of the ridge, the remnant of the battalion "ran directly into a strong and exceptionally well camouflaged enemy position."[47] Tanks and self-propelled guns were concealed in haystacks and intense close-range fire forced the men to ground. Griffin, who may have been the only officer left, ordered a withdrawal—"every man to make his way back as best he could." Not more than fifteen were able to do so. Griffin's body was later found "lying among those of his men."[48]

The Black Watch suffered 307 casualties on July 25. Five officers and 118 other ranks were killed or died of wounds; 101 were wounded, and of the 83 taken prisoner, 21 were wounded. As the official historian has noted, "Except for the Dieppe operation there is no other instance in the Second World War when a Canadian battalion had so many casualties in a single day."[49]

The battle did not end with the destruction of the Black Watch. The brigade message log portrays a scene of confused fighting on the northern edge of May lasting into the early afternoon. At 4:15 P.M. a smokescreen was laid across the front, and Brigadier Megill ordered the Calgaries to withdraw into St. André. Many of the wounded had to be left behind in the fields to the south and east of St. Martin. Lieutenant Leo Dallain, Royal Canadian Army Medical Corps, went forward into this area despite mortar and small arms fire. He located many of the casualties, "organized them into nests and returned with stretcher-bearers to evacuate them." On the twenty-sixth heavy German pressure led to the evacuation of all of St. Martin, and Dallain was

Lieutenant-Colonel S. S. T. Cantlie.

Grave marker for Lieutenant-Colonel Cantlie, who was mortally
wounded during the assault on Verrières Ridge, code-named "Spring."

ordered to cease his attempts to locate further casualties. He was awarded the Military Cross for this extraordinary effort.[50]

Elsewhere on the corps front, prospects were equally dismal. The North Nova Scotia Highlanders and Fort Garry Horse had been mauled in their operation against Tilly-la-Campagne, and in the centre the brilliant success of the Royal Hamilton Light Infantry in capturing Verrières village could not be followed up. The Royal Regiment of Canada and C Squadron of the First Hussars bypassed Verrières heading for Rocquancourt, but they ran into a "hurricane of fire" and took heavy losses. To their right the 1st Royal Tank Regiment encountered accurate long-range fire as soon as it moved forward.[51]

This tentative advance by one British squadron was not part of 7th Armoured Division's planned attack, for Simonds had cancelled the armoured advance. The 1st Royal Tank Regiment was under orders to assist the Royal Hamilton Light Infantry in Verrières and was not part of a larger operation.[52] Despite his caution in committing the armoured division, Simonds still believed that some of the objectives of Phase II could be won. At 5:30 P.M. he issued orders to renew the offensive. Second Division was to capture Rocquancourt and May-sur-Orne, and then at dawn on the twenty-sixth, Fontenay-le-Marmion would be attacked.[53] The Germans had other ideas and throughout the early evening hours pressed a series of counterattacks against 4th Brigade, which made an advance to Rocquancourt out of the question.[54] There was less pressure on the 5th Brigade front, and an attack by the Régiment de Maisonneuve, scheduled for 7:00 P.M., was allowed to go ahead although it is difficult to discern what this move was supposed to accomplish.

The Maisonneuves were to advance down the right side of the road to May, with Major Ostiguy leading C Company on the left flank. D Company under Captain Francois de Salles Robert was to set out at H+15 to clear out the woods on the right flank and then seize the quarry northwest of May. The enemy still occupied the factory area in strength, and the barrage provided by two field and four medium regiments was of little assistance. Indeed, once past the start line, they were fired on from St. André. Ostiguy's men reached the diagonal woods about four hundred yards north of May before enemy fire made further progress impossible[55] At 8:34 P.M. the Maisonneuves reported: "Both forward companies pinned down in line with factory by MGs along road. It is impossible to have artillery engage as target is in our rear."[56] Forty-five minutes later, when it became clear that German resistance was growing, Megill ordered the Maisies to return to St. André, where they were to spend the next four days holding the village and attempting to secure St. Martin. During the course of their relatively small part in Operation "Spring," the Maisonneuves suffered twelve fatal and more than forty non-fatal casualties.

Major F. P. Griffin. LCMSDS

The Calgary Highlanders had been ordered to withdraw to St. André on the evening of July 25, but the companies were scattered and out of touch. Megill ordered Lieut.-Colonel MacLaughlan, who was exhausted by the day's events, to hand over to Major Vern Stott, the second-in-command.[57] Megill told Stott to plan the defence of the area, and this task was quickly accomplished by visiting each company and placing it in an all-around defensive position. Regrettably, Stott was wounded "when a crump of mortar" struck him in the shoulder. "During this same period Major John Campbell staggered into battalion headquarters"[58] seriously wounded. Captain Ross Ellis took over command. That night the Calgaries were sent to join the Black Watch in the rear area. They had lost 5 officers and 172 other ranks killed, wounded, and missing. Every company commander who had gone into battle the previous night was a casualty.[59]

On the morning of July 26, 1944, 5th Brigade began the first day of its second week at the front. More than one thousand men—roughly one-fifth of the total strength of the brigade and more than half of its infantry rifle strength—were killed, wounded, prisoners of war, or exhaustion casualties.

The battles for May-sur-Orne and Verrières Ridge were soon to be rationalized as operations which had greatly assisted the American breakout from St. Lô. But in the immediate aftermath of what had seemed like a week of disasters, the senior officers of II Canadian Corps were forced to think about the events differently. Simonds met with both Montgomery and Dempsey to discuss "Spring" and then talked with his two divisional commanders.[60] The British generals must have had some reservations about Simonds' conduct of the battle, particularly his persistence in continuing daylight attacks which, like Canadian operations on the last day of "Goodwood," had been marked by heavy casualties to infantry battalions. Infantry was a terribly scarce resource in 21st Army Group, and it seems unlikely that Montgomery or Dempsey would have permitted a British general to press such costly operations in the way the Canadians had.[61]

For Simonds, "Spring" was not a failure of command but a demonstration of the inadequacies of individual Canadian units.[62] Brigadier D. G. Cunningham and the commanding officers of two of his Highland Brigade battalions were fired for refusing to press the attack against Tilly.[63] Major-General Keller, whom the British had suggested replacing in early July,[64] was retained in command, perhaps because he had followed orders and demanded that Cunningham mount a new attack. Major-General Foulkes was also left in command. Foulkes had functioned as little more than an observer during the first week of battle. He had received an outline plan from corps headquarters and passed it on to his brigadiers without reference to their circumstances. Communications with the assault troops and even with brigade headquarters were poor throughout the battles, but Foulkes did not go forward to discover what was happening. Much can be blamed on the fog of war, but a divisional commander ought to be more than a conduit for orders from higher formations. Foulkes confined his interventions to orders to "get going."[65]

Second Division's brigadiers had also failed to play a decisive role in the battles of July. Brigadier H. A. Young, commanding 6th Brigade, ignored the problems the Camerons were having in St. André, insisting that the start line for Operation "Spring" was secure. Young did not go forward to determine the situation for himself and does not seem to have grasped how difficult it would be to stage a night attack under these circumstances. Brigadier Megill, who has been much criticized for his role in "Spring," did go forward repeatedly and did attempt to learn all he could about the actual situation. Megill had been appalled by the plan for "Spring," which seemed to have been prepared by someone who could not read a contour map and had never seen the ground.[66] Verrières Ridge, he believed, ought to have been cleared from east to west, not by uphill attacks overlooked from three sides. Megill had discussed this with Foulkes, and after a 7th Armoured Division liaison officer had suggested that his men did not seriously believe that their part in Phase II of "Spring" was possible, Megill returned to Foulkes' headquarters where he sought assurances that the brigades' left flank would be protected by a vigorous British thrust. Foulkes told him that 7th Armoured would go all-out on the morning of July 25, and Megill had to accept this assurance.[67]

Once the operation began and his worst fears were being confirmed on an hourly basis, Megill could not bring himself to intervene. When Foulkes ordered the Calgaries to press their attack and told the Black Watch that speed was essential, Megill simply passed the orders on.[68] When he learned over the "gunners net" that Griffin had arranged an attack for 9:30 A.M., Megill went to see the Black Watch commander but did not overrule his decision.

Later that day Megill learned that Foulkes was going to renew the attack on May using the Maisonneuves and leaving them under 6th Brigade command. Foulkes and Brigadier Young arrived at 5th Brigade headquarters to organize this venture, and Foulkes began the discussion by reporting that Simonds was "furious at the failure which had occurred."[69] Megill protested the decision to order the Maisonneuves into battle, and a shouting match erupted with Foulkes demanding to know whether Megill was challenging his orders. The result of all this was not, however, to cancel an ill-conceived plan but rather to conduct it under the control of 5th Brigade.

Megill offered this explanation of his actions on July 25 in a 1988 interview: "It was perfectly clear that the attack should have been called off at a very early stage in the morning. I suggested this not later than perhaps 8:00 or 9:00 o'clock. Instead the Corps commander was pressing the divisional commander and he was pressing us to get on with an attack which we knew was almost hopeless. Under these circumstances one does not quit. You do as much as you possibly can and hope that someone will see the light and give you some relief."[70] If Phillip Griffin had lived, he would no doubt have offered a similar explanation.

Why did Simonds fail to "see the light"? The message logs suggest that he made the decision to go ahead with the infantry's part in Phase II on the basis of reports that the North Novas and Fort Garry Horse were pressing a new attack on Tilly, the knowledge that the RHLI had captured Verrières, and the information that the Calgaries had troops in or near May. He appears to have used this fragmentary evidence as grounds for launching Phase II while reserving his armoured divisions until more complete information was available. He was wrong, but this was not an unreasonable decision.

After Operation "Spring" failed and it became apparent that the Americans had broken through the German defences, Montgomery changed his plans and issued a new directive. He noted that six of the ten panzer divisions were concentrated in the open country south of Caen so "further large scale efforts in this sector were unlikely to succeed." British Second Army was therefore to regroup and attack with not less than six divisions on the army's right flank at Caumont. This operation, code-named "Bluecoat," drew all three British armoured divisions to the west, forcing a postponement of any armoured thrust east of the Orne towards Falaise, but the Germans did not know this.

The Canadian effort at Verrières Ridge, marred as it was by poor operational intelligence, communication failures, and the kind of mistakes inexperienced troops were bound to make, was nevertheless a successful military operation. The enemy responded to "Spring" with coordinated counterattacks by elements of two panzer divisions. Their attempts to evict the Canadians from Verrières village and St. André cost the enemy heavy casualties and distracted attention from the vital part of the front where an American breakthrough turned into the long-awaited break out.

Fifth Field Regiment, which fired eighty-three thousand 25-pounder rounds during nineteen days of action in July,[71] was heavily involved on the twenty-sixth and twenty-seventh. Canadian and British artillery hammered the German battle groups which now suffered from the same disadvantages. The Canadians had endured, attacking a well-entrenched enemy posted on high ground and in villages. Operation "Spring" may not have been planned as a holding operation, but it certainly became a very successful one.

CHAPTER 5

Falaise

Most of 5th Brigade spent the week after Operation "Spring" near Fleury-sur-Orne. Hundreds of men from the divisional reinforcement unit, already in France, were brought forward to fill in the depleted ranks. All of these were thoroughly trained infantry soldiers, and there was no difficulty in bringing the Black Watch and Calgaries back to a reasonable strength. Unfortunately, there was a shortage of French-speaking soldiers in the reinforcement unit, and neither the Fusiliers Mont Royal nor the Maisonneuves could be reinforced adequately.

The Black Watch faced an incredible rebuilding task. Major Frank M. Mitchell, who as second-in-command had been left out of battle (LOB), took over the battalion on July 26. Of the twenty-seven officers available when Operation "Spring" began, fourteen had been killed or wounded.[1] The surviving officers included Captain E. R. Bennett, who had commanded the carrier platoon throughout the battle; two rifle company 2/iCs, Captains D. Cowans and E. V. Pinkham, who had been LOB; and four lieutenants. Mitchell sent for Major Bruce Ritchie, a veteran Black Watch officer, to serve as 2/iC and "in a moment of inspiration" selected David Law, a young subaltern "who had been eliminated by every commanding officer as an obvious non-runner,"[2] as adjutant. Captain Law and the quartermaster, John Duchastel, looked after the welfare of the officers and men of the battalion with enormous skill.

The reinforcement unit provided several other Black Watch officers, but it also sent a number of what the regiment called "strangers," officers with no Black Watch connection. They arrived from the reinforcement unit in late July and August to take their places in what was really a new battalion. Some were from the regiment's Provisional Officer's Training program and wore Black Watch flashes on their shoulders, but most got their introduction to the "hackle" in the dry fields of Normandy. Lieutenant Joe Nixon, who had joined the Canadian Officer's Training Corps at McGill University as a Black Watch cadet, was one of the new officers who arrived in August. He volunteered for the Scout Platoon and was told by Lieut.-Colonel Mitchell to rely on the experience of Sergeant Barney Benson, who would show him the

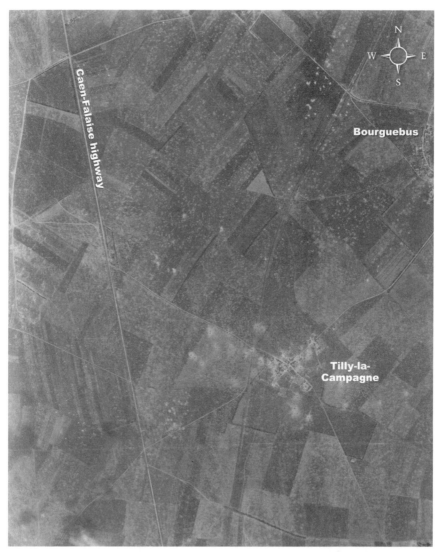

Tilly-la-Campagne. The Calgary attack came from the left along the road into the village from the northwest. Photograph taken on August 4, 1944. LCMSDS

ropes. Nixon quickly realized that this was good advice and they worked closely together until Benson was killed on September 10 at Grande Mille Brugge, outside of Dunkirk. Nixon recalls little discussion of the events of July in his platoon. There was no opportunity to mull things over with his fellow officers as they saw each other only at Orders Groups. The battalion was always dispersed over a wide area, and long periods could go by without any contact with men outside the platoon.[3]

One serious problem the "new" Black Watch faced was the strained relationship between Lieut.-Colonel Mitchell and his commanding officer. Brigadier Megill had regarded the Black Watch as the outstanding battalion in the brigade partly because of the leadership qualities of Stuart Cantlie and his adjutant, Eric Modzfeldt. Megill had a much different opinion of Mitchell, whom he regarded as unsuited for command.[4] Megill felt his doubts were confirmed when a company of the Black Watch was cut off and destroyed on August 5. Mitchell in turn had little confidence in Megill, whom he blamed for the debacle of July 25 and the orders of August 5.[5] Both men were letting the strain of events cloud their judgement. Mitchell did not have the presence of Cantlie or Modzfeldt, but he inspired affection and loyalty among his subordinates.[6] His success in rebuilding the battalion and integrating the newcomers was an impressive achievement. Mitchell, however, contributed to the Black Watch sense of grievance over Operation "Spring," and this helped to poison relations with Megill for the balance of the war.[7]

The Calgary Highlanders had lost their 2/iC and all four company commanders, but in the each case a Calgary captain was available to take over. Lieut.-Colonel MacLaughlan returned to command the battalion despite his shaky performance during "Spring" because Megill did not believe that any of the remaining officers were old enough, or experienced enough, to be promoted and his request for an experienced replacement was denied.[8] The loss of Vern Stott was deeply felt, but the adjutant, Captain Ross Ellis, was beginning to play a major role in the battalion's affairs as a "battle adjutant," and Ellis was a man who inspired great confidence. By July 29 the Calgaries had been rebuilt to their authorized strength.[9]

The Maisonneuves were not relieved in St. André until July 30 when they marched to Etavaux, which was now reasonably quiet. Beer, cigarettes, and chocolate were brought forward, and Lieut.-Colonel Bisiallon tried to reorganize a battalion that was two hundred riflemen short. The Maisonneuves were to operate this way throughout the rest of the fighting in 1944. There was no shortage of officers or NCOs,[10] but for the next fifteen weeks, the trickle of OR reinforcements never made up for the losses in battle, and the Maisies continued as a half-strength battalion.[11]

The period of rest ended for the Calgaries on the last day of July. To the west the American "breakthrough," Operation "Cobra," had become a "break-out," but on the Caen front the enemy was showing no signs of collapse. The Germans were finally shifting most of their armoured divisions to the American flank, but this only reinforced their need to practice "aggressive defence" in the Canadian sector. German fighting patrols hit at various points, and any movement in Canadian lines brought down immediate mortar fire.

The corps commander was, however, required to follow orders. In his directive of July 27, Montgomery had insisted that along the whole eastern flank the enemy "must be worried and shot up, and attacked, and raided, whenever and wherever possible; the object of such activity will be to improve our own positions, to gain ground, to keep the enemy from transferring forces and generally to write off German personnel and equipment."[12]

These orders led Guy Simonds to plan a renewed attack on Tilly-la-Campagne, the village which the North Novas had failed to capture on July 25. Simonds selected this objective because Tilly was on ground high enough to provide better observation of the German defensive positions and thus an ideal jumping-off point for the next offensive. He ordered a night attack by a single infantry battalion, assisted by a squadron of tanks. Foulkes assigned this unwelcome task to 5th Brigade, which meant it would have to be the Calgary Highlanders as neither the Maisonneuves or Black Watch were ready for such a battle.

Simonds' decision to attack Tilly with one battalion, and to repeat this operation with the Lincoln and Welland Regiment a few days later, suggests that he still believed that the failures of July were due to poor execution of a workable battle doctrine. For Simonds the success of the RHLI at Verrières village was proof that it could be done, rather than the exception which proved the rule. The Germans had reacted strongly to the loss of Verrières and were bound to defend Tilly even more vigorously. It was on higher ground and was the start of a good road, the D230, which paralleled the main Caen-Falaise highway for several miles. A battle group of the Adolf Hitler SS Division occupied the village, and the divisional mortars had been registered for every square metre of ground.

The Calgaries formed up at the farm captured by the Essex Scottish and waited for a feint attack by a company of the Lincoln and Welland Regiment. The Lines had barely gotten started before furious mortar fire forced them to dig in.[13] The Calgaries had sent scouts forward with a detachment of the carrier platoon to check on possible minefields, but the route was pronounced clear, and at 2:30 A.M. the artillery began to pound the ground in front of the startline. D Company, under its new commander, Captain Del Harrison, moved first and the other three companies followed, each on its own approach line. The barrage was designed to "walk" the companies into Tilly, lifting at the rate of one hundred yards in five minutes. Wounded began to filter back almost immediately as the enemy "laid down a terrific mortar barrage" and added heavy artillery fire.[14]

The darkened slope was now an inferno, and the Calgary companies still in contact reported that they were being shelled by their own artillery. Lieut.-Colonel. MacLaughlan asked to have the support fire stopped but word was still received that men were still under their own fire. The War Diary insists that this proved that the enemy was "up to his old trick of firing into our own barrage,"[15] but the men on the ground were quite certain they had been shelled from their own rear areas. Some small groups made it into the rubble on the outskirts of Tilly, but no one was going any farther as every move brought increased machine-gun fire. The SS battle group had long years of experience in waiting out barrages before emerging to hit back.

A British squadron from the Scots Grays, assigned to support this operation, was called on to lead the Calgaries, and an additional company from the Royal Regiment of Canada, back to Tilly. One three-tank troop made it to the edge of the village before two of the Shermans were destroyed. The infantry were again subjected to heavy machine-gun fire and what seemed like non-stop mortaring. Captain Mark Tennant's carriers were in constant motion, bringing casualties back and taking ammunition forward.[16] As dawn broke, heavy fog obscured the battlefield helping the Calgaries to dig in and reorganize close to their startline.

As the Calgary companies consolidated, another of those dramas in command was unfolding at corps, division, brigade, and battalion headquarters. Simonds was stern and determined, Foulkes was insistent, Megill was dutiful, and MacLaughlan obedient; a new attack was ordered.[17] The company commanders were called back to battalion headquarters to receive their orders. The mood at the Orders Group was pretty grim, but Captain Ellis had arranged for rations and hot tea to be sent forward, and the Calgary companies were under good control. By mid-afternoon all was ready and the men, together with a squadron of Fort Garry tanks, once more moved forward behind a barrage. After less than two hundred yards and hundreds of rounds of German mortar bombs, the battalion went to ground, dug in, and tried to save itself from destruction. At dusk the men withdrew in good order.[18] The battle continued that night when the Lincs were sent in from the other side of Tilly. They suffered dreadfully before making a disordered retreat.[19] The Calgary dead, including A Company's new leader, Captain John Bright, numbered thirty-four. The wounded, including four platoon commanders and Captain Wynn Lasher, commanding C Company, numbered ninety-seven.[20]

For the Calgaries, Tilly-la-Campagne was a rerun of Operation "Spring" except that losses were even heavier. On August 5 the battalion's weekly field return notes a shortage of 7 sergeants, 25 corporals, and 209 privates.[21] The battalion had been close to full strength on July 31, so losses of around two hundred men are a reasonable estimate. Tilly was a battle which produced dozens of battle exhaustion casualties, a sign of the deep wounds that had been inflicted on the battalion's morale. The Calgaries were to become one of the most effective fighting units in the Canadian army, but at the end of July, they were in very bad shape.

In the early hours of August 5, the Black Watch, with two companies of the Maisonneuves attached, were also sent back into battle. Sixth Brigade had to be relieved so that it could rehearse for its part in Operation "Totalize," a major Canadian offensive, scheduled for the eighth. The takeover in St. André was accomplished smoothly and without any enemy interference. When morning came, there was still no sign of activity from the Germans apart from very light shelling and mortaring. Reports of the withdrawal of panzer units had been intercepted by Ultra, and divisional headquarters decided that the brigade had to "probe forward" to May-sur-Orne.[22] Foulkes explained the necessity of sending the Black Watch to maintain contact with the enemy "so that a larger plan may be successfully accomplished."[23] No armoured support was available.

Lieut.-Colonel Mitchell, understandably suspicious, decided to approach the village with considerable caution. The ground between St. Martin and May had already cost the brigade far too many casualties. He ordered Major Tom Anyon, an energetic young Black Watch officer who had come up from the reinforcement unit on July 27, to take his company to the edge of May-sur-Orne.[24] A Company proceeded carefully. D Company, which followed Anyon's men down the road, maintained a good interval and did not bunch up. The other two companies secured flank positions. Anyon's company took about fifty men into action; the rest were left out of battle.[25]

There was no reaction from the enemy until A Company reached the outskirts of May, then "Jerry started plastering them . . . as fast as he could load."[26] The Black Watch went to ground, and the FOO called for artillery support. Anyon's men were seeking cover in the shallow ditch when a German tank rumbled down the road lacing the ditch with machine-gun fire. There were no Canadian tanks available and no anti-tank gun fire. Anyon was killed along with one of his platoon commanders and three ORs; a dozen men were wounded and an equal number taken prisoner.[27] The German mortar and artillery fire directed from May and the high slope on the west side of the Orne placed a curtain of steel around A Company and effectively pinned D Company down. Battalion headquarters, which had begun to

Burnt-out Canadian Sherman tanks west of Tilly-la-Campagne, photographed in 1946. CFJIC

move forward, was also hit by mortar fire, killing the COs' signaller and Major Edwin Bennett, the support company commander. Bennett, a nephew of former Canadian Prime Minister R. B. Bennett,[28] had played a vital role in organizing the remnants of the battalion on July 25. His death was a heavy blow to the battalion.

The Black Watch withdrew to St. André under fire, and the two Maisonneuve companies took up position on the edge of St. Martin. The Maisies were then ordered forward. They found they could get patrols to the outskirts of May, but anything that looked like a larger effort was deluged with fire.[29] Ironically, the gods of war struck the regiment its hardest blow that day, not on the battlefield but in the apparent safety of St. André when a concentration of artillery fire killed nine men and wounded twenty-one who had been lined up for a hot meal.[30]

The struggle for control of Tilly-la-Campagne, Verrières Ridge, and May-sur-Orne now became part of a much larger operation. Simonds had hoped to secure the ridge before launching Operation "Totalize," but with the Americans racing into the heart of France and British Second Army (Operation "Bluecoat") advancing west of the Orne, an advance down the Falaise road could not be delayed. Simonds had been genuinely surprised by the difficulties his infantry battalions had encountered in July. He was determined to make "Totalize" a success and leave nothing to chance. The great lessons of "Goodwood-Atlantic" and "Spring" seemed to be the need to break through the German defences with both infantry and armour. Many knew this,[31] but Simonds did something about it. In his instructions to his divisional commanders, he explained: "The infantry accompanying the armour to first objectives in Phase One must go straight through with the armour. Arrangement has been made for about thirty stripped 'Priest' self-propelled guns to be available to each of the infantry divisions. . . . The balance of personnel required to be carried through to the first or any intermediate objectives must be mounted under divisional arrangements. The essentials are that the infantry shall be carried in bullet and splinter-proof vehicles to their actual objectives . . ."[32]

This was not the only innovation. Simonds decided to dispense with a preliminary artillery bombardment and to rely on a night attack by Bomber Command to lead the way to the first objectives. The advance would start while Bomber Command was still at work on the flanks. The artillery would begin its tasks after the armoured columns crossed the start line. Once begun the artillery barrage would reach an unbelievable level of intensity; 360 field and medium guns were to fire sixty thousand shells in the first hour of attack. Artificial moonlight would again be tried, and Bofors guns, firing orange tracer, would also assist the formations in keeping direction.

The attack would take place on either side of the Caen-Falaise road. To the left, a brigade of 51st (Highland) Division and 33rd British Armoured Brigade would ride south, bypassing Tilly, to capture the Cranmesnil spur. Its remaining infantry brigades would mop up, taking Tilly, La Hogue, and Secqueville. To the right 2nd Canadian Armoured Brigade, with 4th Infantry Brigade and 8th Recce Regiment mounted on "unfrocked Priests" (Kangaroos) and a miscellany of other bulletproof vehicles would charge through Rocquancourt to capture the high ground at Bretteville-sur-Laize. Sixth Brigade, on foot, would be responsible for May-sur-Orne, Fontenay, and mopping up in Rocquancourt. This was Phase I, the cracking of the main defensive line.

When "Totalize" was originally planned, the second phase of the attack involved an assault by 4th Canadian Armoured Division and 3rd Canadian Infantry Division to break through a second line of German defences, Hautsmesnil–St. Sylvain, immediately beyond the first objectives. Simonds planned to launch this phase sometime on the second day, but only after the Flying Fortresses of the U.S. Army Air Force, plus all available medium bombers, had attacked this second line of enemy defences. In the final stage 1st Polish and 4th Canadian Armoured Divisions were to exploit south to either side of Falaise.[33]

The Germans forced revisions in this plan by withdrawing most of their armour from the eastern sector to fulfill Hitler's wild scheme to cut off the Americans at Avranches. By August 4, 89th Infantry Division, freshly arrived from northern France, had relieved 1st SS Panzer Division. First SS Panzer Division had left two companies of self-propelled anti-tank guns to stiffen resistance, and 89th Division had its own force of self-propelled guns as well as divisional anti-tank guns including 88s.

Though stronger in infantry than the two divisions it was replacing, 89th Division could not readily adopt the kind of defensive scheme based on small, mobile battle groups used by the SS. May-sur-Orne, Verrières Ridge, Tilly-la-Campagne, and La Hogue were strongly posted with two battalions in reserve to protect the rearward artillery and mortar areas which were crucial to defending the gaps. In addition to the divisional artillery of 89th and 12th SS, two heavy artillery battalions with 120mm and 140mm howitzers, and a *Nebelwerfer* regiment with the dreaded six-barrelled mortar projectors were positioned in a semicircle behind the front line.[34]

At eleven o'clock on the night of August 7, the sky over the battlefield was filled with the noise of Bomber Command's squadrons. Few of the enemy's defensive positions were actually hit, but as the farthest targets were bombed, the armoured columns set off due south. It was a night of confusion, lost direction, and growing disorganization; only one battalion, the

Clair Tizon. The village is just north of the crossroads in the center of the photograph, taken on July 25, 1944. The crossroads and Laize River are at the bottom of a valley. LCMSDS

Royal Regiment of Canada, actually reached its objective during the night.[35] It was not until late morning that Phase I of the plan was more or less complete.

Sixth Brigade found that the bombers had not crushed resistance in May-sur-Orne or Fontenay. Only in Rocquancourt, which was on 4th Brigade's main axis of advance and had accordingly been included in the initial artillery programme, was quick success obtained. Here the South Saskatchewan Regiment, which had suffered so heavily in its previous assault on Verrières Ridge, "leaned into the barrage" and was in among the defenders before they had recovered.[36]

For the Camerons in Fontenay and the Fusiliers Mont Royal trying to reach May-sur-Orne, it was a long and bloody night. Daylight brought no relief, and continued enemy possession of the high ground interfered with the deployment of 4th Canadian Armoured Division. Finally, the South Saskatchewans and a squadron of First Hussars swept across the ridge north of Fontenay, capturing 250 prisoners and forging a link with the Camerons in the village. It then took an assault with flame-throwing Crocodiles to break the enemy hold on May.[37]

Fifth Brigade, which had been held in reserve, began to move south in the late afternoon of August 8. They were forced to wait until the B-17s of the USAAF had completed the bombing that was to open Phase II of Operation "Totalize." On the eastern flank of the battlefield, a number of bombers failed to identify their targets, and both 1st Polish and 3rd Canadian divisions were struck by misplaced concentrations. The bombers failed to locate the battle groups of 12th SS Panzer Division which barred the road to Falaise, but the forward positions of 89th Infantry Division were heavily bombed, including 5th Brigade's objective, Bretteville-sur-Laize.[38]

The Calgary Highlanders and a tank squadron of the First Hussars "advanced over open country fringed by evil-looking woods"[39] towards Bretteville. Sergeant Louis Frechette, with one of his men, succeeded in getting behind the machine-gun post that was holding up the lead company and captured it with a wild rush.[40] The Maisonneuves with B Squadron advanced to Quilly across wheat fields which the artillery had set afire "so that the attack was made dramatically from a flaming desert."[41]

The lead section of A Company came under fire from the edge of the town, but a young private, William Cook, worked his way forward, exchanging bursts of fire with the enemy and then charging the last twenty-five yards, firing his Bren gun from the hip. Cook captured six German soldiers including an officer, allowing his comrades to move on into Bretteville.[42] Bren guns, firing at extreme range from the tops of several houses, were used to

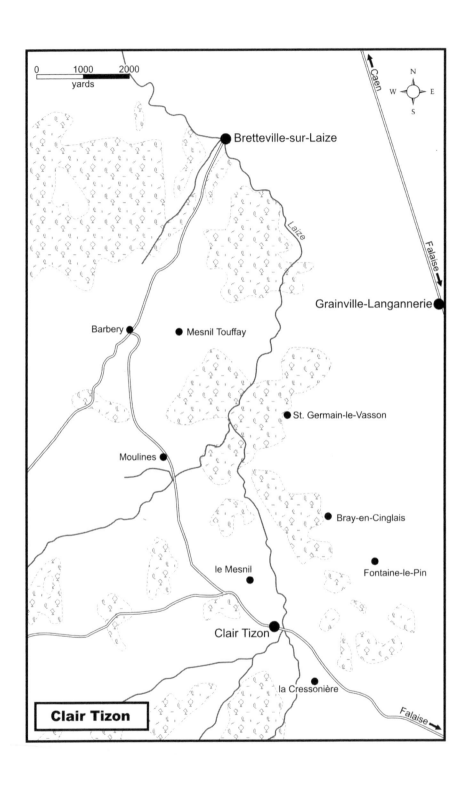

0   1000   2000
yards

N
W · E
S

Caen

Bretteville-sur-Laize

Laize

Falaise

Grainville-Langannerie

Barbery

Mesnil Touffay

St. Germain-le-Vasson

Moulines

Bray-en-Cinglais

le Mesnil

Fontaine-le-Pin

Clair Tizon

la Cressonière

Falaise

Clair Tizon

silence a *Nebelwerfer*. This weapon, called a "moaning minnie" by English-speaking soldiers, was known as *la vache* to French-Canadian soldiers.[43]

The Calgaries, meanwhile, had persuaded a troop of tanks to destroy a large house south of Bretteville which "which sheltered an annoying machine-gun nest."[44] With this accomplished they began to dig in. Lieut.-Colonel MacLaughlan arrived in Bretteville having survived a close call with an anti-tank gun. After surveying the defences he made the extraordinary decision to withdraw the battalion to the high ground north of Bretteville. The four rifle companies marched back up the hill.[45] German artillery observers pounced on this opportunity. The Calgaries who had got through the day with a few minor casualties were caught in the open. Three officers and thirty-one ORs were wounded and eight ORs killed in this episode.[46] Lieutenant Ed Ford, who was briefly evacuated for battle exhaustion, described the scene in an 1987 interview: "We had been taught never to be caught on a forward slope in daylight and at Bretteville we were ordered to come back up over that slope. We were fired upon and we got a lot of casualties and I remember I had to take over from Captain Bill MacQueen to help evacuate the wounded. I stayed with the platoon and was exhausted. I could never understand that; here I was the greenhorn, and I couldn't understand how anybody could order a battalion up over the brow of a hill in broad daylight."[47]

D Company under Captain Wilkes had taken the worst of the shelling, and Wilkes was badly wounded. Captain Ross Ellis "went back through intense fire to carry [him] 250 yards up the hill to safety."[48] Ellis was recommended for the DSO for this action, but nothing came of it. The futility of the whole business was emphasized that night when divisional headquarters ordered the battalion to retake Bretteville the next morning. This was quickly accomplished though A Company had to overcome small groups of German soldiers who had reoccupied the town.[49]

Operation "Totalize" came to end on the night of August 9. Much ground had been gained, and an enemy infantry division had been devastated, but no breakthrough had been achieved, and Falaise was still some distance away. Worst of all, the Canadian and Polish armoured regiments had been severely mauled by the 12th SS. According to Kurt Meyer, Operation "Totalize" had not involved tactical manoeuvre but a "duel between the guns of the Shermans on one side and the Panthers and Tigers on the other."[50] There could only be one outcome in such an encounter, the destruction of all exposed Shermans, but Guy Simonds could not accept such an explanation. He insisted that "Totalize" had been stopped because the two armoured divisions had failed to exploit their opportunities.[51] A new set-piece attack, Operation "Tractable," was scheduled for August 14.

Second Division was not directly involved in "Tractable." Instead Major-General Foulkes was ordered to begin an immediate move south from Bret-teville-sur-Laize to attract enemy attention away from the main thrust which would take place east of the Caen-Falaise road. Fourth Brigade began the attack on the night of the eleventh and moved quickly to the first objectives. The next morning 5th Brigade made a long, dry, dusty march to Mesnil-Aumont.[52] As the brigade dug in, the Calgary Highlanders were warned to be ready for a night march to Clair Tizon, a tiny village astride the River Laize. It would place the battalion behind the German defences on the Falaise road. The Maisonneuves would follow the next day and go through the Calgaries to seize Point 176 near la Chesnaie and Ussy, villages which overlooked Fontaine-le-Pin and Potigny, the main German positions west of Falaise road.[53]

MacLaughlan rejected the "obvious route down the main highway," choosing side tracks close to the River Laize which would take advantage of "every possible bit of cover." The march "was nerve-wracking in the extreme. The route chosen showed on the map as a track through the woods and it was just that." The move was made in the darkness and mist "through deserted woods and empty villages."[54] At Mesnil-Aumont the Calgaries took the first prisoner of the night, a very worried soldier of the 89th Division. The last bound to le Mesnil involved a series of brief fire-fights and the acquisition of more than seventy additional captives.

The battalion had been ordered to rendezvous with a squadron of Hussars tanks at le Mesnil, but the armour had not arrived. Most of August 13 was spent engaging small groups of disorganized German soldiers who found their retreat blocked by the Calgaries. Captain Stuart Moore, the Calgary IO and War Diarist, provided a graphic description of the "queer things" that happened at le Mesnil. "One was the taking over of a Jerry regimental aid post and its medical officer plus casualties. Prisoners simply poured into our cage and looked like a queue going up to the ticket box at a theatre with the IO acting as doorman. Each and every prisoner had an Allied leaflet entitled 'Safe Conduct,' assuring them of good treatment if taken prisoner. . . . They smelled as if a bath had been lacking for weeks and they appeared half-starved as well. Another interesting incident was a young German who jumped out of the bushes into Capt. Mark Tennant's jeep as it passed by and refused to get out."[55]

The Calgaries and the Hussars now set out to capture Clair Tizon and a bridgehead across the River Laize. The companies moved forward carefully, leap-frogging each other. C Company, now commanded by Dalt Heyland, used their battle-drill technique smoothly in taking out an anti-tank gun which "had been giving us hell." By 6:00 P.M. two companies were across the

A patrol from B Company of the Régiment de Maisonneuve passes through the village of Bons-Tassilly, August 16, 1944. LAC

river, but the Germans had begun to recover, and artillery and mortar fire rained down on Clair Tizon and the slopes behind the village.[56]

The Calgaries had performed well, and they knew it. Morale was high, casualties amazingly low. Their carefully organized night move had brought them behind the main German defensive position on the Caen-Falaise road. This action unhinged German resistance on their right flank, assisting 4th Brigade's advance to Tournebu and 53rd (Welsh) Division's movement to Mortainville. Lieut.-Colonel MacLaughlan was awarded the DSO for the achievements of the day.[57]

The Maisonneuves had marched to le Mesnil on the afternoon of the thirteenth. Lieut.-Colonel. Bisiallon had reported that he was 231 riflemen short on the previous day and was functioning with just two companies.[58] Southeast of le Mesnil, the Maisies ran into intense fire from artillery, an 88, and snipers, losing a dozen men including a platoon commander.[59] The battalion needed time to reorganize, but Bisiallon was under pressure to have his men in position by 7:00 P.M. so that they could assist the converging advance on la Chesnaie by the South Saskatchewan Regiment.[60] Unfortunately, the Germans had realized that any further advance down the D6 would unhinge their defence of Falaise. The high ground south of Clair Tizon had been heavily reinforced.

Major Alexander Dugas, commanding A Company, was given the task of taking his men across the bridge at Clair Tizon and attacking directly up the road overlooked from Point 176.[61] Dugas, a thirty-five year old who spent a good deal of the war in staff appointments, had rejoined the battalion in February 1944. An unlikely soldier, he had proved to be a popular, effective company commander, leading A Company throughout the battles of July and August.[62]

The task Dugas faced was quite impossible in daylight, but he did his duty. Crossing the bridge by himself, he began to bring men forward by twos and threes. Suddenly, heavy artillery fire struck, and an 88 knocked out the supporting tanks. Dugas was mortally wounded. The men of A Company took cover where they could, but losses continued to mount.[63]

Captain Edwin Cavendish, the forward observation officer, was able to maintain contact with 5th Field. Cavendish directed fire on a succession of German positions and as the only officer left reorganized C Company in a defensive position and arranged the evacuation of the wounded.[64] All told, the Maisies lost thirteen men killed and forty-one wounded in the day's action.[65]

In the early hours of the next morning, 6th Brigade, "keeping direction in the dark by compass . . . waded across the river and at 4:00 A.M. went forward behind an artillery barrage."[66] The South Sasks got onto the high ground and were joined by tanks of the Sherbrooke Fusiliers. The Camerons fought most of the morning to secure la Cressonniere. In the early afternoon both battalions withdrew their forward elements as being too close to the targets of the heavy bombers that were scheduled to strike at Fontaine-le-Pin and Bons-Tassilly as part of the main attack, Operation 'Tractable." These precautions proved insufficient; the South Sasks suffered sixty-five casualties due to inaccurate bombing, including forty-five in a company withdrawn to a safer area.[67] Fifth Brigade was not involved in further combat in the Falaise area. Drawn into reserve on the fourteenth, it began to move east in pursuit of the retreating enemy on August 20.

The Battle of Normandy was over.

CHAPTER 6

Pursuit

General Montgomery had begun to plan the pursuit of the defeated German armies before the battle of the Falaise Gap was over. On August 20 he issued a directive which was intended to focus Allied energies on his idea for a "single thrust" by the northern route across the Rhine and on to Berlin. Montgomery's argument that a "force of forty divisions" under his command could end the war in 1944 was not accepted by the Supreme Commander, General Eisenhower, but Ike did give Monty priority for Second British Army's advance to Brussels and Antwerp. First Canadian Army was assigned the less glamorous task of cleaning up the left flank, along the Channel Coast. General Crerar was instructed "to advance to the Seine . . . cross the river and operate to clean the Havre peninsula." The port of le Havre was to be captured intact if possible, as was Dieppe. "I have no doubt," Montgomery wrote, "that the 2nd Canadian Division will deal very suitably with Dieppe."[1]

Crerar in turn issued orders to I British Corps to move along the coast and then operate against le Havre. II Canadian Corps was to arrive at the Seine near Rouen and then advance with 2nd Division vectored on Dieppe. Fifth Brigade was to lead the division northwards. The brigade which set out for the Seine was a very different force than the one that had landed in Normandy five weeks earlier. Casualties had devastated the ranks of the infantry battalions, and the losses of officers had been proportionately heavy. Overall, the Allies had suffered two hundred thousand casualties in Normandy, 75 percent of them among the American, British, and Canadian infantry battalions which made up less than 15 percent of the total troops in the bridgehead. In late August the supply of reinforcements and returned wounded had dried up, and almost all Canadian and British battalions were operating at half strength.[2]

Physical casualties are not the only measure of the impact of battle. Thousands of Allied soldiers had been unable to withstand the stress of combat and had been evacuated for "battle exhaustion" during July and August. Second Division had experienced more than five hundred such casualties in July and an equal number in August.[3] Indeed, the division's exhaustion ratio, the relationship between stress casualties and all non-fatal casualties, was

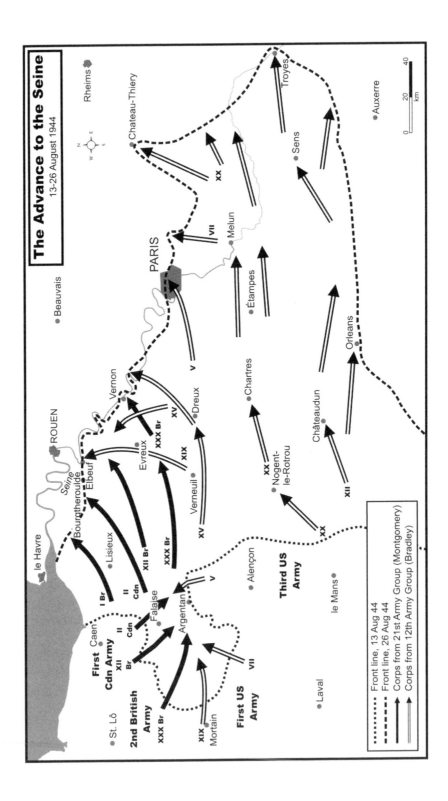

The Advance to the Seine

13-26 August 1944

Rheims

Chateau-Thiery

Troyes

Sens

Melun

VII

XX

Étampes

PARIS

Orleans

Beauvais

Auxerre

Vernon

V

Dreux

XV

XXX Br

XIX

Chartres

Châteaudun

ROUEN

Evreux

Elbeuf

Bourgtheroulde

Seine

Verneuil

XV

Nogent-le-Rotrou

XX

XII

le Havre

XXX Br

XII Br

II Cdn

Lisieux

St. Lô

Caen

XII Br

II Cdn

First Cdn Army

2nd British Army

I Br

Falaise

Argentan

V

XX

Third US Army

Alençon

le Mans

XXX Br

XIX

VII

Mortain

First US Army

Laval

0   20   40
km

	Front line, 13 Aug 44
	Front line, 26 Aug 44
	Corps from 21st Army Group (Montgomery)
	Corps from 12th Army Group (Bradley)

Bourgtheroulde. Lieutenant-Colonel Mitchel brought his battalion through to the northeast end of the town and attacked the German defenders from behind. Photograph taken on August 25, 1944. LCMSDS

thought to be exceptionally high and prompted General Crerar to order an inquiry into the reasons for the loss of such large numbers of men.

Dr. Burdett McNeel, the corps psychiatrist who undertook the study,[4] tried to obtain accurate medical statistics and conducted interviews with Regimental Medical Officers and unit commanders. A particularly careful investigation of 5th Brigade was conducted.[5] Not surprisingly, the Black Watch had the most cases in the division. But this was just one facet of the catastrophe that had scarred the regiment in July, and the ratio of exhaustion cases was about average. The Régiment de Maisonneuve had the highest ratio in the division, but McNeel learned that it continued to function as an effective unit with good morale. The Calgary Highlanders had the highest total casualties in the division. Exhaustion appeared high in absolute numbers but their ratio was not one of the highest. McNeel concluded that heavy stress casualties were an inevitable by-product of the kind of warfare the division had been engaged in; by themselves they told little about the morale or leadership of the battalion.[6]

Fifth Brigade began the pursuit[*] in remarkably good form. The Black Watch, who had been out of battle since August 5, led off and within two days had established a bridgehead over the River Touques. Sixth Brigade then moved through, occupying Orbec after the divisional recce regiment had surprised the defenders by attacking from the north.[7]

Second Division turned north to Thieberville and encountered enemy resistance which caused casualties and imposed delays. The Fusiliers Mont Royal ran into trouble in the village of St. Germain-la-Campagne. The Calgaries, who had themselves been "knocked about by heavy mortar and shell-fire, including 88s," in the centre of Orbec were ordered to assist and MacLaughlan staged a four-company attack which broke German resistance.[8]

The next day the Black Watch led off and were able to move quickly, meeting no opposition. The Calgaries prepared to follow one hour later, but as they crossed the start line in St. Germain, the column of marching troops was fired on by a heavy gun. The sound of tanks led the men to break for the houses on either side of the street while PIAT parties were organized to hunt the enemy vehicles. The artillery "rep," Captain Walter Newman, moved

---

[*] The retreat of the German Fifth Panzer Army was conducted with 86th Corps on the right, or Channel, flank and 1st SS Panzer Corps on the left. Second Division was pursuing elements of the 2nd SS Panzer Division as well as battle groups and stragglers from divisions which had been destroyed in the pocket. 2 Div. Intelligence Summaries, Aug. 20–Aug. 30, LAC.

Lieutenant-Colonel Frank M. Mitchell. LCMSDS

around the "left side of the Cathedral and brought PIAT fire to bear on two enemy half trucks loaded with mines." Stuart Moore completed the story in his War Diary entry. "Orders finally came down to move and at the same time we were promptly told off and reminded that armoured fighting vehicles were not tanks. We stuck to our story that enemy tanks had been in the area—later in the day we found out that the GOC 2 Div had personally been shown a deserted Panther tank near St. Germain . . ."[9]

The twenty-fourth was a day of steady progress, and on the twenty-fifth, the Black Watch were ordered to secure the bridges at Brionne on the River Risle. The Calgary War Diarist recorded the mood of those two days: "We were greeted by a grand presentation of the French people in every town and village as we passed through and were showered with food and drink. . . . Four German prisoners were taken, including two SS men; one is from the 1 SS Pz (Recce) Regiment and this brings our list of SS for the week to representatives of 1, 2, 3, 7, 9, 12 SS Divisions. They are a hateful, arrogant bunch of heartless humanity and they are given no consideration when they are taken by us. The usual procedure is to have them dig slit trenches (for us) exactly to their own measurements."[10]

The Maisonneuves were greeted with special fervour in the villages of the Seine valley. In a letter to his family, acting Lieut.-Colonel Julien Bibeau wrote: "La réception qui nous fut faite est indescriptible. Tout le monde était réuni sur la grande place nous attendant, les cloches de l'église sonnaient a toute volée. Nous avons comblés de fleurs, de vin . . ."[11]

It had rained on the twenty-fourth, but the next day "was perfectly beautiful with bright sunshine and warm wind." The Black Watch occupied Brionne, leaving the rest of the brigade just west of the town around a village named St. Cyr de Salerne. Shortly before midnight the sky above the village was illuminated by a ring of parachute flares. The Calgaries, who were scheduled to move out and lead the next stage of the advance, were caught in the open waiting to mount the trucks. The Luftwaffe attacked in two waves, and the Calgary casualties were appalling: fifteen dead and seventy-two wounded, the worst day for the regiment since Tilly-la-Campagne.[12]

The Maisonneuves were on the edge of the bomb pattern and suffered just fourteen casualties, but Lieut.-Colonel Bibeau and his intelligence officer, Lieutenant Marcel Dussault, were captured by German stragglers. They had been en route to a meeting with the brigadier and had taken cover when the bombs started falling. Hitting the ditch, Bibeau found himself facing the muzzle of a rifle. The second wave of German bombers saved Bibeau and Dussault, for in the confusion, they were able to escape. They reached the Black Watch lines and took a patrol back to the spot. Bibeau's jeep—maps and all—was recovered intact.[13]

The plight of the Calgaries meant that the Black Watch would have to resume the lead. Brigadier Megill arranged for additional trucks from Royal Canadian Army Service Corps, and Lieut.-Colonel Mitchell organized the battalion into four battle groups for the advance. The carrier platoon led the column, followed by a squadron of Sherbrooke Fusilier tanks, then came the four rifle companies each with its own share of anti-tank guns, mortars, and engineers. Mitchell rode with the forward rifle company, and this battle group, together with the carrier platoon and tanks, moved straight through into Bourgtheroulde without meeting any opposition.[14] The rest of the battalion was not as lucky. As the column approached a wood just three kilometres short of the objective, "a German infantry battalion, hidden in the forest, attacked from all sides. For thirty minutes a life-and-death battle was fought with infantrymen and RCASC personnel fighting viciously in the semi-darkness with a determined enemy."[15]

In Bourgtheroulde Lieut.-Colonel Mitchell's contingent was moving through the village when orders to consolidate and establish a firm base were received. The battle group established itself northeast of the main square and began to draw fire from all directions. "The initial phase of the battle in the village resembled an individual battle in which every man carried on his own private war, firing in any direction he heard shots coming from, taking his own prisoners and not knowing in the confusion where to send them."[16] As the other companies entered the village, they came under fire from snipers and a 75mm anti-tank gun which fired on the column at point-blank range. Mitchell decided that it would be impossible to coordinate what was becoming an intense and highly confused battle unless he could concentrate the battalion. He ordered the three companies held up on the southern edge of the village to join him.[17]

Lieutenant William Shea, the battalion intelligence officer, described the events in a 1944 interview: "The rear companies began running the gauntlet of the gun through the centre of the square. About every seventh or eighth vehicle the gun would fire and often would catch a vehicle. Considerable casualties were suffered. The CO as they came rushing along after having beaten the 7.5 gun coolly directed them to their positions despite the MG fire coming on the road from the front and the mortaring and shelling. After 'C' Coy got through it moved to the right flank and 'B' and 'D' Coys went left at which time the gun, being outflanked, withdrew. 'A' Coy still remained ahead near the road. Once through, the other Coys cleared back into the centre of town while the carriers and tanks remained forward as a screen. The effect of the battalion clearing from the NE increased immeasurably the element of surprise, for the enemy was not really expecting an attack that night and were certainly not prepared for it to come from the

Lieutenant-Colonel Julien Bibeau. LAC

NE. Their weapons were turned in the opposite direction. The extent of surprise is shown by the fact that the column ran into an enemy supply vehicle moving through the town in the opposite direction. In addition, an officer and corporal on a motorcycle went by and were taken prisoner or killed. The officer had a marked map showing the location of his battalion HQ and of the gun positions around Bourgtheroulde. Twelve of these gun positions were spotted from this map and were engaged immediately through the wireless of a FOO from a medium regiment. A counterattack on 'C' Coy occurred during the afternoon when about 50 enemy moved in from the N.W. Our tanks fired on them and drove them into 'C' Coy's position. . . . They were dealt with by 'C' Coy at the cost of one casualty. There were actually only two definite and serious counterattacks. All day however, the battalion was heavily engaged with fire from mortars and 88 mm and there was severe shelling on the church and town square."[18]

The Black Watch had run into a significant blocking force of German troops who fortunately had not had time to fully organize their defences. Mitchell's decision to regroup his men outside of the village and attack back into the objective was a bold move which, as he explained, was "justified by the surprise achieved."[19] The battalion had, however, taken serious losses in the day's battle—fifteen killed and thirty-six wounded, not counting casualties in the RCASC transport companies and the RCE pioneer platoon, which had both suffered heavily.[20] The Maisonneuves reached the outskirts of Bourgtheroulde in the afternoon while the fighting in the village still raged. Bibeau mounted a small-scale set-piece attack with an artillery barrage and tank support and quickly cleared out the last area of German resistance on the high ground east of the village.[21]

While the Black Watch was waging its unusual battle in Bourgtheroulde, 3rd and 4th Canadian Divisions had reached the Seine. A platoon of Lincoln and Welland Regiment (4th Division) had gotten across the river, and the battalion quickly expanded the bridgehead. General Crerar was understandably pleased, and he issued new orders on the twenty-sixth that boldly stated, "the enemy no longer has the troops to hold any strong positions—or to hold any positions for any length of time if it is aggressively outflanked or attacked. Speed of action and forcible tactics are therefore required from commanders at every level in First Canadian Army. We must drive ahead with utmost energy. Any tendency to be slow or 'sticky' on the part of subordinate commanders should be quickly and positively eliminated."[22]

Simonds and Foulkes seemed to have shared this view,[23] and understrength units of 4th and 6th Brigades were sent forward into a heavily wooded area known as the Foret de la Londe on the assumption that "it would probably be a non-tactical move and that no, or very few, enemy would be encountered."[24] This view was terribly wrong, but what was worse was that Major-General Foulkes persisted in pressing attacks after it was clear that the division had met significant resistance. Casualties in 4th and 6th Brigades mounted hourly, and on the night of the twenty-ninth, the Calgaries were brought forward to provide a firm base for yet more attacks. Lieutenant Stuart Moore's description of events on August 29 suggests something of the nature of the struggle in the forest:

> Today has been a nightmare for the battalion in our hazardous position in the Foret de la Londe. All day long we were subjected to heavy MG, rifle, Schmeiser fire and to continuous harassing long range shellfire interspersed with 88 from the village of le Chenaie. We were dug in on the reverse slope of the high feature west of le Chenaie and had little protection from the type of fire that was directed at us.
>
> Six prisoners were taken and strangely there were only from ersatz battalions. The fire that rained on us certainly couldn't have come from this bunch of scruff because they are certainly not the type. The day was probably the most hectic one the Bn has had, bar none, and this includes Tilly la Campagne and St. André sur Orne. The fire was no heavier than any time before, but was certainly more constant.
>
> During the day the 6th Bde on our right flank had a very bad time as well as ourselves and finally at 1800 hours the SSR misinterpreted an order and withdrew from their vital position. Shortly afterwards the Camerons followed suit and it took considerable trouble and worry to get these two battalions back into position. In the evening the CO. was called toth Brigade and was greeted with the excellent and very welcome news that 5 Bde was to pull out . . .
>
> We moved by transport to a new and very much quieter area near Elbeuf. It was a wonderful relief and also a terrific shock to find our casualties for the day from the shelling totalled 43 ORs and 3 officers.[25]

Two brigades of 2nd Canadian Infantry Division had been decimated during the three-day battle in the Foret de la Londe, suffering 577 casualties. They had come up against a well-organized enemy blocking force which was under orders to buy time for the units, struggling under air attack, to get across the Seine. The 331st Infantry Division, reinforced with a battle group from 6th Paratroop Division and elements of 2nd SS Panzer Division, had fulfilled their mission. But what was the mission of 2nd Canadian Division?

Rouen Cathedral, August 30, 1944. LAC

With both 3rd and 4th Division across the Seine on the twenty-seventh, the decisions to order 2nd Division to continue fighting a costly infantry action for three more days made no military sense. Given the serious manpower shortages in 2nd Division before the battle, the further wasting of five of its infantry regiments seems especially difficult to understand.

The next morning 5th Brigade was ordered to cross the Seine at Elbeuf and proceed to the staging area for Operation "Fusillade," the capture of Dieppe. The columns moved quickly through Rouen, where cheering crowds had emerged from the ruins. The brigade War Diarist reported that there "was considerable evidence here of the successful efforts of the Air Force to destroy both the German escape routes and bridges, as well as his transport. Fortunately the beautiful churches and buildings of the town had not been badly damaged and particularly the magnificent cathedral was an impressive sight."[26] Loaded in vehicles, the brigade moved quickly north. Captain Mark Tennant of the Calgary Highlanders, who had earned a notable reputation in the battalion for his handling of the carrier platoon, was one of the few to encounter any German resistance. Tennant, known as the "Green Hornet," was fired upon as he led his recce party into a farm yard. His men quickly overcame this resistance, taking ten prisoners. When a truck loaded with German soldiers "dashed madly away from the scene of the fracas," Tennant and his crew set off in pursuit and succeeded in shooting out a tire, causing the truck to crash. The recce party then took on a tank which was "shelling the crossroads at Cote." The tank "blew itself up," and the crew took off.[27]

As the brigade settled in for the night, the 8th Recce Regiment (14th Hussars) pressed on towards Dieppe, and at 7:30 A.M. Major D. F. S. Butt-Francis, who had been wounded in the 1942 raid, led his squadron into a town which erupted in a spontaneous demonstration of joy. The Germans, after destroying the harbour, had left for their new defensive line on the Somme. The determination of 8th Recce Regiment to reach Dieppe paid enormous dividends, for they were able to report the city clear just in time to prevent RAF Bomber Command, whose planes were already in the air, from blasting the town.[28]

Fifth Brigade now began its longest period of rest since entering France. Given the condition of the battalions, the five days were largely spent absorbing replacements and reorganizing companies and platoons, but there was time to take part in celebrations of Dieppe's liberation and the return of the Canadians. No soldier who participated in the parade could forget the thrill "of coming round the Z-bend in the road in Dieppe and being greeted by

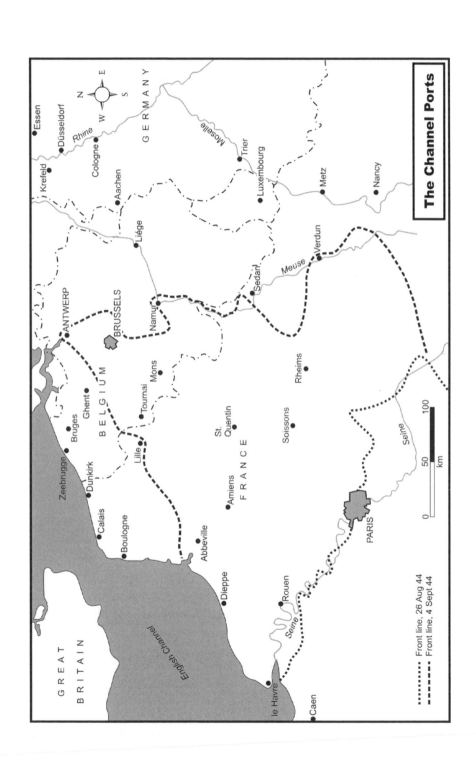

The Channel Ports

GREAT BRITAIN

English Channel

GERMANY

BELGIUM

FRANCE

Essen
Düsseldorf
Krefeld
Cologne
Aachen
Liége
ANTWERP
BRUSSELS
Namur
Mons
Tournai
Ghent
Bruges
Zeebrugge
Dunkirk
Lille
Calais
Boulogne
Abbeville
Dieppe
Caen
le Havre
Rouen
Amiens
St. Quentin
Soissons
Rheims
Sedan
Verdun
Meuse
Trier
Luxembourg
Metz
Nancy
Moselle
Rhine
Seine
PARIS

N
W E
S

Front line, 26 Aug 44
Front line, 4 Sept 44

0   50   100
km

the sounds of massed Pipes and Drums. Canada Week became an interval of freedom from the agony of war."[29]

The Black Watch received a draft of more than one hundred men and seven new Lieutenants to take over the rifle platoons. Major Ritchie, the 2/iC, was promoted to lieutenant-colonel and given command of the Royal Hamilton Light Infantry. His replacement, Major Alan Stevenson, was a familiar face; he had been wounded crossing the Caen Canal with the battalion. Perhaps the most important change was the appointment of Lieutenant William Shea as intelligence officer. A young lawyer from North Bay with no previous Black Watch connection, Shea, according to Lieut.-Colonel Mitchell, was "a remarkably fine fellow—highly capable. Can see in the dark. Best map reader I ever came across."[30] He became a key figure in the battalion.

The Calgaries had a more substantial rebuilding task before them. After Foret de la Londe they were short 283 men, 30 corporals, 10 sergeants, 1 captain, and 4 majors. Their losses in platoon commanders had also been high, but they had been keeping a surplus of lieutenants in the battalion and were able to use them as replacements. Fortunately, all the company commanders were veterans of the Normandy campaign, and this helped to see the unit through the enormous task of absorbing almost two hundred replacements, more than one quarter of the battalion's normal strength, in one week.[31]

The Maisonneuves would have been delighted to face the Calgaries' problems. On September 2 they were short 272 riflemen, but only seventy replacements were available.[32] This did allow the restoration of a four-company system, but companies had an average strength of sixty. The biggest change for the Maisonneuves was the impact made by the new commanding officer. Lieut.-Colonel Bisiallon had been invalided out of the battalion on August 15, after Clair Tizon. Julien Bibeau became acting CO and was later confirmed in command.

The new CO was a very different character than his predecessor. Bibeau was thirty-six years old in 1944. He had joined the Canadian Officers Training Corp (COTC) while at the University of Montreal and became a lieutenant in the Maisonneuves in 1937. An outgoing, gregarious, bilingual individual, he rose from salesman to assistant sales manager of a large milling company. When war broke out, he immediately went active with the regiment. The long years in England did not dampen Bibeau's enthusiasm, and in 1943 he was promoted to major and sent to a Senior Officers School at Brasenose College, Oxford. Bibeau came third in a class of twenty-six, his fluent English helping him to overcome the barrier that frustrated so many French-Canadian officers in the unilingual world beyond the French-Canadian battalions.[33] The Maisonneuves might be a half-strength battalion which could not be used in the same way as their sister regiments, but Brigadier Megill was

A convoy of vehicles from 2nd Division passes through Rouen to the delight of the liberated citizens of the city. LAC

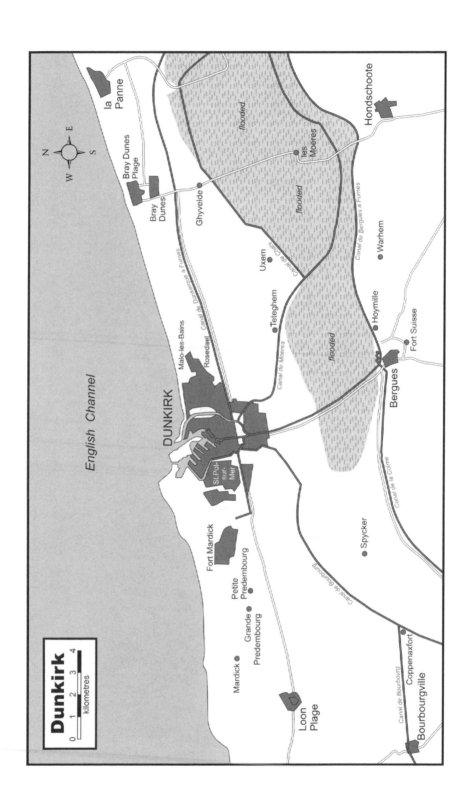

stating the simple truth when he spoke of the determination of the Maison-neuves. They were, he insisted, "one of the [division's] best and most reliable units in battle."[34]

The order to go back to war arrived on September 6. Montgomery, still convinced that the war could be won in 1944 if Eisenhower would give him the resources for "one really powerful and full-blooded thrust toward Berlin," wanted the Canadians to capture the Channel ports. "I want Bou-longe badly," he told Crerar, but he also wanted operations to capture Calais and Dunkirk to begin as soon as possible. Antwerp, liberated on September 6, could not be used until the Germans had been evicted from the banks of the Scheldt estuary which led to the port. Boulonge or any other good Chan-nel port could serve as a supply base until Antwerp was freed.

Third Division was assigned to capture Boulonge and Calais; Second Division was to clear the coastal strip between Dunkirk and the Dutch fron-tier. Fifth Brigade, which had been spared the worst of Foret de la Londe, was to spearhead the division, moving to an assembly area in the Foret d'Eperlecques. The recce regiment, probing ahead, ran into the German positions in Bourbourgville and Gravelines, two villages which appeared to be part of the outer defences of the "fortress" of Dunkirk. Montgomery had not yet decided to avoid Dunkirk, which was to remain in German hands until the end of the war, and Fifth Brigade was ordered to begin the task of liberating the area.[35]

The Black Watch led off, seizing a bridging site south of Bourbourgville, and establishing a base for the advance. There was heavy rain all morning with a high, cold wind. The Germans had flooded much of the area "by blowing the canal banks . . . the ditches were full of water and the ground very spongy. "[36] The Maisonneuves now moved through the Black Watch, securing a canal crossing and advancing to the northeast edge of the town. Captain Pierre Fafard gave the following description of the initial stages of the attack to the divisional historical officer in 1944. "The town of Bour-bourgville is remarkable for having a canal completely around it and because the church is centrally located and all the approaches across this canal can be covered from the market-square in the centre of town. The bridges were all blown by the enemy and a search had to take place for canoes and boats with which to cross . . ."[37] The approach had been difficult due to harassing fire from 75mm and 88mm guns but the 5th Field Regiment was soon ready to deal with this, and the Maisonneuves entered the town using boats sup-plied by the eager citizens, by swimming or, in the case of Major Ostiguy's C Company, by crossing over an improvised plank footbridge.

The German defenders withdrew only under intense pressure, and they seemed determined to hold the north end of town. The railway station was strongly defended with two 20mm anti-aircraft guns deployed as anti-infantry weapons. No one was eager to face this barrage until Sergeant J. P. Leblanc dashed into the centre of the street, lay down, and provided enough covering fire to silence the guns and get his men moving forward.[38] The town was not finally freed until several hours before dawn, but this did not stop the population from beginning to celebrate liberation in the parts of the town which were clear.

While the Maisonneuves conducted their house-by-house clearance of Bourbourgville, the Calgaries were attempting to attack the railway station at the north end of the town. Their approach route from the west was over an open road with no cover, and they came under non-stop shell fire. Megill ordered them to hold where they were, wait for the Maisonneuves to finish their work, then move north to Loon Plage the next morning. They were underway shortly after first light. Les Planches, a handful of houses halfway to the objective, was taken quickly by the lead company under Major Dalt Heyland, but when the next "bite," a road junction, was reached, enemy artillery pounded the area. It was difficult to dig in and impossible to move forward. D Company moved around the flank to approach Loon Plage from the west, but they were halted at a farm five hundred yards outside the village. The Calgaries were under enormous pressure and taking heavy casualties. Their War Diary reports, with some emotion, that "The Régiment de Maisonneuve were then ordered to assist us moving three companies northwards along the road parallel to our axis. . . . They took five hours to even get to a point 1500 metres up the road . . . we had to continue without help."[39]

The Maisies had started north quickly enough, but A Company's lead platoon, commanded by Lieutenant Leclerc, had gone less than half a mile when it ran into a carefully concealed German position. The platoon got into some farm buildings, with carefully controlled fire and movement, and an all-around defensive position was created. The company commander, Major Alexander Angers, was wounded along with a dozen others. Leclerc's group was surrounded, unable to move without attracting artillery and direct fire. Fifth Field Regiment was contacted and responded quickly bringing down a barrage and allowing the Maisonneuves to withdraw from the burning buildings in which they had taken cover.[40]

The Maisonneuves, like the Calgaries, were trying to invest the Dunkirk perimeter against formidable odds. The enemy had ample supplies of artillery shells—enough, as it turned out, to defend Dunkirk till the war was over—good observation of all daylight movement, and an intimate knowledge of the terrain. The infantry battalions, without any armour or air support and without a clear mission, were pressing forward without taking time

Troops of 2nd Division march triumphantly into Dieppe, September 1944. LAC

for reconnaissance and without making full use of intelligence from the French resistance forces in the area.

The Black Watch on the right flank of the brigade were also attempting to carry out an attack without adequate support. Major Alex Pinkham's C Company was teamed up with a troop of armoured cars from 8th Recce Regiment. Their objective, Coppenaxfort, lay some five thousand metres east of Bourbourgville along a single straight and elevated road on the bank of a canal. No trees, no shrubbery, no cover of any kind existed. Because of the ground the company could only move in single file taking care to space out considerably. The first armoured car remained about one hundred yards behind the lead troops, but it was soon knocked out by a hidden anti-tank gun firing from long range. Mortars and field guns struck at the infantry who tried to dig in. Fifth Field Regiment was short of ammunition and fully committed to the Calgaries and Maisonneuves, so the Black Watch had to wait for dark to withdraw and regroup. The next morning a single platoon of C company, assisted by one armoured car, rushed the bridge leading into the town only to discover that the Germans had withdrawn.[41]

These gains meant little to 5th Brigade, for they now found themselves occupying positions the Germans had carefully surveyed as artillery targets. Throughout the following week the brigade used fighting patrols to harass the enemy and battalion attacks to compress the perimeter. The Black Watch captured Spycker on September 11 in a furious battle which engaged two RHC companies. Spycker was evidently a sensitive spot, for the Germans counterattacked in strength, inflicting considerable casualties. Lieutenant Joe Nixon and his scout platoon played a crucial role in stopping the counterattack. Nixon personally handled a PIAT gun while his sniper-scouts took a heavy toll of the enemy infantry. One sniper, Private Frank de Lutio, won the Military Medal for his efforts that day, but the cost of holding the village was too high, and Megill withdrew the Black Watch on the night of September 13.[42]

The Maisonneuves took over the area and attempted to maintain some degree of pressure. Division was pressing brigade for information, but patrols could be costly. Lieutenant Charles Forbes of the Maisonneuves dealt with one request by donning a priest's cassock and beret. He walked up to and through the German position and returned with a full report.[43] Major Ostiguy, ever aggressive, brought elements of his C Company to within two hundred yards of the German defensive perimeter without being seen and was able to plot the enemy positions, which were harried with Bren and rifle fire when night fell. The Maisonneuves also acquired the services of a troop of light anti-aircraft guns and tried them out as super-heavy machine guns.[44]

The Calgaries had it much easier. They occupied Loon Plage on September 9 and used it as a base for patrols to probe the perimeter. Battalion headquarters was besieged by the resistance forces, including two rifle-toting, teenage boys who arrived with three German prisoners. The War Diary also describes a cocktail party at Monsieur Le Maire's home which MacLaughlan and Ellis attended. "Here they were surrounded by bevies of beautiful girls and glasses of champagne plus of all things a large, beautiful bouquet of fresh flowers."[45]

Reinforcements, more than two hundred of them, arrived while the battalion was at Loon Plage, and each company was brought up to full strength. Major Vern Stott, who had been wounded in Operation "Spring," arrived to take up his post as 2/iC of the battalion and immediately made his presence felt. Stott had always believed that a soldier's life should be as comfortable as possible, and both officers and men benefited from his energy and enterprise.[46] Ten days later Stott left to take command of the South Saskatchewan Regiment.

"Market Garden," Montgomery's great September gamble, required the support of all available elements of Second British Army. He therefore assigned the holding operation at Antwerp to First Canadian Army. On September 15 the Dunkirk perimeter was handed over, and the 2nd Canadian Division began its move to Antwerp.

The Belgian White Brigade had played a crucial role in securing Antwerp and its vital port for the Allies. Eugene Colson, a merchant navy officer and resistance leader, had led his men into the dock area and, with the arrival of the British, urged an assault on Merxem, the industrial suburb east of the docks and north of the Albert Canal. The British had no orders to move north from Antwerp, and the best they would attempt was a three-company crossing of the Albert Canal which was aborted after suffering 150 casualties.[47] The next day, September 6, the bulk of the British forces left Antwerp in preparation for Montgomery's attempt to bounce the Rhine. The 53rd Welsh Division was left temporarily in the city with the task of defending the docks.

Antwerp was a strange place in September 1944. The civilian population was caught up in the euphoria of liberation and seemed almost oblivious to the presence of the Germans in the northern suburbs of the city. Some civilians went about their affairs to the point of crossing back and forth over the Albert Canal from the German to the Allied sector. The Belgian resistance, on the other hand, was active in attempting to extend the dock area perimeter. The Essex Scottish and the Royal Hamilton Light Infantry took over the defences, and on the night of September 20, the Essex were hit hard by a German attack which was apparently intended to seize and destroy a railway bridge. Heavy fighting raged through the night, but the enemy was beaten off.[48]

A signpost welcomes a soldier from 2nd Division back to Dieppe. LAC

The area around the 4th Brigade positions had been flooded by the Germans until White Brigade patrols supported by Canadian artillery secured the sluice gates, allowing the tidal water to be drained. The Royal Hamilton Light Infantry moved its lines forward to protect this site on September 22.[49] From that date until October 2, no major initiative was taken by either side.

Fifth Brigade made the trek to Antwerp on September 18. The ride across the newly liberated Belgian countryside was an exhilarating experience:

> The route laid down . . . was marked throughout by 2 Cdn Inf Div arrows. What a marvellous treat to be able to sit back and enjoy the scenery along the way. Arriving at the Belgian border, it was a relief to know there would be no customs' inspection. We left French soil, some with a sigh, but soon we were engrossed with the beauty of the Belgian countryside. All agreed that the roads were the best that had been seen for a long time. So different was the sight that greeted our eyes, that one almost forgot that we were at war. Beautiful, rolling, lush country could be seen for miles. Arriving at the cities, great was the amazement to see three-lane boulevards, smart modern shops and streetcar networks. Nearing such famous places as Ypres, St. Julien, Passchendaele, Poelcappelle, Calgarians began to experience a certain well-known lump in their throats. The Canadian Battlefield Memorial at St. Julien stands significantly in mute and solemn dedication to our valiant dead. . . . At various points along the way, the entire convoy was showered with gifts of fruit, bread and of course at times with liqueurs. Hand-clasping was just as prominent, a practice as in France, and the familiar 'Cigarette for Papa' slogan greeted us. One very pleasant experience was hearing so many people speaking English. The "pubs" reminded one of some of the ones in England. The sight of beautiful poppies caught the eye of many and the full meaning of Flanders fields became self-explanatory. Considerable attention was paid to the members of the fair sex. With few exceptions the majority of women and young girls were healthy and good looking. From all early reports, it was the general opinion that a reasonably lengthy sojourn in the country would not be too great a hardship on the troops.[50]

Fifth Brigade was given little time to get its bearings in the new area. The 53rd Welsh Division departed before 5th Brigade arrived, leaving no useful information. The brigade made contact with local elements of the resistance and Megill planned to begin sending patrols across the canal. General Foulkes, however, wanted "a more formidable force to go across" because intelligence was (as usual) reporting an enemy withdrawal.[51] The Black Watch were therefore ordered to place a fighting patrol over the canal. If this could be accomplished without provoking strong resistance, the Calgaries were to push three companies across to establish a bridgehead.

The operation did not go well. According to the Brigade War Diary, "the Black Watch fighting patrol was not successful in getting over the canal. They got fourteen men onto the locks, but they were pinned down by machine-gun fire and were eventually withdrawn."[52] Was this a normal mishap or a badly executed operation? Brigadier Megill was uncertain, but when he met Mitchell, the tension between the two men led to an explosion. Mitchell refused to accept any criticism of his battalion.[53] The outcome, if not the details of the encounter, are clear. Mitchell was no longer in command.

In a letter written a month after the event, Mitchell offered an unusual explanation of his behaviour. "I greatly regret," he wrote, "that I found it necessary to take the actions I did on September 22, 1944 but I'm afraid that then when I arrive at a calculated decision, it is providential that it be carried out. I assure you that I have made no mistake other than possibly the method of handling, and I tried to be loyal to both the Regiment and higher authority."[54]

With Mitchell gone, Megill was anxious to obtain a new commanding officer from outside the list of regimental officers. When told that the veteran Black Watch officer Lieut.-Colonel Bruce Ritchie, who had been commanding the Royal Hamilton Light Infantry,[55] would be appointed, Megill protested strongly. He urged Foulkes to place Vern Stott or Denis Whitaker, two proven combat leaders, in command of the Black Watch. Foulkes would not agree, and Ritchie took up his duties the next day.[56]

The incident quickly faded into the background because, on the night of the twenty-second, the Calgary Highlanders got a fighting patrol and then three companies across the canal and quickly established a solid bridgehead. The Calgary success was made possible by the extraordinary coolness and bravery of Sergeant C. K. "Ken" Crockett. A corporal who accompanied Crockett on the patrol gave this account of the night's events shortly afterwards:

On the night of 22 Sep. 44 a party of ten men were picked to cross over the Albert Canal and establish the initial bridgehead on the

North side, through which the remainder of the battalion could move to enlarge the bridgehead for the brigade assault. I was a Bren gunner in this detachment. It was an extremely dark night and although we knew from fire which had come from the North bank during the day that it was strongly held, there was not a sound at the time we prepared to go across. About an hour after midnight, carrying our weapons and extra ammunition, we moved from the company position down to the bank of the canal where a footbridge connected the mainland to a small island about thirty feet out in the canal. Sgt. Crockett crossed to the island alone and then as all remained quiet returned and lead us slowly and carefully out to the island. There was still no sound and signalling us to follow he started across the top of the lock gates between the island and the North shore, a distance of about ninety feet. Feeling our way carefully so as not to make a sound we inched along until Sgt Crockett stopped and sent back word that we were to wait where we were. He had come to a point where the lock gates had been broken away and ahead of him stretched a thin pipe about six inches in diameter. He went along this pipe until he reached the shore where he found a heavy wire barricade blocking his path. Still there was not a sound. Sgt Crockett returned along the pipe and started forward once more, we following. With Cpl Harold's help he lifted the barrier and moved slowly ahead. Almost immediately I heard a sentry challenge him, then the sound of Sgt Crockett's sten gun, followed by enemy machine gun and small arms fire from close range. We all crossed the pipe as quickly as possible and took positions as ordered by Sgt. Crockett. There seemed to be three machine gun positions, very close, firing on us and Sgt Crockett, firing his sten gun from the hip as he walked towards it, silenced the nearest one. He then crawled forward with the PIAT man to a position from which they could fire on the second post with the PIAT. Two bombs silenced it after which, rejoining his detachment, Sgt Crockett directed them onto the third machine gun post. When it was silenced we moved through these positions to make sure they were cleared and were posted by Sgt Crockett in positions forming a small bridgehead and from which we could fire on the enemy ahead of us to assist the remainder of the platoon to cross, followed by the remainder of the company and the battalion. Sgt Crockett, throughout this entire action, remained cool and did not at any time display the slightest hesitation and fear, neither in the deathly silent crossing nor after we reached the north bank and came under intense, enemy machine gun and small arms fire which continued all that night and the following day.[57]

Crockett was recommended for the Victoria Cross (he received the Distinguished Service Medal) for his exploit.

The Maisonneuves followed the Calgaries into the bridgehead, and the advance to Bergen-op-Zoom and the Beveland peninsula began. The pursuit of the German army was over; the enemy had dug in and would fight with all its energy to postpone the opening of the port of Antwerp. The Canadians now forced a new battle, every bit as challenging as Normandy.

CHAPTER 7

October

On October 2 Guy Simonds, who had temporarily replaced an ailing Harry Crerar, issued his first directive as acting commander of First Canadian Army. The task of clearing the approaches to Antwerp, the banks of the Scheldt Estuary, was assigned to 2nd and 3rd Canadian Infantry Divisions. Third Division was to attack "Scheldt Fortress South,"[1] which the Canadians called the "Bresken's Pocket," while 2nd Division was to "clear the area north of Antwerp and close the eastern end of the Zuid Beveland Isthmus."[2] After these tasks were accomplished, both infantry divisions would develop operations to clear Beveland and capture "Scheldt Fortress North," Walcheren Island.

Simonds assumed that 2nd and 3rd Divisions could complete their tasks in one or two weeks, and he focused his attention on Operation "Infatuate," the capture of Walcheren Island. He persuaded Bomber Command to "sink" Walcheren by bombing the dykes. With the support of Admiral Ramsay he won approval for two seaborne assaults on the island using 4th Special Service (Royal Marines) Brigade and 4th Commando Brigade. But these elite troops would have to wait until the Canadians had captured the Bresken's Pocket and cleared South Beveland, operations which would take close to five weeks of intense combat.

Fifth Brigade was heavily involved in combat well before Simonds issued the formal orders. After the Calgaries had crossed the Albert Canal, 6th Brigade launched a series of costly and unsuccessful attempts to force the Turnhout Canal.[3] Second Division was temporarily under the control of I British Corps, and it was decided to pass 5th Brigade through the bridgehead across the Turnhout that had been won by 49th (West Riding) Division. To attack west along the north side of the canal was an excellent idea, but the brigade met strong resistance from small battle groups of the 711th and 346th Infantry Divisions supported by armour. The Calgaries again took the lead. Captain W. J. "Bill" Riley, the 5th Field Regiment FOO who normally worked with the battalion, went forward to establish an observation post in a brickworks just three hundred yards from the enemy position. Riley brought

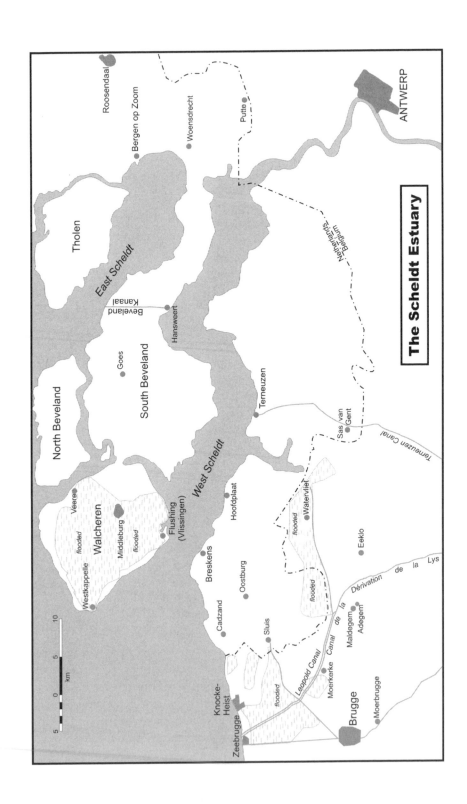

The Scheldt Estuary

Roosendaal

Bergen op Zoom

Woensdrecht

Putte

ANTWERP

Tholen

East Scheldt

North Beveland

South Beveland

Goes

Beveland Kanaal

Hansweert

Terneuzen

Netherlands
Belgium

Walcheren

Veere

Middelburg

Flushing (Vlissingen)

Breskens

Hoofdplaat

flooded

flooded

flooded

Westkappelle

Cadzand

Oostburg

Sluis

Knocke-Heist

Zeebrugge

Brugge

Moerbrugge

Moerkerke

Maldegem

Adegem

Eeklo

Watervliet

flooded

flooded

flooded

flooded

Sas/van Gent

Terneuzen Canal

Derivation de la Lys

Canal de la

Leopold Canal

West Scheldt

km

0   5   10

down carefully observed fire, correcting it as enemy anti-tank guns sniped at him.[4] The Germans were forced to abandon Eindhoven, which the Calgaries quickly occupied.

The Black Watch took over the advance, capturing the village of St. Leonard in a night attack. Lieut.-Colonel Ritchie positioned his four companies along a three-quarter-mile perimeter with the 6-pounders of the anti-tank platoon in forward positions.[5] At four in the morning, the first of a series of counterattacks began. Gordon Bourne, then a lieutenant serving with the anti-tank platoon, described the scene: "Our two flanking companies received a bad mauling but the two centre companies managed to hold out. . . . When dawn broke and the results of the early morning fighting could be seen, it was apparent the German casualties were very heavy. The sprawling bodies that littered the surroundings were mute evidence of the bitterest tussle . . ." Daylight also brought artillery fire and an attempt to move a towed anti-tank gun into position covering the main square. Bourne "grabbed a rifle and killed two of the Jerries before they could bring the gun into position. The others took to their heels."[6] The Calgary Highlanders attacked through the Black Watch and worked systematically to expand the bridgehead, making contact with the Fusiliers Mont Royal on the south side of the canal. The Maisonneuves, who had fought their way forward on the open north flank, took seventy-four prisoners, but their own casualties were high.[7]

The Black Watch were told to plan an attack on Brecht and Lieut.-Colonel Ritchie organized a textbook operation. Ritchie was determined not to move until the start line and the approaches to it were securely held. One of the most serious single problems confronting Allied commanders in Northwest Europe was the tendency of rifle companies to report that they controlled an area when it was simply in range of their light weapons and under observation by the artillery FOO.

The Calgary War Diary for October 1, 1944, describes a typical situation. During the night the Calgaries had beaten off several counterattacks including a wild engagement with a single German tank that "slipped into a pocket," making it impossible to use anti-tank guns "without endangering our own troops." Major Kearns' A Company engaged the tank with PIATs, and it withdrew. The presence of the tank and the fact that the Calgaries were involved in small fire fights all along their front convinced Ritchie that the Calgaries did not control the area, and he insisted that they physically occupy a number of buildings overlooking the startline. MacLaughlan was furious at this implied criticism. The Calgary War Diary records his views that "It became annoyingly evident that the RHC wanted Calgary Highlanders to provide a guaranteed safe approach and passage beyond the start line."[8] This is exactly what Ritchie did want, and he got it. The Calgary forward compa-

Lieutenant-General Guy Simonds with Admiral Bertram Ramsay, October 1944. LAC

nies occupied the buildings until the Watch were in place, then "pulled back to their previous positions."

The attack on Brecht went as planned. The companies moved quickly forward, closely followed by a squadron of Fort Garry tanks. Nighswander had developed a fire plan which integrated a medium regiment and the brigade's heavy mortars with his own field regiment. "Such was the accuracy of the barrage that when the riflemen reached the point where the enemy mortars were sited they found all six of the mortars out of commission and in the area over forty craters from our medium and field artillery shells." The enemy had "put up a determined resistance" within the town, but the Watch, having followed the barrage closely, were in among them quickly taking prisoners and forcing the Germans to evacuate the furthest edge of the town "hurriedly," leaving behind "stacks of ammunition."[9]

The next day Ritchie again demonstrated his determination to take no chances with the battalion placed in his charge. A platoon of D Company was cut off by a German force. "They were in no immediate danger and had suffered no casualties, but Lieut.-Colonel Ritchie laid plans for a full-scale attack. It was necessary to go from house to house to reach them and in conjunction with the infantry our Universal Carriers, equipped with flame throwers were used for the first time, while our 17-pounders fired from the flank upon houses known to be occupied by the enemy. B company consolidated the position and the total result was a 300 yard advance, some minor casualties, eight prisoners, and many enemy dead left on the field."[10]

Ritchie and his battalion took great pride in their conduct of the battles of St. Leonard and Brecht.[11] This was the kind of action they had trained for, and the contrast between these encounters and the kind of hastily improvised battles that they and other 2nd Division units had been forced into previously was obvious to all. But there is a price to pay for tactical success as well as failure; the battalion lost twenty-four killed and ninety-six wounded during the week ending October 4.

While 5th Brigade fought its way west, 4th Brigade occupied Merxem and began to probe towards the divisional objective. Today, the area north of Antwerp is crisscrossed by highways linking the city with new suburbs and towns which were small villages during the war. It is still possible to follow the old road from Antwerp to Bergen-op-Zoom, but some imagination is required to see the countryside as it was in 1944. The area east of the highway was then thickly set with woods. On the left towards the Scheldt estuary, the land was below sea-level with the fields, or polders, protected by dykes. Houses straggled along sections of the main roads, but there were long gaps between each cluster. The Germans had flooded as many of the polders as they could, so movement on the left had to be confined to the raised roads.

Fifth Brigade began to move into this strange landscape ready to take over the advance. Hundreds of German soldiers had surrendered in the final days of October, and now with the canal defences broken, the enemy appeared to be in full retreat. Divisional intelligence reported "definite indications of enemy withdrawal" and noted that prisoners were from a wide variety of units and included many low-category personnel. The main enemy force barring the route forward was thought to be the 70th German Infantry Division, an unusual unit made up of men who suffered from ulcers. This "stomach" division had garrisoned Walcheren Island where an ample supply of milk and soft bread was available. Some of its battalions had been sent to fight along the Antwerp canals, but had been withdrawn to defend Walcheren and Beveland when it proved impossible to hold that line. Divisional intelligence reported that other German troops had apparently fallen back to Bergen-op-Zoom, leaving "outposts which will have to be dealt with in our push forward."[12]

Back at corps headquarters the same optimism prevailed. The Intelligence Summary for October 7 boldly insisted that the enemy had "given up any plan he might have had to stand on the approach to Walcheren."[13] Unfortunately, Allied intelligence had failed to grasp German intentions. On the same day that II Canadian Corps distributed its appreciation, General Gustav von Zangen, commanding fifteenth Army, issued an order which declared that, "the defence of the approaches to Antwerp represents a task which is decisive for the further conduct of the war."[14] Von Zangen did not just offer words, he ordered his army reserve, "Battle Group Chill," including the 6th Parachute Regiment and several battalions of self-propelled guns, to his right flank with orders to bar access to Beveland.

Fifteenth Army was able to switch its reserves to the Antwerp sector as a result of a decision by Field Marshal Montgomery to go over to the defensive on the western side of the Arnhem salient. Montgomery was concerned with a crisis that had developed on his eastern flank and wanted to clear that up before renewing the attack north to the River Maas.[15] He failed to recognize that this would leave 2nd Canadian Division as the only unit between Antwerp and Nijmegen engaged in offensive operations.

Lieut.-General Erich Diestel, who was commanding the mixed bag of divisional fragments defending the area north of Antwerp, described the arrival of the reinforcements when he was interviewed in 1945. "On October 2nd the Canadians attacked north from Merxem and in three days had driven the division's right flank back to Putte, a distance of some 7 kms. . . . There was no regular line to hold at this time, but rather a series of tactical points. . . . The division had lost over 800 men in the battle for the Turnhout and Albert Canals and was in a very tired state. About 7 October, in almost melodramatic-

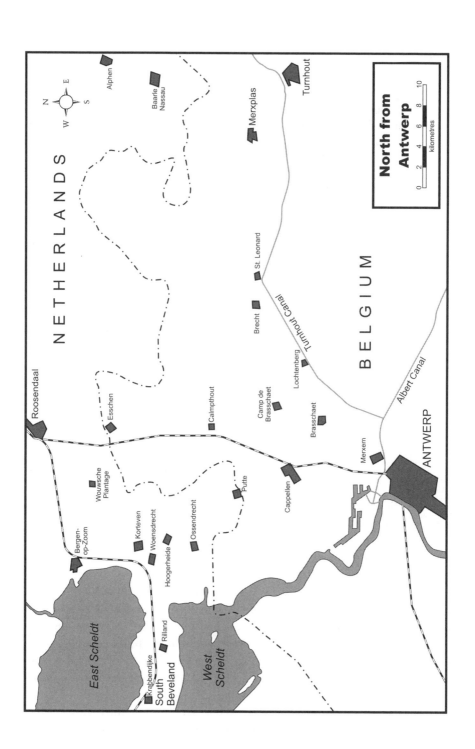

North from Antwerp

kilometres

0 2 4 6 8 10

NETHERLANDS

BELGIUM

ANTWERP

Roosendaal

Alphen

Baarle Nassau

Merxplas

Turnhout

St. Leonard

Brecht

Lochtenberg

Turnhout Canal

Albert Canal

Esschen

Calmpthout

Camp de Brasschaet

Brasschaet

Merxem

Cappellen

Putte

Wouwsche Plantage

Korteven

Woensdrecht

Hoogerheide

Ossendrecht

Bergen-op-Zoom

Krabbendijke

Rilland

South Beveland

East Scheldt

West Scheldt

fashion, aid came in the form of the 15 Army Assault Battalion consisting of about 1000 men from the Army Battle School and the Von der Heydte Parachute Regiment of about 2500 fanatical and eager young parachutists."[16]

The Canadians did not learn of von Zangen's decision until the German reinforcements arrived, but the acting corps commander, Major-General Foulkes, and the acting divisional commander, Brigadier R. H. Keefler, were well aware that the division was running a great risk by moving north with an unprotected eastern flank. They had decided to commit 6th Brigade and most of the one understrength armoured regiment available, the Fort Garry Horse, to that sector.[17] This meant that only two brigades with one squadron of tanks were available to push on to the villages of Ossendrecht, Huijbergen, Hoogerheide, and Woensdrecht.

On the morning of October 7, the Calgary Highlanders took over the lead. They had been briefed to work within an elaborate artillery fire plan that assigned code names to a large number of pre-arranged targets. Instead of relying on a creeping barrage, the company commanders, through the FOO, called down fire and, when satisfied, "simply lifted artillery to other positions and watched results." The Calgaries spent most of the day working forward to Hoogerheide by this method, and with the assistance of tanks. Lieutenant Alex Keller won the Military Cross for his part in one excellent example of infantry-tank cooperation. Emerging from a wooded area, his platoon met intense fire from a shrub-covered rise surrounded by open ground. Keller pinpointed the enemy positions and arranged to have the tanks provide supporting fire. When the Fort Garry troop opened up, Keller "with a terse 'follow me' proceeded at a fast walk straight across the open ground. His platoon, after a short startled pause, quickly followed . . ." Sixteen prisoners were captured without a single Calgary casualty.[18]

The Régiment de Maisonneuve had been ordered to parallel the Calgary advance, securing the village of Huijbergen. There were fewer identifiable targets in their section, and the whole attack broke down fifteen hundred yards short of the objective when the part of C Squadron, Fort Garry Horse assigned to the Maisonneuves, "ran into 88 and 20 mm fire: the infantry went to ground and the attack bogged down, never to get started that day."[19] The night of October 7–8 was a grim one for the Calgaries and Maisonneuves. Heavy shelling and mortar fire was fairly continuous, and patrols reported enemy movement indicating a major build-up in the roads north of Hoogerheide. The Calgaries were especially hard hit by the wounding of Captain Mark Tennant,[20] a superb soldier who had used the battalion's Bren gun carriers as if they were light tanks.

The Maisonneuves attempted to renew their advance the next morning, but they confronted an anti-tank ditch strongly defended by 20mm small-

Men from the scout platoon of the Regiment de Maisonneuve talk about future operations, Ossendrecht, Holland, October 17, 1944. LAC

arms and mortar fire. Lieutenant Charles Forbes, who had a well-earned reputation for daring, led his platoon in a flanking movement but they were
quickly driven to ground. Forbes charged the position by himself, firing his
sten gun and yelling at his men to follow. He personally "rushed two posts,
killed two crew members and captured five more."[21] With this position
cleared the Maisonneuves were able to move forward several hundred yards,
relieving the pressure on the Calgary flank.

The Black Watch moved into position in Hoogerheide, hidden by an early
morning mist. Their task was to move up on either side of the Korteven road
to the junction with the Dool Straat. At 10:30 A.M. the advance began with C
Company inching its way up the left side of the road and D Company the
right. A troop of Fort Garry tanks followed cautiously. Major Alex Popham, a
veteran company commander who had fought in every battle since St. André,
reported that D Company would have to fall back to the start line. Despite the
flexible artillery, the company was taking too many casualties from troops who
were "well dug in, in well-sited positions, and supported by artillery, mortar,
heavy machine guns and scores of snipers."[22] Seventeenth Platoon, under the
command of Lieutenant "Beau" Lewis, actually crossed the Dool Straat and
"had established themselves in three houses in the street when they received
orders to pull back. The withdrawal was well executed and this platoon took
up their new position without incurring any casualties."[23]

Counterattacks began before the withdrawal was complete. "One enemy
self-propelled gun charged down the street firing blindly" but was knocked
out by a Fort Garry tank mounting a 17-pounder.[24] The Black Watch carrier
platoon, with its Bren guns, dealt with a company-size attack, holding fire
"until the enemy was from 50 to 60 yards away and then they opened up
everything they had, killing over fifty."[25] The Germans continued to press
along the Canadian perimeter throughout the afternoon before deciding
that these encounters were far too costly.

Dutch civilians and air reconnaissance had provided fairly detailed information on the arrival of major German reinforcements, and both division
and corps intelligence accepted an estimate of between two thousand and
three thousand troops. Brigadier Keefler reacted to this information by
ordering 4th and 5th Brigades to go over to the defensive and prepare for a
major attack which the army intelligence section, probably on the basis of
Ultra decrypts, had predicted for the night of the eighth.[26]

The German attack began with intermittent mortaring and shelling
which seemed to be designed to cover the infiltration of patrols. Scouts from
both 5th Brigade battalions sent in a steady stream of reports of enemy
movement. The Black Watch captured one group of twenty-four young soldiers. The War Diary notes that they belonged to parachute battalions,

Major-General Charles Foulkes. LAC

ranged in age from twenty to twenty-six, and were "fine physical specimens, keen to fight and with excellent morale." This had not prevented them from advancing into a trap, suggesting that inexperience and overconfidence were also characteristics of the parachutists.[27]

The battle began in earnest around 4:00 A.M. Major Deb Kearns, commanding A Company of the Calgaries, had just requested help to deal with infiltrators when a general attack began. Colonel Nighswander had arranged to have FOOs with each company commander, and for the next three hours, 5th Field Regiment fired a number of pre-arranged tasks, "shooting continually upon targets directed by the companies." In the slit trenches the riflemen fired at anything that moved and drenched the battle zone with Bren guns firing on fixed lines. Shortly before 8:00 A.M. Major Ross Ellis, commanding the Calgary reserve company, launched a limited counterattack of his own. A troop of Fort Garry Horse "put intense fire for ten minutes on a small wood on the west side of Hoogerheide," and just as this ended, 11th Platoon swept through the woods, emerging quickly with "31 walking prisoners and three wounded."

The enemy paused to regroup, but in the late afternoon A Company, now commanded by Lieutenant Don Munro, was attacked from three sides. Part of the company was cut off, and the balance withdrew into D Company's position, abandoning a crossroads which was important to the defence of the battalion position. At first light the Calgaries counterattacked. Major Bruce Mackenzie, D Company's commander, had joined Major Kearns in the medical evacuation stream and Captain Bob Porter now had the company.[28] His job was to advance directly on the crossroads while B Company attacked from the flank. B Company's commander had labelled the objectives "Ross" and "Ellis" and worked his men forward in the traditions of the Calgary Highlanders' battle-drill school. Ellis and some of his men seemed to be actually enjoying their role as the battalion's "fire brigade." Both objectives were taken and twenty-three more prisoners captured.

By mid-day of the tenth, the German counterattack seemed to be spent. Von der Heydte's regiment had suffered heavy casualties, estimated at 480 men, in addition to more than fifty prisoners of war.[29] Much is made in the secondary literature of the prowess of the German officer corps and the fighting power of the German infantry. Yet the battle for Hoogerheide demonstrated major deficiencies in German strategy and tactics which were not uncommon in Northwest Europe. Von der Heydte had launched a frontal attack against forces which had gone over to the defensive. He persisted in pressing forward despite heavy losses. To attack in this manner, when reconnaissance would have shown the weakness of the Canadian right flank, suggests overconfidence and doctrinal rigidity. The texture of the bat-

tle also indicates that both in their defensive positions and in tactical counterattacks the Calgary Highlanders were more than a match for the enemy.

In his postwar memoirs von der Heydte recalled:

> It must have come as a considerable surprise to the Canadian Com-
> mand that after the successful crossing of the Scheldt they should
> meet with a battle ready and battle worthy reinforced German Para-
> chute Regiment. Nevertheless the Canadian Command decided to
> make an immediate attack on a wide front. . . . When the first attack
> shattered as a result of the resistance of the Parachutists, the Cana-
> dians, within three hours, attempted to launch a new attack, clearly
> with fresh troops: this attack also came to a halt immediately before
> our main positions.
>
> I decided to make a counter-attack with limited aims, which
> brought us to the outskirts of the villages of Woensdrecht and
> Hoogerheide. The Canadians—I say that as a German—fought bril-
> liantly: to the rank of Brigadier, the officers stood side by side with
> their men on the front lines.[30]

Fifth Brigade was pulled back into reserve on the evening of October 10
with orders to prepare for another attempt to seal off the Beveland Isthmus.
The acting corps commander had arrived at brigade headquarters during
some of the heaviest fighting on the ninth with new instructions for offensive
action. Brigadier Megill was able to persuade him that the "amount of opposition concentrated on this front"[31] meant that this would at least have to be
postponed, but Foulkes was insistent: a breakthrough of the German defences
had to be achieved as soon as possible.

Foulkes informed Keefler that the South Alberta Regiment, 4th Division's armoured recce unit, would come under his command, to protect the
still vulnerable flank. Other 4th Division units were promised later that week.
This would allow Keefler to use all three brigades in offensive operations.
Several plans were developed, but the events of the next few days were probably determined by the unexpected success of a company of the Royal Regiment of Canada, which forced its way forward through the difficult
polderland between Woensdrecht and the coast to reach the embankment
carrying the railway from Beveland to the mainland.[32] The next day, October
11, the Germans struck all across the front in a renewed attempt to overwhelm the Canadians. Since Foulkes had ordered 4th Brigade, with both the
Maisonneuves and South Sasks under command, to maintain pressure, 4th
Brigade and the 6th Parachute Regiment flailed away at each other throughout the day. The Royal Regiment fought off six separate counterattacks—

Captain B. S. "Beau" Lewis (left) and Lieutenant Joe Nixon, Black Watch, November 1944. LCMSDS

"No ground was given and heavy casualties inflicted,"[33] but its own attempt to seize the railway embankment was beaten back. The RHLI and South Sasks improved their positions in the Hoogerheide-Huijbergen area, but movement attracted well-placed mortar fire, and no serious advance was attempted.[34]

Foulkes met with Keefler and Megill that night and outlined a plan which called for 5th Brigade "to plug the neck" of the isthmus by attacking through the Royal Regiment of Canada position. One battalion would seize the railway embankment, the other two would then go through to seal the approaches to Beveland.[35] Megill again protested that the enemy forces in the area were too strong and too well dug-in. The terrain, he insisted, offered the defender too many advantages. His battalions, which had now been in action for two weeks, had lost a large number of experienced officers, NCOs, and men, and there had been no time to integrate the reinforcements.[36] Foulkes had heard all of this before, and his only concession was to promise that the attack would have all available support, including whatever ammunition the artillery and mortar units required.[37] Fifth Brigade was given twenty-four hours to prepare.

Foulkes had little choice in the matter. On October 9 Field Marshal Montgomery had issued a directive which emphasized offensive action by Second British Army in the Nijmegen sector. First Canadian army was told to use "all available resources on the operations designed to give us free use of the port of Antwerp,"[38] but only 2nd and 3rd Divisions were available. Montgomery did promise reinforcements. The 104th U.S. and the 52nd (Lowland) Scottish Division would both be allotted to Simonds, but neither would be available for at least ten days. There could be no question of waiting for these substantial reinforcements, and the Canadians would have to get on as best they could.

When Eisenhower received a copy of Montgomery's directive, he had on his desk a report from Admiral Bertram Ramsay, the British naval commander, which criticized the pace of operations to clear the Scheldt and noted that the Canadians were being handicapped by an ammunition shortage. Eisenhower, unhappy with Montgomery's conduct of operations, used this information in a message to Monty which concluded, "I must emphasize that all of our operations on our entire front from Switzerland to the Channel, I consider Antwerp of first importance and I believe that the operations to clear up the entrance require your personal attention." Montgomery was furious at this reprimand, accusing Ramsay of "wild statements" and denying there was an ammunition shortage. The field marshal also insisted that Eisenhower had agreed to his policy of making the "main effort" against the Ruhr.[39]

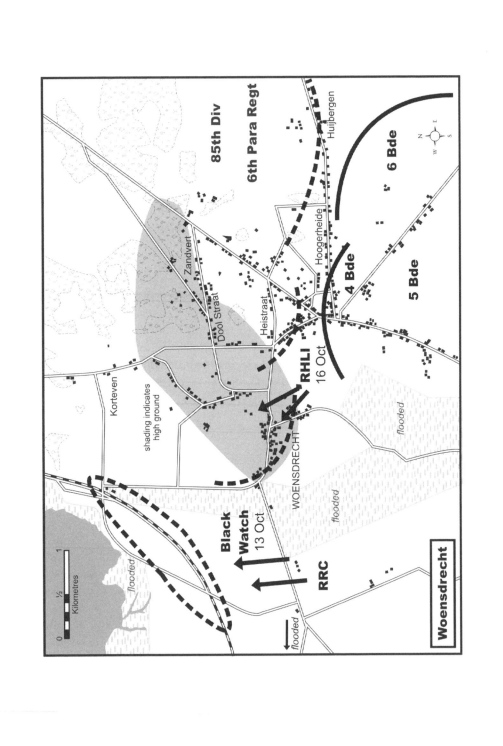

Woensdrecht

The most important immediate effect of this high-level confrontation was to put enormous pressure on the two Canadian infantry divisions. On the night of October 9, 2nd Division was informed that "the limit to artillery ammunition expenditure [which Monty had denied existed] has been removed."[40] The battle was to be continued with new intensity, and there was little that any brigade or divisional commander could do about it. When, on the night of October 11, Foulkes allowed Megill to postpone the brigade's attack until the thirteenth, he went about as far as he could go.

The extra twenty-four hours were put to good use. The first phase of the assault, code-named Operation "Angus," would have to be undertaken by the Black Watch; the Maisonneuves were still more than two hundred riflemen short, and the Calgaries had borne the brunt of the fighting at Hoogerheide. The Black Watch had done well since Ritchie had taken charge, and each company was led by an experienced commander.[41] The attack was built around an elaborate scheme to shoot the battalion on to the dyke, one company at a time. Two field and one medium regiments, as well as the heavy mortars and machine guns of the Toronto Scottish,[42] would provide the basic firepower. A Royal Marine heavy anti-aircraft regiment with 3.7-inch guns was also available, but it was short of ammunition.[43] The Fort Garry Horse supplied a troop of tanks, but given the field of fire available to enemy anti-tank guns, it could be used only to provide an initial shoot on the dyke junction, code-named "Angus 1."[44] The Spitfires and Typhoons of 84th Group would also participate, weather permitting. Ritchie examined the ground from an artillery spotter plane on the afternoon of the twelfth and at 7:30 P.M. called his final Orders Group—"Angus" would begin at 6:15 A.M. on Friday the thirteenth.

For the Black Watch October 13 was "Black Friday," the second worst single-day disaster in the history of the Royal Highland Regiment of Canada. It was not so much total casualties, 145, but the ratio of dead-to-wounded that marked the day's fighting. Fifty-six Black Watch soldiers were killed or died of wounds, and twenty-seven were taken prisoner.[45] What had happened?

The plan called for C Company, under Captain N. G. Buch, to make the first bound to the dyke junction. The fire plan attempted to neutralize the enemy by targeting positions back to Korteven and drenching the dyke embankment with high explosives. According to the divisional artillery commander, much of the effect of this was lost when C Company, "held up by small-arms fire from dug-in positions," was thirty minutes late on the start line and lost much of the benefit of the initial artillery program.[46] At 6:45 A.M. the company passed through the RRC positions, but after less than three hundred yards, perhaps halfway to the objective, the advance faltered in the face of well-aimed small-arms fire. B Company, under Major D. H. Chapman,

Angus 1. The Black Watch objective was at the junction of the railway embankment and the dyke at the upper left. The start line was the road from Woensdrecht at the bottom of the photograph, taken on October 6, 1944. LCMSDS

had moved forward in preparation for the second bound and were heavily mortared while waiting to go in. By 7:30 A.M. both Buch and Chapman had been wounded and other casualties plus stragglers were filtering back. At first the Black Watch tried to use the mortars and artillery to suppress the enemy fire, but "owing to the nature of the country it was extremely difficult to indicate a target with any degree of precision."[47] It was then decided to use smoke to mask the area and set the forward companies onto "Angus 1" as soon as possible. At 9:00 A.M. the objective was smoked, and some sections of C Company made it to the objective, only to find themselves pinned against an embankment twenty feet high. As the men tried to dig in, grenades were lobbed over the dyke at them. Most of these men were subsequently taken prisoner, many of them with shrapnel wounds. The balance of C Company had withdrawn to the start line.[48]

Although two attacks had now failed, Operation "Angus" was not called off. Even before the results of the second attack were known, divisional headquarters had issued warning orders for the preparation of a third assault "led by WASP flamethrowers."[49] This could not take place before mid-afternoon, and all that could be done in the meantime was to request air support from 84th Group. The records indicate that six requests for air strikes against prearranged targets were forwarded by 5th Brigade, and four were flown. At 11:45 A.M. twelve Spitfires bombed the brickworks west of Korteven, and in the later afternoon twelve Spitfires and sixteen Typhoon sorties were flown against the same target.[50] The long curving dyke between "Angus 1" and "Angus 2" was a difficult target for fighter bombers, and was not engaged.

Ritchie called his Orders Group for 3:00 P.M. The battalion was not in good shape. C Company now consisted of twenty-five men while B Company was down to forty-one, including company headquarters. Ritchie concentrated his remaining resources on the task of capturing and consolidating "Angus 1." A and D Companies were to move in behind the WASPs which would flame the embankment from left to right. A squadron of 17-pounder anti-tank guns and a troop of tanks were to engage enemy observation posts. The WASPs moved quickly when the artillery barrage began and were able to complete their task, losing one carrier which bogged down in the mud. D Company lost its CO, Major Chapman, in the advance, but Lieutenant Lewis, who had again done a "marvellous piece of work" in getting his platoon onto the objective, took command, and the rest of the company "pancaked on the objective."[51] A Company, which had drawn the more exposed right flank, suffered the heaviest casualties of the day. Lt. Alan Mills, who led one of the platoons, described the attack in a letter to his father written from a hospital in England: "We formed up behind a dyke and advanced over open ground. When we got practically to our objective (six hundred yards away) the

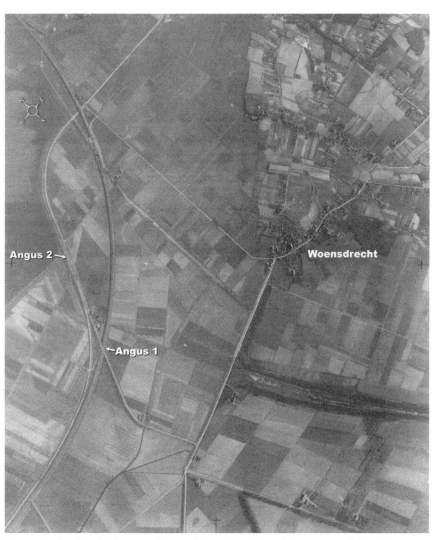

Woensdrecht. The high ground east of the village (top-right corner of the photograph, taken on September 12, 1944) can be identified by the shape of the fields.

machine guns and mortars became too hot and we began to drop right and left. Somehow a few managed to get to the objective. Those of us who were hit lay out in an open field with no cover. . . . The Battalion seems to have horrible shows periodically and this was one of them. A couple of NCOs who lived through May-sur-Orne told me that this was just as bad as that."[52]

Lieutenant Lewis and his men could be said to have captured "Angus 1," but they were quite unable to carry out the order to consolidate. As darkness fell all Jeeps and carriers in the battalion were mobilized to get the wounded out. The Black Watch diary reports that "many acts of heroism were performed in the dark which will never come to light. No words can pay sufficiently high tribute to those of our men who went out in the dark searching through flooded fields to ensure that all possible had been taken out to proper medical attention." Shortly after midnight Brigadier Megill ordered the battalion to withdraw; Operation "Angus" was over.

The post-mortems on this engagement began almost immediately. Lieutenant William Shea, the battalion intelligence officer who had watched the battle unfold from an observation post, suggests that there were three reasons for the failure of the RHC attacks: "first, the great natural defensive strength of the obstacles attacked; second, the determined opposition of the enemy who were paratroops; third, and most important, the poor quality of reinforcements received by the battalion." According to Shea the reinforcements were "mainly from the RCASC [service corps]," who had little or no infantry training and exhibited poor morale. They had, he noted, arrived "a matter of hours before an attack" and there had been no time for infantry training. "Furthermore, most of these reinforcements were not interested in infantry work to begin with, and did not want to fight." They did not understand the need to keep up with the barrage and took cover when their own artillery fired.[53] Shea's observations are but one example of such complaints from 2nd Division units in October.[54] With the Minister of National Defence, J. L. Ralston, visiting corps and divisional headquarters amidst rumours of the possible dispatch of conscripts from Canada for active service, it was natural that hard-pressed infantry officers would seize on this explanation, but the available evidence does not provide unqualified support for Shea's interpretation.

The Black Watch, by all accounts including their own, had fought with conspicuous success in early October at St. Leonard and Brecht, using reinforcements obtained in September. Casualties, 119 all ranks, had been evenly spread, and it must be presumed that the fifty-five OR reinforcements received on October 9 were shared among the companies. The fighting at Hoogerheide, which was also successfully handled, produced eighty-one casualties, most of them in D Company which under ordinary circumstances would have received the bulk of the forty-nine additional replacements who

A group of Calgary Highlanders passed by a knocked-out German self-propelled gun, Krabbendijke, Holland, October 27, 1944. LAC

arrived after October 6.[55] It was normal practice to leave new men out of battle, particularly one as difficult as "Angus," but if D Company did take its reinforcements forward, they must have shared in the one considerable success achieved by Lieutenant Lewis that day. Veterans will find this argument difficult to accept, but it is supported by the available evidence from personnel files[56] and may be more accurate than impressionistic evidence, even from those who were there.

The Black Watch were not the only Canadian unit to suffer from Montgomery's hesitation in assigning priority to Antwerp. Despite a series of sharp counterattacks on the South Sasks at Hoogerheide, the weekend was spent preparing for the Royal Hamilton Light Infantry to assault Woensdrecht and the low ridge behind the village. The RHLI attack on October 16 was initially successful, as the Germans withdrew from the village when the barrage began. All four companies were dug in when the inevitable counterattacks began. For the next four days, the RHLI defended the village in an action which cost them 167 casualties.[57] Companies from the Essex Scottish and Maisonneuves were also drawn into the battle as 6th Parachute Regiment repeatedly attacked despite its own mounting losses.

On October 16 the War Diarist of 5th Brigade headquarters recorded a view shared by everyone in 2nd Division: "Cannot understand why they do not put more troops in the area and finish the job once and for all instead of playing about, shifting first one battalion and then the other. This is beginning to look like a winter campaign unless something breaks soon." Help was in fact on the way, for as the battle for Woensdrecht raged, events at SHAEF, Supreme Headquarters Allied Expeditionary Force, were transforming Allied strategy and the role of II Canadian Corps. Montgomery, still angry at Ramsay and Eisenhower over the criticism of his strategy, had written a paper entitled "Notes on Command in Western Europe." This document contained a biting critique of the entire conduct of Allied operations since Normandy, as well as a renewed call to place Montgomery back in charge of land operations. Even General Eisenhower, who consistently sought to avoid confrontation and preserve the unity of the Allied coalition, could not ignore such a direct attack upon his leadership. He informed Montgomery that if the field marshal continued to believe the command arrangements were unsatisfactory, "it is our duty to refer the issue to higher authority." Eisenhower had lost his patience; he told Montgomery that the real issue was Antwerp, and "it does not involve the question of command in the slightest degree."

Montgomery received Eisenhower's letter on the fifteenth, and the next day, warned that Ike had had enough and was seriously considering demanding his removal, he wrote a conciliatory note promising to give Antwerp "top priority in 21 Army Group." The note was signed, "Your very devoted and

Sherman tanks of the Fort Garry Horse near the Beveland Canal, October 30, 1944. LAC

loyal subordinate, Monty." That afternoon Montgomery called his army commanders to his tactical headquarters and issued a new directive giving operations to open Antwerp "complete priority." The eastward-directed operations of Second British Army were closed down and it would now attack to the northwest in support of First Canadian Army, which "would be pulled over towards Antwerp."[58]

As the official historian C. P. Stacey wrote, "As soon as the new orders took effect the situation north of Antwerp was transformed. The 4th Canadian Armoured Division . . . was to be used as a hammer to loosen the German formations confronting 2nd Division."[59] Fourth Division was to clear the country northeast of Woensdrecht and free 2nd Division's flank. It in turn would be supported by 49th West Riding, 1st Polish Armoured, and 104th U.S. "Timberwolf" Divisions in an operation which was certain to force a rapid German retreat to the Maas.[60]

For 5th Brigade evidence of the change in fortune was not long in coming. The Calgary Highlanders were putting the finishing touches on their plans for a replay of Operation "Angus" when word came that the attack was postponed until the right flank was clear. Second Division staff now turned their attention to Beveland and the approaches to Walcheren Island. A two-brigade push to Korteven was planned, with 5th Brigade ordered to close the isthmus. Fourth Brigade would then begin the advance into South Beveland, where they would be joined by a brigade of the 52nd (Lowland) Scottish Division who were to stage an amphibious attack on the south coast of the isthmus.

With the Black Watch in reserve and the Maisonneuves still engaged at Woensdrecht, the brigade's part in the push north was carried out by the Calgary Highlanders. For the Calgaries, alone among 2nd Division units, October had been a month of triumphant achievement. However, the strain of battle had begun to affect the commanding officer, and for much of the month, Major Ross Ellis had run the battalion. MacLaughlan had been a strict disciplinarian and a good administrator. At age thirty-seven he was very much the old man, a nervous, sometimes irritable, task-master who led the battalion by issuing detailed orders. Ellis, at twenty-nine, was a soldier's soldier, handsome, dynamic, immaculately turned out, recklessly brave. As battle adjutant he had done much to make the battalion effective. As commanding officer he infused it with his own energy and intensity.[61]

The regimental newspaper, *The Glen*, which was published regularly throughout the campaign, printed a tribute to Ellis in its October issue. It is quoted here as an indication of the kind of response Ellis evoked:

It is not enough merely to welcome him and to say how downright proud we are to have him. Because, you see, most of have known him for a long time, and every time we think of him, we are more than proud. In fact, there is a warm feeling for him deep down inside us. He's not merely the finest soldier in the Battalion; he's a man among men, a man who has been through everything with us and knows us even better than we know ourselves.

Ellis represented the brigade at the planning conference called by Major-General Foulkes on October 22. Foulkes began the meeting not with words of praise or encouragement, but with the announcement "that there would be no discussion of when the operation would take. . . . A large scale appreciation had been made and all risks pertaining to the situation were understood." Regardless of such risks the effort, Foulkes stated, would be made. "The task for 2nd Div was set so that before the last hour on the 23rd some forces would be started out in the South Beveland peninsula."[62]

If Foulkes had waited twenty-four hours until the full effects of 4th Division's pressure had been felt by the Germans, Operation "Mac" would have been relatively easy.[63] As it was, the battalion began to meet serious opposition at "Angus 3" and fought all day to control the area. By morning on the twenty-fourth, resistance was "softening," and the battalion was able to move forward to seal off the isthmus. The Calgaries were then required to follow up any signs of enemy withdrawal, and in this role they pushed forward to the northern extension of the Woensdrecht ridge. Major Dalt Heyland and C Company drew the task of taking out the main pillbox, and when this was accomplished, the last of the German defenders at Woensdrecht were marched into captivity. Major-General Foulkes came forward to the Calgary tactical headquarters for the first time since operations had begun in July, to thank the battalion "for the damn fine job they had done for the division." The issue of fifty cigarettes per man was more warmly received.

With the route into South Beveland open, Operation "Vitality I" was launched on the morning of the twenty-fourth. In the early hours of "a rainy, pitch-bleak morning two 'Jock Columns' of Essex Reg't Infantry, 8th Recce Armoured Cars, and Fort Garry tanks"[64] set out for the Beveland Canal. Progress was slow, and when three recce cars and three tanks were knocked out, the armoured thrust ended. The next day, a conventional infantry attack with the artillery pouring fire on two crossroads brought complete success. That night "Vitality II," an amphibious assault across the Scheldt carried out by a brigade of the 52nd (Lowland) Scottish Division, forced the enemy to abandon their new defensive line at the Beveland Canal and conduct a hasty retreat to Walcheren. The Scots, their advance slowed by mud, mines, and

A Canadian truck bearing the Red Cross negotiates a Bailey bridge over the Beveland Canal, October 29, 1944.

the natural caution of green troops, failed to prevent this exodus. The 52nd, trained initially as an elite mountain unit and then converted to a specialized "air transportable" division, was not happy with its new assignment in land below sea level.

The Canadians found their new partners more than a little strange.[65] An officer of the Royal Regiment of Canada left an account of his first meeting with the Scots which has become a classic Canadian military anecdote:

> In the early hours of the 29th I was out with a unit of carriers, maintaining a standing patrol on the left flank of the battalion. In order to complete our patrol, we utilized some Dutch bicycles to patrol down a dyke to the bank of the West Scheldt. All our men were desperately tired and in a filthy, wet, muddy condition. On our way we were terribly surprised to find a party of what were obviously Allied troops landing in a small boat. Then forth from the boat onto the shore stepped what seemed to me to be the finest soldier I had ever seen in my life, a fine figure of a Scottish gentleman, carrying the shepherd's crook affected by some senior Scottish officers in place of a cane or a swagger stick. He had a small pack neatly adjusted on his back. (I had absolutely no idea where mine was and couldn't care less.) His gas cape was neatly rolled. (I had last seen mine somewhere around Eterville.) He had his pistol in a neatly blancoed web holster. (I had mine in my hip pocket.) He had a neatly kept map case. (I had mine stuck in my breast pocket.) He was a Colonel and I was a Captain. His boots were neatly polished and I was wearing turned-down rubber boots. I did manage to salute, although I think it must have been haphazard. He politely enquired if we were Canadians. (Although who else could have looked as we did?) I assured him we were. He asked if I could direct him to battalion headquarters. I did better than that. I escorted him to battalion headquarters. I was taking no chances on losing such a beautiful specimen to the German Army.[66]

Fifth Brigade entered the battle for Beveland with orders to capture the main town Goes, and then push on to the causeway which linked Beveland to Walcheren Island. The amphibious assaults on Walcheren could not begin until 2nd Division had cleared south Beveland and was positioned to invade Walcheren from the east. The Black Watch and Maisonneuves crossed the Beveland Canal in the early hours of the twenty-ninth, encountering resist-

The Walcheren Causeway. The Canadians were attacking east to west (right to left) against well-prepared German defenses. The barren nature of the causeway is evident from this photograph, taken on November 4, 1944, with only shell craters and shattered trees to offer protection; the shadows of the trees are visible across the causeway. The two large craters to the left of center were blown by German engineers to deny the causeway to vehicles. LCMSDS

ance at several strongpoints. The Maisonneuves advanced to Kloetinge along a road bordered with large trees. The fields on either side were flooded and the village isolated behind a destroyed bridge, but the strongpoint, with a battery of five 40mm guns, surrendered quickly when Lieut.-Colonel Bibeau launched an attack from both flanks. One Canadian soldier was killed in the attack, and Padre Marchand buried him in the local cemetery, with the villagers in their traditional costume dress looking on. No one could fail to be moved by the gratitude of the Dutch civilians for whom liberation was not just a word.[67]

Goes had been evacuated by the enemy when Kloetinge fell and the Black Watch carrier platoon was given a tumultuous reception. "Orange flags were being flown everywhere. The people clambered all over our vehicles and the riflemen had to fight their way through the civilians to get to their areas in the town. When they heard that the men had nothing to eat since early morning they brought out tea, coffee, hot chocolate, bread, biscuits, cake and all sorts of fruit. One old lady brought out a bottle of 'Old Mull' and handed it to the boys telling them she had been saving it for four and a half years for this day."[68]

To the south the Essex Scottish had advanced all the way to the west shore of Beveland. The acting divisional commander, Brigadier Keefler, responding to the constant pressure from corps headquarters, "asked" Brigadier Cabeldu "to try and exploit further and push a bridgehead over the causeway."[69] Cabeldu protested, arguing that only very fresh troops could accomplish the task. The alternative, a proper assault crossing of the water obstacle, would require some time to mount. Keefler agreed to relieve Cabeldu of responsibility for the crossing, but ordered him to seize the enemy positions at the Beveland end of the Walcheren causeway. The Royals accomplished this task in a finely controlled night action which pinched off all the defenders by moving along the water's edge. They also captured 153 prisoners and a great deal of equipment.[70]

At 9:30 on the morning of October 31, Simonds decided to go ahead with the amphibious attacks on Walcheren Island and informed the acting corps commander of this decision. Foulkes immediately sent a signal to 2nd Division headquarters which read, "No interference on Walcheren by guns or air. Most desirable we get on with it."[71] The hazardous amphibious attacks on Flushing and Westkappelle were scheduled for dawn on November 1, and it was important to persuade the enemy that the attack would come from the Beveland area. The Scottish brigade had been scheduled to perform this task, but it was so slow in arriving.[72] That evening, Foulkes ordered Brigadier Megill to begin the operation by seizing a bridgehead on Walcheren which could then be turned over to the Scots.[73]

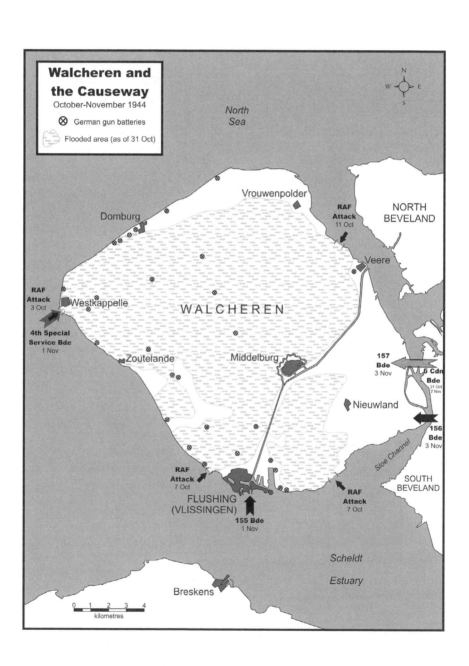

Walcheren and the Causeway

October-November 1944

⊗ German gun batteries

  Flooded area (as of 31 Oct)

North Sea

Vrouwenpolder

RAF Attack
11 Oct

NORTH BEVELAND

Domburg

Veere

RAF Attack
3 Oct

Westkappelle

WALCHEREN

4th Special Service Bde
1 Nov

Zoutelande

Middelburg

157 Bde
3 Nov

5 Cdn Bde
31 Oct
2 Nov

Nieuwland

156 Bde
3 Nov

Sloe Channel

SOUTH BEVELAND

RAF Attack
7 Oct

FLUSHING (VLISSINGEN)

RAF Attack
7 Oct

155 Bde
1 Nov

Scheldt

Estuary

Breskens

0 1 2 3 4
kilometres

Megill, whose troops were every bit as weary and understrength as Cabeldu's, accepted his new instructions without protest. He had argued with Foulkes in Normandy and attempted to persuade him that an October 13 attack was badly conceived, but he had no such objections to the task outlined for the brigade early on October 31.[74] The plan called for the Calgaries, who still had officers and NCOs trained for amphibious assaults, to cross the water obstacle in storm boats and tracked landing vehicles. The Maisonneuves would then be ferried over to join them. This action, coming hours before the seaborne invasion, would prevent the enemy from shifting troops to the Flushing or Westkappelle and might result in the rapid occupation of Middelburg.

The Calgary War Diary records in detail the preparation for the crossing. B Company was "put through its paces in handling the assault boats," and two privates were given instruction in driving "Weasel" LVTs which were to be used to ferry ammunition. While the preparations went ahead, the Black Watch tried to advance along the causeway. Megill had told Ritchie to conduct a "quick operation" to try to "push a strong fighting patrol on to the other side."[75] Ritchie planned a much more deliberate attack using all four companies. Unfortunately, the leading troops were stopped cold some seventy-five yards before the end of the causeway, leaving the whole battalion strung out behind. The War Diary describes the situation: "The enemy had his guns sited to give crossfire on the causeway with one tank dug-in and an anti-tank gun firing down the centre of the road. Enemy snipers had positioned themselves in the marsh bordering the causeway and were very accurate. . . . The enemy was firing one gun, the shells of which raised water two hundred feet high when they fell short. He was also ricocheting A.P. shells down the causeway which was hard on the morale of the war." The battalion suffered losses of ten killed and thirty-four wounded before it was able to withdraw.[76]

While the Black Watch were digging in, the engineers sent to reconnoitre the water-crossing reported that "there was not sufficient water even at high tide to permit such an operation." They further reported that "the ground was too saturated for movement on foot and there were too many runnels in the mud flats to permit 'Weasels' to operate."[77] There was no time for further reconnaissance; if an attack was to divert attention away from the main landings, it would have to take place across the causeway.

The Calgary scout officer, Lieutenant Gordon Sellar, had been detailed to observe the Black Watch attack. He was able to provide information on the nature of the enemy resistance and the location of the main defensive line. Ross Ellis proposed to use the darkness and the barrage to get B Company "to traverse the causeway and fan out north, south and west."[78] The other com-

Looking east along the causeway. Photograph taken in 1946. CFJIC

panies were to pass through, establishing a substantial bridgehead including the village of Arnemuiden. The Maisonneuves would then cross to join the Calgaries. A comprehensive artillery scheme was arranged with 5th Field and a medium regiment being joined by a newly arrived artillery regiment from 52nd Division. Captain Nobby Clarke got his men moving forward early, as they were "complaining of sore feet" in the intense cold. At 11:40 P.M. the shooting began. Ten minutes later battalion headquarters was informed "Baker Company reports Merry Christmas"—the attack was underway.

The fire plan had been designed to blanket the enemy positions on the island, but with the withdrawal of the Black Watch, the Germans had moved well out onto the causeway. Captain Clarke quickly realized the futility of the situation, and Megill accepted the request to withdraw and start again. Clarke and Ellis went to brigade headquarters to advise on a new fire plan which would sweep the enemy off the causeway and suppress opposition from the island. Megill and Nighswander decided to use two field regiments on a frontage of 750 yards. The barrage was made tight by arranging "lifts" of just fifty yards every two minutes.[79]

The Calgaries' D Company moved out at 6:05 A.M. It was still very dark, but the men were able to work forward quickly using the barrage to reach the western end of the causeway. D Company was held up there for the next several hours, but the FOO directed fire on a succession of targets, and by 9:30 A.M. the initial objectives to the south were secure and prisoners were on their way out. Major Bruce Mackenzie advised Ellis that another company could be sent through them "although care should be taken because of the high velocity gun firing down the road."

A Company crossed quickly and turned north. B Company followed and moved south, making good progress against light opposition. C Company also crossed but could not move ahead as there was now heavy shelling of the area. Ross Ellis and his scout officer Gordon Sellar set out across the causeway at 3:45 P.M..[80] Sellar can still remember the impression Ellis made on him that afternoon. Freshly shaven, neatly dressed, and apparently calm and good humoured, Ellis checked C Company's forward positions, chatting to the men in the slit trenches. Sellar recalls, "It was amazing to see them brighten up and grin broadly when they saw the Colonel." Ellis and Sellar then "slowly walked back down the causeway talking to the men dug in there."[81]

The Calgaries had seemed in control of the bridgehead, but the shelling intensified, and B Company, hit by a heavy counterattack, was forced to retreat all the way to the edge of the causeway. A Company's only officer, Captain Wynn Lasher, was wounded, and the situation seemed to be deteriorating. The brigade major, George Hees, volunteered to take Lasher's place, and the spare artillery FOO Captain Walter Newman asked to go along as

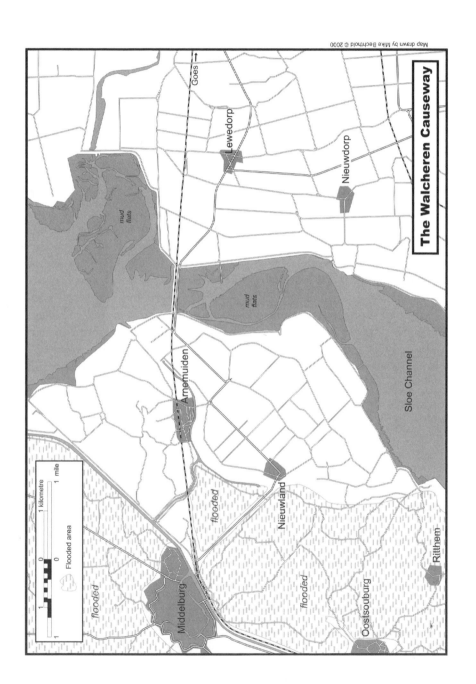

The Walcheren Causeway

Goes →

Lewedorp

Nieuwdorp

mud
flats

mud
flats

Sloe Channel

Arnemuiden

Nieuwland

Middelburg

flooded

flooded

flooded

flooded

Oostsouburg

Ritthem

0   1 kilometre
0   1 mile

Flooded area

2/iC. While Newman had a well-deserved reputation for risk taking, Hees was a staff officer without combat experience, and so his offer was quite extraordinary. Ellis, on his way back to the island to obtain first-hand information, took the two men across and settled them in. The situation had deteriorated further, and it was clear that the enemy was determined to prevent a breakthrough to Middelburg.[82] Ellis once again walked back to Beveland and brigade headquarters. Megill listened to his report but had to tell him to hang on until "division decided what to do."[83] At divisional headquarters Keefler was under considerable pressure from Foulkes. At 4:30 P.M. corps sent a signal which reported the interception of a German wireless message announcing that all German troops on Walcheren were "ready to surrender." The corps commander ordered his men "to push on and establish our bridgehead as soon as possible."[84]

Detailed instructions did not arrive from division until shortly before midnight. The landings at Flushing and Westkappelle were going well after some initial problems, and Megill was told to be prepared to hand over to 52nd (Lowland) Brigade at 6:00 A.M. the next morning. It was stipulated however that a further attack would be necessary and the end of the Walcheren causeway firmly controlled before the relief took place.[85] Megill had already developed a plan to pass the Maisonneuves through the Calgary position, but Keefler "ruled that this attack would continue one hour only and the relief would take place in the position reached at that time. In consequence it was decided to commit only two companies of the Régiment de Maisonneuve since it was not considered possible to deploy more men along the defile of the causeway in that time."[86] Ellis had withdrawn both D and C Companies to Beveland, so that not more than fifty men were left holding the dyke at the edge of the island.[87]

The lead Maisonneuve company, commanded by Captain Camile Montpetit, was in position at 4:00 A.M. Unfortunately, the barrage, fired by 52nd Division artillery, began three hundred yards short, striking the Calgary positions and delaying the Maisonneuves who were still three hundred yards from the end of the causeway when the guns stopped. Megill ordered the Maisonneuves to dig in where they were and wait to be relieved by the Glasgow Highlanders, but Montpetit's company did not receive the order. They had made contact with the Calgary Highlanders and moved forward onto the island assuming that their B Company was close behind.[88]

The Maisonneuve force consisted of about forty men, including six volunteers from the Belgian White Brigade who had been with the battalion since September.[89] Lieutenant Charles Forbes, heading 18th Platoon, and Lieutenant Guy de Merlis, commanding 16th Platoon, were skilled and

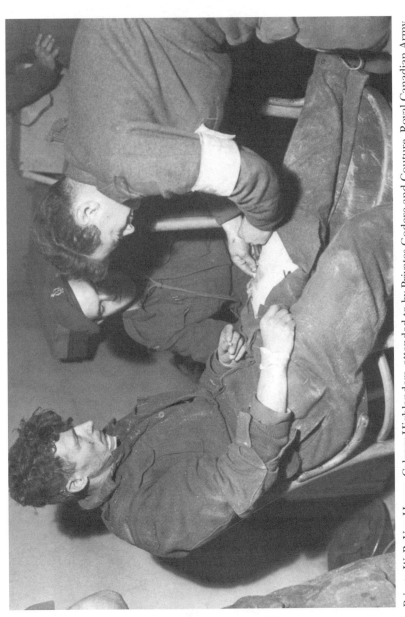

Private W. R. Van Herne, Calgary Highlanders, attended to by Privates Godere and Couture, Royal Canadian Army Medical Corps, November 1, 1944. LAC

Black Watch pipers play a lament during a burial service of men from the regiment, Ossendrecht, Holland, October 26, 1944. LAC

aggressive leaders, and the Maisonneuves worked their way forward to a position some five hundred yards inland. A farmhouse became company headquarters, with the two platoons deployed back-to-back along the main road on both sides of the railway underpass. They were, however, totally isolated because the Calgaries had been withdrawn and B Company of the Maisonneuves was well back along the causeway.

For the next eight hours, this small battle group fought with extraordinary courage. Lieutenant D. G. Innes, a FOO with 5th Field Regiment, maintained contact with Montpetit's men, calling down defensive fire.[90] Rocket typhoons were also in action , but it was rather the efforts of individuals, such as Private J. C. Carriere, who took out a 20mm gun with a PIAT, that epitomized the day's brave and heroic deeds. Carriere, a signaler, volunteered to stalk the gun. After crawling four hundred yards along a shallow ditch partly filled with water, "he reached a point from which he could bring fire to bear from his PIAT." Carriere was wounded, but he managed to knock out the gun and return to his comrades.[91]

Brigadier J. D. Russel, commanding the Scottish brigade, had arrived at Megill's headquarters on the night of October 31. Russel was understandably unhappy at the prospect of sending one of his battalions into this chaotic battle. The divisional commander, Major-General E. Hakewill Smith, had urged him to find an alternate way onto the island, and his engineers were searching for a route well to the south of the causeway. This sensible plan has been somewhat misrepresented in postwar accounts. Hakewill-Smith was planning to mount a carefully organized two-brigade attack as part of the overall battle for Walcheren Island. This action was expected to take some time, and it is not difficult to understand why he challenged Charles Foulkes, the acting corps commander, when Foulkes ordered him to attack across the causeway.[92] This dispute involved an issue quite separate from the decision to commit 5th Brigade on October 31.

Russel agreed to take over the causeway bridgehead, but only with a minimum of troops. The Glasgow Highlanders sent two platoons forward, but they were forced to dig in at the western edge of the causeway. Private (later Sergeant-Major) Charles Ouellet of the Maissonneuves volunteered to contact the relieving troops and with a companion attacked the position holding up the Scottish soldiers. He was able to lead elements of one Scottish platoon to Captain Montpetit's headquarters.[93] At noon on November 2, the Maisonneuves and the Scottish troops were ordered to withdraw under cover of a fire plan laid on by Lieutenant Innes.[94] The Glasgow Highlanders dug in at the end of the causeway and held the position until the Germans were forced to withdraw. The 52nd's divisional engineers found a crossing near Nieuwdorp, and by dusk on November 3, they had outflanked the enemy.[95]

Black Watch funeral service, October 1944. LCMSDS

Fifth Brigade was by then on its way to Belgium for a long overdue rest. The causeway had cost the Calgaries seventeen killed and forty-six wounded. The Maisonneuves, with their companies of less than sixty men, had just one fatality and ten men wounded. The battle for the causeway was not the ill-conceived disaster that it is so often portrayed as. The acting corps commander's orders to mount an attack and maintain pressure were a necessary part of the overall plan to capture Walcheren Island. The operation itself was carried out with considerable skill and relatively small losses. If 157th Brigade had been ready to take advantage of the successful Calgary assault on the morning of November 1, a large bridgehead might have been established and Arnemuiden captured. The 52nd Division would play a significant part in the battles of 1945, but in October 1944 its performance was not impressive. The Canadians had crossed the Beveland Canal and reached the west coast of Beveland in two days. The Scottish troops landed on the south coast on October 26 but took six days to move the short distance west. Their inexperience and caution meant that the 2nd Division was forced to provide the necessary diversion for the commando landings. On October 20 Field Marshal Montgomery, who had belatedly recognized the importance of the Scheldt, wrote a letter to Guy Simonds which was as close to an apology as Montgomery could offer:

> I think everything you are doing is excellent, and your troops are doing wonders under the most appalling conditions of ground and weather. I doubt if any other troops would do it so well and I am very glad the Canadians are on the business. Please tell your chaps how pleased I am with their good work.[96]

CHAPTER 8

Victory

The battle of the Scheldt formally ended with the surrender of Middelburg and the evacuation of the last German bridgehead south of the River Maas. The next day, November 9, II Canadian Corps relieved British troops in the Nijmegen bridgehead. Second Division was brought forward to occupy the eastern flank of the salient, facing the Reichswald Forest and the northern extension of the Siegfried Line. The division's task was to defend the area against a possible German attack and to "inflict casualties and undermine the morale of the enemy by patrolling, raids and limited offensive use of artillery."[1] First Canadian Army was to consider plans for a major offensive along the west bank of the Rhine, but Montgomery had not yet set a date for this operation.

The brief rest and the promise of time in a quiet sector did wonders for the morale of the division. Reinforcements arrived in sufficient numbers to bring all battalions, even the FMRs and the Maisonneuves, up to strength and there was time to integrate them properly. On October 28 Simonds had issued a directive on "Absorption of Reinforcement Personnel" which addressed complaints about the quality of replacements. "I do not believe," Simonds wrote, "that Commanding officers have given enough consideration to the human aspects of the problem." They must realize "that when the reinforcement officer or soldier joins the unit with which he is going to fight, it is one of the great moments of his life comparable with birth, marriage or death. . . . The reinforcement (unless he is a recovered casualty returned to his own unit) comes as a stranger. Regardless of how thorough his preliminary training may be, in the stress of his first battle, he may react in a way contrary to his training unless steps have been taken to win his confidence."

Simonds reminded commanders of his previous instructions "that every infantry battalion and armoured regiment will have a strong 'left out of battle' party, including 2/iCs and selected officers, NCOs and men." These men should form a "unit reception school" to "test and initiate the new soldier." Except in an emergency, he insisted, "reinforcements will *not* be posted into fighting echelons . . . until they have spent a minimum of forty-eight hours in LOB school." Simonds, perhaps anticipating the anger of battalion commanders who had fought through much of October with companies of less than half strength, concluded on a conciliatory note. "I fully appreciate that during the period of intensive activities through which we have been going that commanding officers have had little time to think about things other than the battle in which they are engaged. But, once proper arrangements have been made for reinforcement absorption, and a unit reception school formed, the senior LOB officer can command it."[2]

The recommendations in Simonds' directive may seem to fall in the category of the obvious, but a number of battalions were failing to provide any organized method of absorbing reinforcements. It is possible to have a good deal of sympathy for harried battalion commanders who had rushed men into action, but Simonds was surely right to insist on the creation of unit reception schools.

Simonds did much more for 2nd Division than lecture to it. During the summer Crerar had insisted that infantry divisions were to be commanded by infantry officers despite general agreement that none of the infantry brigadiers in Normandy were suitable. This policy brought a Permanent Force infantry officer, Brigadier Dan Spry, back from Italy to take over 3rd Division even though no one thought he was ready for such an appointment.[3] Simonds had opposed this policy, and in November he was instrumental in the selection of Bruce Matthews to replace Charles Foulkes.

The new general officer commanding 2nd Division had begun his army career as a militia officer artillery officer. Between 1939 and 1942 Matthews served as battery commander, counter-battery officer, and regimental commander. He also served as CO of the 7th Canadian Medium Experimental Battery, gaining experience in sound ranging and helping to prepare the gun drill and range tables for the new 5.5-inch gun. Matthews did not go to staff college or to a senior officers' course, but he had a quick mind, enormous energy, and considerable self-confidence. Matthews was an early exponent of the artillery-based battle doctrine which he "learned from British officers with experience in the desert."[4] When 1st Division was selected for Operation "Husky," the invasion of Sicily, Matthews was promoted brigadier and CRA of 1st Division. Simonds insisted on the appointment of Matthews as Corps CRA when he took command of II Canadian Corps.

Matthews was one of the brightest and most competent officers in the Canadian army. Like many other men of ability, he was appalled by the decision to promote inexperienced officers to divisional command because they were infantrymen. When Simonds offered him 2nd Division, he did not hesitate. As a senior artillery officer, he had often watched infantry commanders

Lieutenant-Colonel Ross Ellis leads the Calgary Highlanders in review. Major-General Bruce Matthews is taking the salute. Brigadier Megill stands to his right. LAC

put troops into battle around a fire plan he had devised. "Fire and movement meant artillery and infantry and artillery officers knew more about
planning proper infantry operations than any infantry officer,"[5] he insisted.

Second Division's brigadiers might not have agreed with this estimate of
infantry officers, but they could not help respecting and admiring Matthews'
professionalism and style of leadership. Brigadier Megill found that it was
now possible to discuss operations and actually have some input into planning.[6] Under Foulkes, brigadiers had been little more than a conduit for passing on orders; Matthews set out to consult brigade commanders about all
aspects of training before major operations began again. Fortunately, there
was ample time. Battle-drill schools were re-established and special attention
was focussed on the battalion's own support units. Fighting patrols, which
Simonds described as "the best school for junior leadership,"[7] provided much
needed experience for the large number of reinforcements received since
the fighting in October.

Early in December, D Company of the Black Watch was selected for a
large-scale raid code-named "Mickey Finn." Major E. W. Hudson, a veteran
of the Italian campaign who had joined the battalion in late October, led his
men through six rehearsals planned around a carefully timed artillery program. Platoons were briefed to "get as close to the fire of supporting 25-
pounders as possible," and urged "to work as sections and not to bunch up."
The raid was successful in the sense that the company got to its objective,
inflicted losses, and returned with a prisoner. But significant casualties, five
dead and twelve wounded, were suffered, and as usual it was enemy mortar
fire which caused most of the wounds.[8]

Simonds and Matthews, in common with most Allied commanders,
believed that the artillery-based battle doctrine used throughout 1944 was fun-
damentally sound. If men stayed close to the barrage, they could get to their
objective. If there were also enough guns to seal the area with fire and prevent
the enemy from counterattacking while the infantry consolidated, the position
could be held and losses inflicted on the Germans as they counterattacked.
Allied casualties in such attacks came primarily from enemy mortars which
were registered to ensure a rapid response on any line of approach.

"Mickey Finn" was intended to test new techniques in overcoming this
problem. Major J. M. Watson, the counter-mortar officer of 2nd Division,
and the members of the Operational Research Section attached to 21st Army
Group had created an experimental scheme to detect and deal with enemy
mortars. Five forward-observation posts were established to report locations
by sound ranging, and the recently formed 1st Canadian Radar Battery
attempted to locate mortars with its radar sets. Air observation pilots were
also sent aloft to try to spot mortar flashes. None of these efforts proved

immediately successful. The flash of mortars was not visible to the pilots and the hastily positioned radar sets picked up the falling mortar shells, but not the first part of the mortar trajectory. As usual the enemy shifted location two or three times, so even those positions spotted by visually retracing the line of flight were not necessarily hit.[9]

The counter-mortar exercise demonstrated a characteristic failing of the Allied war effort. In radar, as in many areas of technological development, the needs of the air force and navy had taken priority over the army. Experiments with the use of radar on the battlefield were long overdue, and it is not surprising that the first attempts to employ it were unsuccessful. By February 1945 1st Canadian Radar Battery was well trained and played a significant role in spotting German mortar and gun positions in Operation "Veritable."[10]

First Canadian Army had been gearing up for a large-scale operation, code-named "Veritable," to be launched "as soon as possible after January 1, 1945,"[11] but on December 16 von Rundstedt's Fifth and Sixth Panzer Armies crashed through the forward line of First U.S. Army in the Ardennes. The Battle of the Bulge had begun, and all Allied operations were put on hold until this unexpected threat was dealt with. The Canadians were not drawn into any part of the battle, or into the counter-offensive which forced the Germans back to their start line. Concerns about a second converging attack from the north kept Crerar's troops on the alert, but 2nd Division spent December and January in a static role in the Nijmegen area.

On January 21, 1945, Field Marshal Montgomery issued a new directive. "The enemy," he wrote, "has suffered a tactical defeat in the Ardennes with severe losses in men and material." It was time to launch a strong offensive "south-eastwards between the rivers Rhine and Meuse." The target date for "Veritable" was February 8, less than three weeks away. First Canadian Army would have British XXX Corps as well as II Canadian Corps under command, and if the weather was poor, with the terrain soft and wet, both corps would be employed in what was bound to be a slow, deliberate operation.

Second Division was scheduled to play a small but important role in the opening stages of "Veritable." A triangular wedge of ground north of the Siegfried Line defences was still in enemy hands, and the German border village of Wyler had been transformed into a strongpoint to defend this area. Matthews ordered 5th Brigade to capture Wyler, securing the flank for 15th Scottish Division, which would attack the main defences at the edge of the Reichswald Forest. Brigadier Megill gave the task to the Calgary Highlanders and the Régiment de Maisonneuve.

The plan for the advance on Wyler emphasized the need for speed, as control of the road to Kranenburg was essential to the rapid advance of 15th Division. The battalions attacked after a preliminary bombardment which

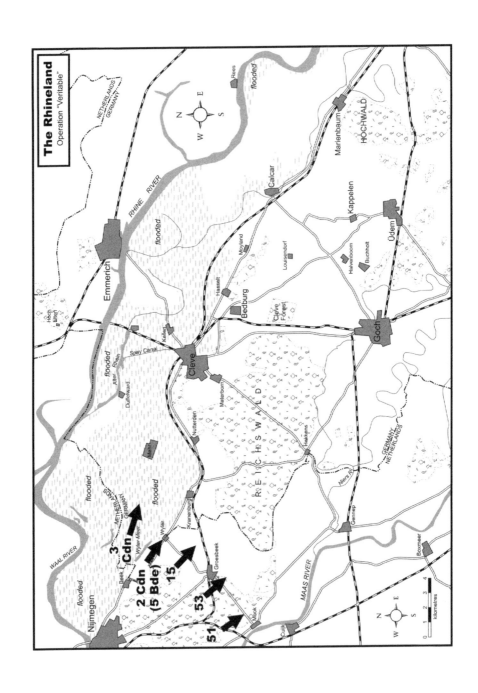

The Rhineland
Operation "Veritable"

directed a minimum of six tons of high explosives on each target. During February 8 over half a million artillery and mortar shells were fired in support of "Veritable," many of them in counter-mortar programs which virtually eliminated enemy interference with the initial advance.[12]

The Calgaries surprised the defenders of Wyler by breaking through west of the village. Mines were the principal obstacle in this first phase. The Germans had laid rows of small *Schuhmine*s "quite openly on the surface of the ground, with other mines interspersed and hidden below the surface. In attempting to avoid the visible mines troops were caught by the hidden ones."[13]

Lieutenant Ed Ford, who had passed on his responsibilities as intelligence Officer and War Diarist, led 14th Platoon, with fixed bayonets, in behind the barrage. As they began the left pivot that would bring them into Wyler from the flank, the enemy came to life, raking the platoon with machine-gun fire. Ford "had his mortar man fire smoke bombs" and, shouting "follow me" crossed the last few hundred yards to the edge of the town creating a "mini-barrage of Bren and Lee-Enfield fire."[14]

The Maisonneuves, attacking on the right flank, used two companies to secure Den Heuvel and Hochstrasse. They had carefully surveyed the route and studied a sand table model, but their rapid success on February 8 was due mainly to the way companies "crowded the barrage"[15] and got in amongst the defenders before they had recovered. Lieutenant Louis Fontaine "led his platoon to the destruction of many sniper nests and M.G. posts" even though he was wounded on the start line. He and Private Hector Lefebvre, who attacked an enemy dugout single-handedly, were awarded medals for their part in the day's work. With Den Heuvel secure, the reserve company was sent through to assist the Calgaries in the second phase of their attack.[16]

The situation south of Wyler was in a confused state. Major John Campbell, the Canadian army's first battle drill instructor who had been wounded in Normandy, was killed in this, his first action after returning to the battalion. His company had taken heavy casualties, and Lieut.-Colonel Ellis went forward to reorganize the battalion. Ellis won what many regarded as a long overdue DSO for his efforts that day. The citation reads, "LCol Ellis went forward through a heavily mined area which was covered by a devastating small arms fire to get information and re-organize. Finding that no further progress could be made by the first Company he went forward and cleared a start line for the reserve company to pass through, then moved to the second Company on the left to co-ordinate the plan. To deal with the exceedingly heavy mortar, machine gun and small arms fire which constantly swept the entire area, he drew up a fire plan for a creeping barrage and personally supervised the advance to the objective, his battalion capturing 287 prisoners including the regimental commander and his staff." The citation goes on to summarize the role played by Ellis since the Calgaries landed in France and concludes, "his enthusiasm and complete disregard for his own personal safety, coupled with sound judgement and tactics and his exceptional leadership, are reflected in the aggressive, proud spirit of the men in his battalion, and its record of achievement."[17]

The Calgaries lost two officers and eleven other ranks killed, one officer and sixty other ranks wounded in the battle for Wyler. Once they entered the village, it was evident why the strongpoint had held out despite the overwhelming fire support. The Germans had positioned most of their troops in the northern end of Wyler, "constructing very strong dug-outs in the banks of the Wyler Meer to form a complete network of communication trenches throughout the area."[18] Artillery or infantry alone could do little against such a position, but by working together they could readily accomplish the task.

After the battle for Wyler, Fifth Brigade was withdrawn to join the rest of 2nd Division in reserve. It returned to the front lines on February 20, relieving 7th Brigade, which had suffered almost five hundred casualties in a six-day struggle for Moyland Wood. There was some immediate mopping up to do in the village of Moyland, and the nearby chateau was liberated by the Maisonneuves. A British journalist who visited the chateau described the scene: "Inside was a vast confusion of wreckage. In the principal bed-chamber the curving walls embellished with paintings of flamboyant nudes, the cooking stoves of a French Canadian company roared under pans of frying fat. Here Frederick the Great, at ease in a canopied bed on the raised dias, had once held morning levee. In the magnificently appointed bathrooms of the state apartment, groups of soldiers washed and shaved . . ."[19]

The brigade had not been brought forward to enjoy the delights of a chateau. Crerar had decided on a new operation to complete the tasks outlined in "Veritable." This enterprise, code-named "Blockbuster," called for all three Canadian divisions to conduct a series of assaults against the right flank of the German defences. But on February 23 the Ninth U.S. Army, in Operation "Grenade," crossed the River Roer and turned north in a manoeuvre intended to eliminate all German units west of the Rhine. Since Ninth U.S. Army had ten fresh divisions available, a German retreat was inevitable. Nevertheless, Montgomery and Crerar decided not to wait until the Americans arrived. "Blockbuster" was scheduled for the twenty-sixth, and it began on time.

Fifth Brigade was assigned a supporting role in the first stage of "Blockbuster." Sixth Brigade attacked the main defences on the Calcar ridge, with

Major-General Bruce Matthews. LAC

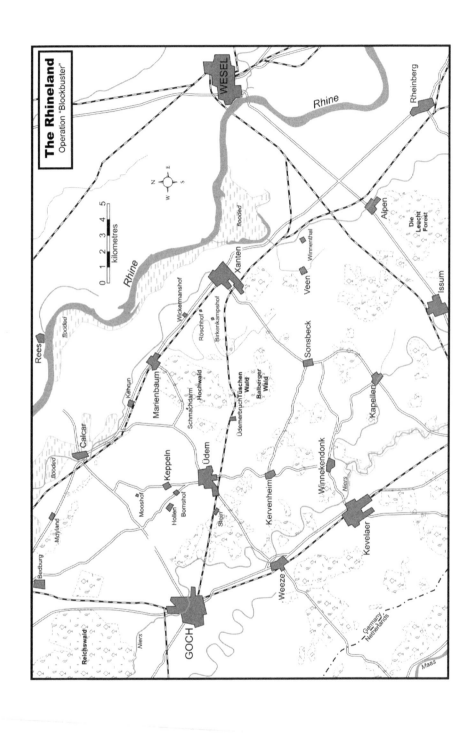

The Rhineland
Operation "Blockbuster"

WESEL

Rhine

Rheinberg

Rhine

flooded

Alpen

Die
Leucht
Forest

N
E
W
S

kilometres
0 1 2 3 4 5

Winnenthal

Xanten

Veen

Issum

Rees

flooded

Wickelmanshof

Röschhof

Birkenkampshof

Sonsbeck

Kehun

Marienbaum

Hochwald

Schmachdarm

Tüschen
Wald

Balberger
Wald

Udemerbruch

Kapellen

Calcar

flooded

Keppeln

Moitland

Mooshof

Hollen

Bornshof

Üdem

Stein

Kervenheim

Winnekendonk

Niers

Bedburg

Kevelaer

Reichswald

Niers

Weeze

GOCH

Germany
Netherlands

Maas

the Black Watch and Maisonneuves advancing to fill in the left flank of the crest of the ridge. Only one squadron of tanks was available, and this was kept in reserve to be used in a separate operation against the final objective, "Raven." The artillery plan was designed primarily to get 6th Brigade onto its objectives, and two of the areas, "Gull" and "Eagle," to be seized by the Black Watch, were "swept by a fast barrage" which was over well before the troops could possibly attack. A third position, "Ottawa," which could be dealt with by a "slow barrage," was easily captured by C Company, but "Gull" and "Eagle" were vigorously defended.[20]

Ritchie ordered his men to withdraw, and a new attempt, using a squadron of the First Hussars and an artillery program with some tricky timings, was organized. The after-action report of the Hussars describes the events. "Before the attack started it was necessary to regroup the squadron into two troops of 4 tanks and a headquarters troop of 4. . . . Platoons were allotted to each troop. . . . Due to the soft ground, tank speed and therefore infantry speed was much reduced. A further reduction in speed was caused by three of 1st Troop's tanks being knocked out by mines. . . . While the tanks were still 400 yards from the final objective the artillery concentration lifted so a repeat of five minutes was asked for and obtained. This lifted at the correct time. The time lag between the cessation of artillery fire and the moment when the infantry entered the houses was covered by a heavy fire from all guns and machine guns in the tanks. The infantry dug in on the forward slope while the tanks took up defensive positions covering all approaches."[21] This superb example of all-arms cooperation demonstrated what could be done when the resources were available.

The day's action had demanded a great deal from everyone. For example, CSM L. Frost led the carriers forward on foot, guiding them around mines. He then searched a group of buildings which he found to be occupied by enemy troops. Returning quickly to company headquarters, he briefed Major R. MacDuff, who organized a flanking attack on the buildings which led to the capture of seventy prisoners. Frost won the DCM and MacDuff the DSO for these actions.[22]

The Maisonneuves also ran into trouble. Only one of their four objectives, a woods designated "Robin 2," was defended, but it had been heavily reinforced, and when D Company began crossing the open ground in front of the woods, it was "shot up from all sides and the struggle developed into a very slow infantry fight in close contact with the enemy which made artillery support difficult to arrange."[23] Lieutenant Guy de Merlis' platoon was in reserve about a hundred yards behind, and he was able to make a left-flanking attack along a side road occupying a house and forming a firm fire base.[24]

Brigadier Megill told the Hussars to send first one and then two troops to aid the Maisonneuves. Bibeau decided to use the tanks and some WASP flamethrowers to provide close support for an advance by his reserve company. The CO led the attack himself, directing the WASPs in overcoming stubborn resistance in well-concealed dug-outs. Bibeau won the DSO at Calcar ridge. The citation read in part: "Throughout the entire action this commanding officer's cool, clear thinking, sound judgement and complete disregard for his own safety were worthy of the highest praise."[25]

Bibeau was not only brave, he was deeply concerned with his officers and men. He had arranged for Major Ostiguy to serve as a liaison officer at brigade HQ when the effects of six months' continuous action were becoming evident. After the battle for Calcar ridge, he sent for Lieutenant de Merlis to England to take an intelligence officers' course. During the battle de Merlis, "after escaping scratchless for six months," was hit by a grenade fragment and bullet in the leg. This seemed "sufficient warning." He avoided medical evacuation and the danger of missing his chance to go to England by convincing the regimental medical officer to patch him up at the unit and look the other way, "in exchange for a bottle of champagne!"[26]

Maisonneuve losses for the day totalled thirteen killed and thirty-three wounded; the Black Watch had eleven dead and twenty-three wounded. This made February 26 the bloodiest day of battle for both battalions in 1945. Fifth Brigade had nevertheless been relatively lucky. The battles of February had cost the Anglo-Canadian army 490 officers and 8,023 other ranks killed, wounded, and missing. More than a thousand other soldiers had been evacuated as battle exhaustion casualties. The psychiatrists noted that many of these were either veterans who had used up their last ounce of courage or a large number of recovered psychiatric or surgical casualties sent back into combat. Few of these could be returned to their units.[27]

The Calgary Highlanders had been in reserve on the twenty-sixth, but that night, they were brought forward to join in the assault on the next German fortified position, the Hochwald Layback. This line of anti-tank ditches and concealed dug-outs stretched from the Rhine to the Meuse. In the north it was situated on the western edge of the Hochwald Forest, where it was particularly difficult to identify the sources of enemy fire. The Calgaries broke through the outer defences and penetrated into the woods, but enemy mortar and artillery shells exploding in the trees made further advance impossible and consolidation difficult. The last objective was taken in mid-afternoon when C Company, now commanded by CSM Harold Larsen, used "very good artillery support" to clear the area. "The night ended with the battalion in position with three companies across the line of woods. . . . At 2230 hrs the meal came up and for the first time in 24 hours, all boys received food. . . .

over 200 PWS were taken"[28] but at a cost of eleven killed and forty-four wounded. The Black Watch tried to advance through the Calgaries on the twenty-eighth, but this attempt to work forward through the woods turned into an all-day struggle which produced losses of seven killed and thirty-five wounded, without appreciable gains.

The lead Black Watch company would have suffered more casualties were it not for the extraordinary actions of Private J. J. Koropchuck. His company came under heavy fire from "a number of Germans in a long communication trench and hollow in the ground." His corporal reported what happened next: "Koropchuck without waiting rushed up to the position firing his Bren gun. Once he seemed to stumble and I think he was hit. I yelled to him to get down behind a tree. He went a little further, knelt down and fired again, again he was hit but he managed to throw three grenades. The German fire lessened a lot and none of the machine guns fired again. I think he knocked them out. The wounds he received throwing the grenades killed him."[29] While Koropchuck was attacking, Private Albert Fromstein, a battalion stretcher-bearer, "organized stretcher parties and personally aided in evacuating casualties over a distance of several thousand yards" despite continuous mortar and machine-gun fire. He was recommended for a Military Medal for "saving the lives of several of his comrades."[30]

Crerar was now attempting to put pressure on the entire German perimeter in hopes of forcing a breakthrough which would cut off the enemy before Hitler gave permission to evacuate across the Rhine. The Canadian and British advance from the north also made things easier for the American divisions racing towards the last bridges at Wesel. Whether this was sufficient justification for pressing a series of battalion attacks in the dense Hochwald Forest is another matter.

The first days of March were miserable beyond belief. The Calgaries tried to expand their "bridgehead" in the forest but failed to do so. On the third, the brigade was pulled out to take on a new task: "clearing a startline, astride the Udem-Xanten railway line, for a thrust to be made by 4th Canadian Armoured Division."[31] This was the infamous "Hochwald Gap" in which the armoured division had already suffered horrendous casualties.

Fifth Brigade's operations in the gap began at 3:00 A.M. on March 4 with the Maisonneuves and Black Watch attempting to advance on either side of the railway line. Both battalions ran into snipers and were subjected to repeated mortaring. The night was cold and dark with no moon, and it was impossible to keep direction out of sight of the railway line. The leading Black Watch company took less than fifty men forward. By early morning twenty-two were casualties, and the remainder were widely scattered. Two veteran NCOs, Sgt. P. V. H. Cicerci and CSM A. F. Turnbull, were able to bring

Major Jacques Ostiguy, Régiment de Maisonneuve, receives the Distinguished Service Order from Field Marshal Bernard Montgomery, Ossendrecht, Holland, October 17, 1944. LAC

their platoons, with the wounded, back to the start line,[32] but Black Watch casualties in the Hochwald now numbered close to 150. The Maisonneuves, with ten killed and twenty-six wounded, were not as severely hurt, but their War Diary records a deep sense of frustration with this forest fighting against an enemy who couldn't be seen.

Major-General Matthews tried to limit the commitment of his brigades to the Hochwald, but corps headquarters was adamant; close contact with the enemy had to be maintained.[33] The Calgaries pushed through to the north-east during the night of the March 4, and the Maisonneuves were ordered to stage a full-scale attack on a defended locality the Calgaries had identified. The Maisonneuves used a barrage to place all four companies well forward, but patrols quickly discovered an anti-tank ditch with the enemy dug in on the other side. No further advance was attempted.[34]

The relentless Allied attacks of the first few days of March had forced the German command to withdraw to a new defensive line known as the "Wesel Pocket." This had been organized on March 1 and was initially manned with supply troops who scrambled to construct strong points, lay wire and dig deep, narrow, anti-tank ditches. The Germans withdrew to this last position on the west bank of the Rhine during the night of the fourth. In the south the withdrawal resembled a rout, and the Americans were clamouring for orders to cross the Rhine and exploit the near-total defeat of the enemy in their sector.[35] Montgomery refused permission to "bounce" the Rhine. He ordered Ninth U.S. Army to move into First Canadian Army's sector and capture Wesel, but stuck rigidly to his "master plan" which called for Second British Army to cross the Rhine in a set-piece attack scheduled for late March.

Montgomery's decision to bring Ninth U.S. Army up to Wesel instead of keeping to the original boundary lines, was taken in the context of the "very hard and bitter fighting" taking place on the Anglo-Canadian front. As he told Field Marshal Alan Brooke, "The enemy up here seems to be quite unaware of what is happening in the south and he is holding to his positions with tenacity and is counterattacking savagely. . . . We have made little progress though we have killed a good many enemy."[36] Common sense suggests that in such a situation Montgomery ought to have waited until the Americans cut off the German escape route at Wesel before renewing the advance from the north. But this option was rejected, and a new converging attack by both British and Canadian troops was ordered for March 8.

In the Canadian sector this decision led Crerar and Simonds to organize a new operation, "Blockbuster II," to capture Xanten and the high ground which overlooked the Alter Rhine. Simonds ordered 2nd Division to carry out this plan, but a brigade from 43rd Wessex Division was also brought forward to assist in the first phase. This addition allowed Matthews to plan an elaborate set-piece attack using 129th British and 4th Canadian Brigades to capture Xanten, with 5th Brigade held back to advance through to the high ground. The artillery of two divisions and the corps artillery group were the key to the advance, but the Sherbrooke Fusiliers and two squadrons of flame-throwing crocodile tanks from 79th Armoured Division were also available to provide the infantry with close support. Smoke was used to mask the operation from the enemy artillery spotters on the east bank of the Rhine.

All of this careful preparation was not enough to prevent the battle from deteriorating into a costly slugging match. The German artillery ignored the smoke, firing continuously from the flank of the Allied advance. The weather prevented effective air support and, in combination with the smoke, reduced visibility for counter-battery operations. Fourth Brigade had a very difficult time in Xanten, and 129th British Brigade found its attempts to control the eastern part of the city were equally costly. Casualties to the Royal Hamilton Light Infantry were so heavy that Matthews considered using 5th Brigade to help out in Xanten. The Royal Regiment had, however, been more fortunate. As darkness fell, the Royals linked up with British troops and Matthews decided to send 5th Brigade on to their original objectives in a night attack.

Brigadier Megill had watched the day's events closely. It was apparent that the worst problems stemmed from the attempt to advance with an open right flank. Megill persuaded Matthews to place the South Sasks under command. "They were instructed to take up positions along the north-eastern edge of the forest to protect the right flank of 5 Cdn Inf Bde."[37] With this arranged, the Maisonneuves were ready to move off before midnight on the eighth. Mounted in Kangaroos, supported by tanks and mine-clearing flails, the Maisonneuves charged forward down the main road, reaching their objective, a wooded hill south of Xanten, and collecting 118 prisoners. The Black Watch followed up this advance on foot, taking a further fifty prisoners. The Maisonneuves again took over the lead, moving south shortly after 9:30 A.M. to secure a crossing of the canal at Birten.

Resistance was now growing. The enemy put in an "exceedingly heavy mortar bombardment" and counterattacked the lead company. Prisoners reported that some three hundred German troops were forming up in Birten Woods. Megill, whose tactical headquarters was well forward, arranged an immediate attack on the woods using Crocodiles, Sherbrooke tanks, and the battalion's WASPs as an assault force. This attack began to bog down, but Bibeau ordered Major LeAndré Lacroix, commanding the reserve company, to take his men around the right flank.[38] Lacroix had an anti-tank gun brought up and "taking a Bren gun from one of his men, fired twenty-five magazines to cover his gun crew and permit them to get in position." With

Major Ostiguy after receiving his Distinguished Service Order. LAC

the six-pounder providing fire support, the company, led by Lacroix firing the Bren gun from the hip, overwhelmed the enemy. More than two hundred prisoners, including the colonel commanding 18th Parachute Regiment, were captured.[39]

Casualties had been heavy in the attacking force, and in the darkness "the situation became confused and the chain of evacuation between forward companies and the casualty collecting post was strained to the breaking point." Private Robert Champagne, Royal Canadian Army Medical Corps, went forward to re-organize the battalion stretcher-bearers and recced a new evacuation route. Champagne had served as an ambulance orderly in every battle fought by the battalion since Normandy. He was awarded the Military Medal in June 1945 for his consistent contribution to the medical services of the battalion.[40]

The Calgaries had been paralleling the Maisonneuve advance, gathering in prisoners but taking casualties from mortar fire. They watched with relief as Birten fell, but orders now came to push across the canal. "Small parties of German paratroopers were taken by surprise in farms and houses, many of them still cooking their breakfast in the early morning."[41] Megill had withdrawn the Black Watch back to Xanten and informed them that they were part of a new plan to "bounce" the Rhine. The battalion was to use Kangaroos to "dash" south to Ginderich, "whereupon the Calgary Highlanders would rush across the Wesel bridge followed by the RHC and Maisonneuves." Fourth Brigade were to follow up the crossing.[42]

Whether this was a genuine plan concocted by Megill and Matthews in the context of the collapse of German resistance, or a "pep talk" designed to encourage weary men to make one more effort, is not clear.[43] Either way, nothing came of it, for the next day Calgary patrols met units of the 52nd Lowland Division. The Canadians were pinched out of the action just as the Germans blew the last bridge at Wesel. The battle of the Rhineland was over.

The defeat suffered by the German army west of the Rhine, coupled with the enormous losses on the eastern front, made the continued defence of Germany impossible. In the west the Allies had taken their millionth prisoner, and victory could now be only a matter of time. In his dispatch to the Canadian government, General Crerar summarized the experience of his army in the recent battles:

> During the concluding stages our own infantry suffered heavy casualties from shelling, mortaring and rockets. This was consistent with the enemy's tactics throughout the whole of the operation. His firepower, particularly from machine-guns, mortars and cannon had been more heavily and effectively applied than at any other time in

the Army's fighting during the present campaign. Not including self-propelled guns, I estimated that at the beginning of March over 700 mortars and more than 1,000 guns of various calibres were available to the First Parachute Army. Only rarely did there appear to be any shortage of ammunition, and on a narrow front, the enemy gunners were able to concentrate their fire on our points of penetration in the natural defiles along the line of advance. The combined effects of guns and tough going made themselves felt in the loss to us of some 300 tanks . . .

Our material superiority was not without its effect, but the state of the ground and the prevailing wet and overcast weather prevented the full deployment and exploitation of our strength . . .

In late March General Eisenhower wrote to congratulate Crerar:

Dear Crerar,

I have previously sent out general messages of congratulations to the several parts of this Allied force, covering our more recent operations. The purpose of this note is to express to you personally my admiration for the way you conducted the attack, by your Army, beginning February 8 and ending when the enemy had evacuated his last bridgehead at Wesel. Probably no assault in this war has been conducted under more appalling conditions of terrain than was that one. It speaks volumes for your skill and determination and the valor of your soldiers, that you carried it through to a successful conclusion.

With warm personal regard.

Sincerely,
Dwight D. Eisenhower.

Crerar's reply included this tribute to his men:

I believe that no troops could have put up a finer exhibition of enduring gallantry and determination than was demonstrated during those weeks of bitter, bloody and muddy fighting. With such soldiers, British and Canadian, no Commander could ever fail in the tasks he had been set to accomplish.

Crerar's salute to the men who had endured the weeks of bitter, bloody fighting was entirely appropriate. Second Division had been used in "Blockbuster" as a diversionary threat; its attacks intended to persuade First Para-

The area of the Hochwald Forest attached by 5th Brigade. Photograph taken on February 22, 1945. LCMSDS

chute Army that the direct route from Calcar to Xanten was the focal point of the Canadian offensive. The Germans do not appear to have been influenced by this scheme and were able to shift vital reinforcements to the south to block the approaches through the Hochwald Gap and at Sonsbeck. In the end "Blockbuster," like "Veritable," was a battle of attrition; the elaborate plans for an armoured breakthrough did not work, and success depended upon the skilful coordination of artillery and armour in support of conventional infantry attacks.

Second Division played a minor part in "Veritable," but its role in "Blockbuster" was very demanding, and it suffered the heaviest losses of all the Anglo-Canadian divisions engaged. Close to three hundred officers and men were killed and more than eleven hundred wounded in the twelve days from February 26 to March 10.[44] These losses were considered to be "light,"[45] given the ground conditions and the enormous weight of enemy artillery and mortar fire, but no one in the rifle companies reacted with such detachment.

Battle exhaustion, which had taken such a large toll in the rifle companies in Normandy and the Scheldt, had been evident throughout the Rhineland battle. Almost 700 men were treated for battle exhaustion in Canadian medical units, including 237 from 2nd Division. A number of those who broke down in combat were individuals who had been previously wounded or evacuated for battle exhaustion. The corps psychiatrist noted that he was seeing more men who were "war weary" and those who had become "chronically exhausted." Very few of the recent reinforcements, including the conscripts, had suffered breakdowns.[46]

Fifth Brigade had done very well in "Blockbuster." The attack on Calcar ridge and the advance south of Xanten were successful, well-coordinated operations. The heavy casualties came in the forest fighting, but even here Matthews did not allow the situation to deteriorate into another Foret de la Londe. One of the biggest changes in the pattern of the brigade's actions was the new role of the Régiment de Maisonneuve. From the first days at Verrières Ridge through the battle of the Scheldt, the Maisonneuves were constantly understrength and could not take their turn leading brigade advances. They had been effective in a supporting role and in smaller actions, but "Blockbuster" was the first operation the brigade fought using three full-strength battalions. The Calgaries were especially grateful for this change in fortune. On March 14 the officers held a mess dinner in a Nijmegen restaurant. "The pipers played, champagne was served and Lt.-Col. Ross Ellis revealed the popular news that Brigadier Megill, the guest-of-honour, had been awarded the D.S.O."—a tribute to both Megill and the brigade.

The Canadians waited in the Nijmegen area for the Rhine crossings scheduled for March 24. Ninth Brigade joined the assault under British command, and the rest of 3rd Division followed it into the bridgehead. Second Division was kept back until March 31 when the advance into Holland began. First Canadian Army was assigned three tasks in early April: to open up a supply route through Arnhem, to clear northern Holland and the coast of Germany towards the Elbe, and finally to begin the liberation of western Holland.[47]

Crerar assigned the Arnhem problem, and the liberation of the old provinces of Holland, to I Canadian Corps which had been brought up from Italy. II Canadian Corps was to move quickly north with 4th Division on the right maintaining contact with the British, and 3rd Division on the left coordinating its actions with I Corps. Second Division was given the relatively straightforward task of advancing to Groningen, an ancient university town and the largest city in northern Holland. The main enemy forces in the area were withdrawing to the Twente Canal, where a new defensive line was to be established.

Sixth Brigade took the first bound north on March 31. The next day the Black Watch advanced to Terborg. The battalion was now commanded by Major Eric Motzfeldt, who had been wounded in the preparatory stages of Operation "Spring." He returned to the battalion as second-in-command for the Rhineland battles and replaced Ritchie at the end of March. Motzfeldt, a Danish-born Canadian, had joined the regiment in 1939 and was widely regarded as an outstanding leader. As 2/iC Motzfeldt had worked with enthusiasm to train and integrate the new replacements; as acting CO he led from the front, infusing the battalion with his own energy.

The Black Watch, with a squadron of Fort Garry Horse, cleared Terborg in an all-day operation which required careful control. The Calgaries drew the next bound to Doetinchem, where the enemy had fortified the centre of the town using cement-filled railway cars as roadblocks. The next morning the battalion 6-pounders, WASP flamethrowers, and three companies fought their way into the two town after Royal Canadian Engineer specialists blew the roadblocks. Doetinchem was the most difficult action fought by the Calgaries in the last weeks of the war. The casualties—six killed and forty-one wounded—demonstrated that some elements of the German army would still resist strenuously even when they were surrounded and cut off from any hope of relief. The Calgaries collected more than sixty prisoners in Doetinchem, but the snipers continued to harass the troops. A deliberate and deadly search of the town was made. Corporal Frank Potts and the scout platoon accounted for four snipers, all of whom were killed.[48]

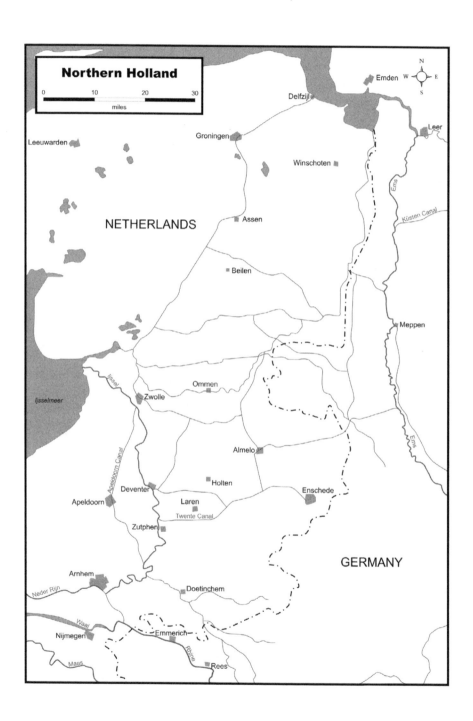

Doetinchem was the last battle the Calgaries fought with Ross Ellis in command. Ellis was ill with a high fever, and the regimental medical officer intervened to hospitalize him. Fortunately, Major W. D. "Dalt" Heyland, who had been with the battalion throughout the campaign, was able to take over immediately. Heyland's role in the history of the Calgary Highlanders has been overshadowed by the memory of Ellis, but Heyland's contribution as a platoon commander in Normandy, and as a company commander and 2/iC from September to April, was quite outstanding. In April 1945 he was one of only four officers who had been with the battalion in July, and he and Ellis were the only ones to have served continuously.[49] If Ellis was out, there could be no doubt about who would succeed him.

The Twente Canal line was breached on the morning of April 4 by 4th Brigade. The Maisonneuves were ordered to enlarge the bridgehead to the north while the Calgaries worked east towards Lochem. The Maisonneuves ran into well-organized resistance just north of the canal, but the men of B Company were able to use their practised battle-drill skills in a converging attack supported by the battalion 6-pounders. The Calgaries entered Lochem without difficulty, using their PIATs as cannon to force the rear guards to "up anchor." The Black Watch moved through the Maisonneuves to assault Laren, and another of those bitter, costly, small engagements that marked the campaign to liberate Holland erupted.

The German battle group in Laren included a self-propelled gun and several armoured vehicles fitted with 8cm rocket projectors. C Company suffered quite heavy casualties when the enemy unleashed a heavy bombardment. Major Motzfeldt and his command group were about three hundred yards behind the leading troops when several rockets landed in their midst, wounding Motzfeldt and his scout officer. The senior company commander, Major V. E. Traversy, took charge and "after consultation with the 5th Field Artillery rep and the Squadron commander of the Fort Garry Horse, formulated a new three phase plan" which required a "heavy concentration of field and medium artillery on the town of Laren." The day's battle cost the Black Watch fourteen killed and twenty-eight wounded—their worst day of the last phase of the war.

The loss of Motzfeldt was a serious blow to the battalion. The remaining senior Black Watch officer was Major V. E. Traversy, who had been 2/iC of a company in Normandy before he was wounded. Traversy had returned to the unit in time to command a company in "Blockbuster," but Megill did not believe he was ready to lead a battalion. The brigadier persuaded Matthews to appoint Lieut.-Colonel Syd Thomson, D.S.O., M.C., as the new CO. Thomson had established an outstanding reputation commanding the

A tank of the Fort Garry Horse with men of the Régiment de Maisonneuve aboard are welcomed in Rijssen, Holland. LAC

Seaforth Highlanders in the Italian campaign. The Black Watch "seniors" were not happy that an "outsider" had taken command, but Traversy reassured the regimental commandant that if it had to happen, they "couldn't have asked for a better one." "Thomson," he wrote, "is young, keen, and enthusiastic and has settled in very quickly. He has only concerned himself with operations and left questions of policy, promotions, administration and internal regimental affairs to the 2/iC and Adjutant."[50] Thomson quickly resolved the tension between battalion and brigade. He found "that he was working with Megill as opposed to for him. Megill, like Hoffmeister in Italy, frequently came to my tactical headquarters. . . . Furthermore Megill would listen to a battalion commander's opinion."[51]

Thomson's knowledge of operations was evident to all on April 8 when he organized a successful ad hoc attack to liberate Holten. The Black Watch reached their first objectives on the outskirts of the town by noon, but the Maisonneuves on the left flank were experiencing very heavy machine-gun fire from a railway embankment. Thomson decided to take the battalion into Holten and cut off the force fighting the Maisonneuves. "D and A Coys., each with tanks in support, moved off at 2000 hours. The tanks . . . set a few buildings on fire and when D Company advanced they were surprised to find the inhabitants jubilantly dancing near the burning buildings—Sniper activity was extremely heavy until Captain B.S. Lewis, in command of D Company, countered by using all 2-inch mortars . . . firing literally hundreds of rounds and the anti-tank gun attached to his company which fired in the neighbourhood of 200 rounds with excellent results." With the centre of the town under control, Thomson ordered A Company to clear out the top end. Further rapid exploitation took the pressure off the Maisonneuves and liberated the rest of Holten. The Maisonneuves had two killed and twenty-two wounded, including Major Gerry Brosseau, one of their veteran company commanders. The Black Watch had one killed and nine wounded in the battle for Holten.

The struggle for Holten was the last serious engagement in early April. Army headquarters had agreed to a proposal to use two airborne battalions of the Special Air Service in an operation designed to prevent the enemy from forming a new defensive line. The 2nd and 3rd Regiments de Chasseurs Parachutistes were dropped in a wide area of northeast Holland on the night of April 7. Organized into small groups, they were able to make contact with the Dutch resistance and create considerable confusion in the rear areas.[52] This may account for the relative ease with which 2nd Division reached Groningen.

Groningen, with a 1939 population of 115,000, was the largest city in the northeast and the sixth largest in the Netherlands. The old town is protected

by a moat, and canals encircle much of the new built-up area.[53] Fighting for
the city was not an inviting prospect, but if Groningen and the port of Delfz-
ijl were liberated while 3rd Division cleared the enemy from the Emden
area, the Royal Navy could quickly open up a direct route for relief supplies
and end the threat from U-boats based in the Ems estuary.[54]

Matthews ordered 4th Brigade to begin clearing the city on the night of
April 13. He had no solid information about the garrison, but it soon became
evident that the enemy were fighting aggressively. Prisoners revealed that in
addition to ad hoc battle groups of German soldiers, a battalion of Dutch S.S.
troops were involved. Fourth Brigade approached the city from the south
where the main defences were located. The fight for the railway station area
involved "fierce hand-to-hand encounters" which absorbed all three battalions. The Essex found a bridge intact over the water-barrier, and 6th Brigade
crossed to begin clearing the old town on the fourteenth.[55]

Fifth Brigade had been kept in reserve, but the ferocity of the street
fighting in Groningen led Matthews to commit the brigade to a new attack
from the western edge of the city. The Calgaries seized the village of Hoog-
kerk on the afternoon of the fourteenth and, after consolidating, moved
toward Groningen. The scout platoon crossed the canal returning with prisoners and a detailed report. D Company, under Captain Mark Tennant, used
a precise artillery and mortar plan to cross the canal and overwhelm the
defenders, "suffering no casualties." Heyland had seen that the rest of the
battalion was fed while this attack went in, and the Calgaries advanced into
Groningen that night.[56]

The Black Watch were brought forward to clear the northern sector of
the city. The Calgary Highlanders "had managed to find a means of crossing
the canal and they decided to take advantage of it. . . . A barge was swung
across the canal leaving a gap of about four feet which the men were able to
jump with comparative ease, heavy laden though they were . . ." There
seemed to be no enemy in the area, and the Black Watch decided to check
all houses by the simple expedient of "ringing the doorbell and then standing on the doorstep waiting admission." The first signs of opposition—sniper
fire—came at dawn, and shortly thereafter the canal crossing was raked by
20mm fire, preventing the rest of the battalion from advancing into the town.
"Some Dutch bargees brought along another barge, with decks lower than
the first, and lashed it into place behind the higher barge thus affording
cover to the men who now crossed on the second barge."

The Black Watch were directed to clear the area around a large park.
"On approaching the path it became necessary for all the companies to take
cover and edge their way forward through the back gardens until they
reached the houses facing on the park itself. Here a pitched battle ensued,

lasting over two hours, with our men using PIATs and Brens, rifles and grenades, as well as 2-inch mortars against an enemy dug-in in bunkers and slit trenches returning our fire with 20 mm and small arms fire. At 1555 hours all the 2-inch mortars in the companies laid fire down heavily on the park and the flame section fired a few bursts. Then the rifle companies assaulted the park. The enemy gave ground reluctantly . . ." The battalion captured 247 prisoners. Its own losses were one killed and eleven wounded.[57]

Brigadier Megill came forward to Thomson's tactical headquarters and decided to pass his reserve battalion through the Black Watch to maintain momentum. The Maisonneuves swung south to put pressure on the defenders, resisting 6th Brigade in the old town. The last phase of the battalion's attack required B Company to capture a bridge over the inner canal. The leading section commanded by Corporal Jean Marie Beaulieu was pinned down by two 20mm guns. Beaulieu, armed with a Sten gun, raced across the bridge and outflanked one of the guns, taking the crew prisoner. He engaged the second gun while his section crossed the bridge, ending resistance and securing the company objective.[58] The next day the battalion moved to the eastern edge of Groningen with the Black Watch paralleling their advance to the north. The German garrison commander surrendered that afternoon.

The division was not to complete the task of liberating the province of Groningen. Montgomery wanted another infantry division to protect Second Army's flank during the battle for Bremen, and 2nd Division was rushed into Germany to join in the battle in the Oldenburg area. The Maisonneuves made the journey without their commanding officer. Lieut.-Colonel Julien Bibeau was ordered to England to take up a training appointment. Bibeau had commanded his battalion longer than any other CO in the division and was very tired. He had requested replacement after the Rhine crossings but remained in command until he was confident that Major Lucien Lalonde, a staff officer who had joined the battalion in March, was "fit for command." Lalonde's obvious intelligence and energy had won the confidence of the company commanders, so the news of Bibeau's sudden departure did not affect the battalion's morale.[59]

The last few days of the war in Germany brought a small but steady drain of casualties from mortar fire. The Calgaries had six men killed and twenty-seven wounded in the struggle for Delmenhorst. German resistance was not well organized, but there seemed to be no shortage of mortar rounds. The last Maisonneuve fatalities occurred in the same battle when two were killed and twenty-seven wounded. The Black Watch, which had led the brigade into action in Caen, led off in the last battle of the campaign in the area of Hude, Germany, suffering four fatal and sixteen non-fatal casualties before completing their tasks. These last days of the war were a miserable period for everyone. It rained steadily, and the tired, bedraggled and soaked men, who were asked to maintain pressure without taking too many chances, collapsed into deep sleep when they were rotated out of the action. The Calgaries were in contact with an enemy blocking position at Berne when suddenly, on May 3, the defenders were gone. The next morning rumours that the war was over swept through the brigade, and a BBC news bulletin confirmed the news. All German forces in Northwest Europe would surrender as of 8:00 A.M. on May 5. It was over.

Epilogue

The collapse of German resistance and the ceasefire caught the soldiers by surprise. Lieut.-Colonel Thomson, who was acting brigadier, confirmed the news with divisional headquarters and then visited each battalion. Few cheered, and there were no signs of celebration. Rumours about a surrender had been current for several weeks, but the fighting had not stopped, and the steady drain of casualties had sapped the energy and morale of the men in the rifle companies. To be killed or wounded in the last days of the war seemed a particularly cruel fate, and the predominant emotion on May 5, 1945, was simple relief at having survived.

The soldiers now faced a very different future. Some volunteered for service in the Pacific and it was these adventuresome souls who got home to Canada first. The rest faced the prospect of occupation duties or long periods of waiting for their turn to be sent home. The professional soldiers, and those who hoped to make a career in the postwar army, spent time analyzing the "lessons learned" in the campaign and developing recommendations for new equipment and doctrine. The vast majority wanted little more than a quick return to civilian life and said so, loudly and often.

Repatriation was organized on a point system, which initially emphasized the principle of early in, early out, so there was a steady exodus from the battalions through the summer of 1945. Those who remained took courses, learned about their options through the Rehabilitation Training Programme, and went on weekend leaves in the friendly cities of Holland. They also tried to make sense of what they had been through. The Calgary Highlanders published a souvenir issue of their regimental journal, *The Glen*, which included brief histories of each component of the battalion and some reflections on what it all meant. In *The Glen*, as in other regimental publications of the period, the soldiers of the Canadian army expressed pride in their achievements, a determination to remember fallen comrades, and hope for a better way of living in a world without war.

What was left of the brigade moved to England in September, and two months later all three battalions and the 5th Field Regiment sailed for home. Civic and military authorities in Montreal and Calgary were determined to organize a proper reception with bands playing and crowds cheering. The soldiers gladly accepted this tribute and then broke ranks, rushing to embrace their families. In a moment the brave battalions were just memories.

In the first decade after the war, Canadians had little difficulty in giving meaning to the achievements and sacrifices of the men and women of the armed forces. The horrors of the Third Reich were fresh in everyone's mind, and no one doubted that Canadians had made a major contribution to the defeat of the "monstrous tyranny" which had threatened the survival of Western civilization.

This view came under attack in the 1960s from a generation influenced by the war in Vietnam and the rise of a new a historical revisionism. All wars were suspect, and the kind of patriotism that had formed the context for Canadian participation in the Second World War seemed too closely tied to Britain to be acceptable. History came to be written and taught as though the only important events of the war years were the conscription crises, the internment of Japanese Canadians, and the rise of labour unions.

Historians who did write about the Canadian army relied on the work of C. P. Stacey and the other official historians. Stacey had no doubts about the significance of the cause for which we fought or the value of Canada's contribution. He was, however, a professional historian writing during a phase of the Cold War when British writers were echoing Liddell Hart's effusive praise of the combat effectiveness of the *Werhmacht* and the brilliance of its generals.

Stacey's first sketch of the army's story, *The Canadian Army, 1939–45*, published in 1948, included some sensible comments about Canadian inexperience and consequent difficulties on the battlefield. By 1960, in *The Victory Campaign*, he had developed a much more sweeping critique. In a chapter entitled, "Normandy: The Balance Sheet," he offered a version of what had become the standard interpretation of the performance of the Allied forces in Normandy. "The Allies," Stacey wrote, "owed their victory in great part to numerical and material superiority." He went on to emphasize the role of "very powerful naval forces" and "tremendous air forces" in the defeat of the German armies. "Even on the ground," Stacey noted, "the Germans were, as time passed, considerably outnumbered."

Stacey also believed they were out-generalled, especially by Montgomery. But Allied superiority "on the higher levels" was not matched in the conduct of operations on the battlefield. "Man for man and unit for unit," Stacey insisted, the German army had been tactically superior to its Allied counterparts. He offered a number of specific criticisms of the Canadians, carefully noting that these comments could be "applied with little change to the British and American forces."

Stacey's critique of the Canadian army has been broadly accepted since it appeared in 1960. His view that the army had "not got as much out of our long training as we might have" (what army ever has?) has been greatly embellished by other historians. The comment that the army suffered from "a proportion of regimental officers whose attitude towards training was casual and haphazard" has been extended to include brigade, division, and corps commanders, most of whom were severely criticized by the next generation of historians.

Stacey specifically endorsed the views of Major-General Charles Foulkes, who insisted that 2nd Division was no match for "battle-experienced German troops" in its first two months of combat. Stacey went further than Foulkes, contrasting the difficulties of the Canadian divisions with the superior performance of the equally inexperienced 12th SS Division and other untried German formations. He briefly considered the possibility that the apparent superiority of the enemy "may have been due in part to the fact that the German formations were on the defensive while ours were attacking . . ." but made no attempt to develop this vital point. The evidence presented in the pages of *The Brigade* suggests that far more attention ought to be paid to this factor and to other specific circumstances which influenced the battles the Canadians fought.

The 2nd Canadian Infantry Division was required to enter combat in the midst of a deadly struggle for vital terrain. The German commanders knew that if the Anglo-Canadian forces could stage a breakthrough in the open country south of Caen, then the entire German army in Normandy would be trapped. They used their armoured divisions to prevent this possibility and in the process lost not only the battle of Normandy but the battle for France.

The struggle for Verrières Ridge, which cost 5th Brigade so many casualties, had to be fought. The enemy, forced out of Caen, withdrew to high ground which provided an equally effective blocking position. Armchair strategists, operating with hindsight, may argue that there had to be better ways of capturing the ridge than the ones tried, but there are few grounds for believing that any alternate operational plan or tactical innovation would have made much difference. The simple truth is that the Allies' "numerical and material superiority," "powerful naval forces," and "tremendous air forces" meant little at the tactical level. What really mattered on the battlefield was that the Allies were seldom able to concentrate enough troops to obtain the kind of force ratios necessary to overcome a well-equipped, well-dug-in defending army. Airpower allowed the Allies freedom to manoeuvre behind their own lines but could not change the fundamental realities of the battlefield. The enemy had to be drawn into combat, not simply struck by high explosives. The Germans could not trade space for time in France, so Allied advances were inevitably met with fierce counterattacks. It was in these clashes that the army of the Third Reich was destroyed, and the battalions and regiments of the Canadian army played a major role in its destruction.

After Normandy the character of the war changed for a few brief weeks, but north of Antwerp, as elsewhere along the front, the autumn recovery of the German army was soon evident. The battles to clear the Scheldt estuary were some of the most trying and difficult engagements fought by the Allied armies in Northwest Europe. Mistakes were no doubt made here, as they had been in Normandy, but given the limited resources available, the Canadians functioned with skill and determination. The same must be said for the Rhineland campaign of February–March 1945.

I began the research for this book because I had become convinced that historians, myself included, had placed too much emphasis on strategic and operational plans and too little on what actually happened in battle. This study has focused on the details of actions at the battalion and company level. The evidence confirms my belief that historians have greatly under-rated the achievements of the Allied combat troops who inflicted a series of defeats on the German army and thereby played the major role in the liberation of the people of Northwest Europe. I have developed this argument further in two books that analyze the role of the entire Canadian army in Northwest Europe: *Fields of Fire: The Canadians in Normandy* (2003) and *Cinderella Army: The Canadians in Northwest Europe, 1944–1945* (2006), both published by the University of Toronto Press.

Notes

CHAPTER 1

1. *Calgary Herald*, 1 Sept. 1939.
2. Roy Farran, *The History of the Calgary Highlanders 1927–54* (Calgary, 1954), 23. David Bercuson, *Battalion of Heroes: The Calgary Highlanders in World War II* (Calgary, 1994), 6-11.
3. Ibid.
4. Interviews, Calgary Highlander veterans.
5. *The Glen*, 1968, 1.
6. *Calgary Herald*, 18 Sept. 1939, 9. Farran, Chapter I.
7. Ibid., 24 May 1940.
8. *Calgary Herald*. 23 May 1940, 14.
9. Three militia lieutenants from the Light Horse, O.H. Mace, S.O. Robinson and Donald Munro, resigned their commissions to join as private soldiers. They later became officers in the regiment. Farran, 25, and letter Donald Munro to T. Copp, 6 Nov. 1990.
10. *The Calgary Herald* for 18 Sept. 1939 carries a story which reads in part, "Calgary's 'Jungles' which once housed hundreds of jobless single men on the banks of the Bow River have practically disappeared and the tiny settlements of men have disbanded. Quietly and unnoticed the jobless have drifted into the harvest fields or joined the army as recruits."
11. Personnel Records of Calgary Highlanders Killed in Action, LAC.
12. War Diary, Calgary Highlanders (WD CH), Sept.–Dec. 1939 (WD CH). The minimum age for recruits was raised from 18 to 19 in November 1939. Sixty eighteen-year-olds were transferred to the strength of the regimental depot. *Calgary Herald*, 24 Nov., 15.
13. Farran, 30.
14. Ibid., 28.
15. *Calgary Herald*, 13 Oct. 1939, 16.
16. Ibid., 20 Oct., 10.
17. This weapon too must have moved on for in February 1940 "A/T rifles were not available, so the instruction regarding this weapon is only theoretical." WD *CH*, Feb. 1940.
18. The arrival of supplies of battle dress ended the last hopes of preserving the kilt. Highland regiments had been informed that the kilt would be reserved for dress occasions in November 1939. Now the only apparent dress distinction was headwear, either Balmoral or Glengarry.
19. WD *CH*, May 1940.
20. Personnel Records.

21. On April 29, 1940, the Calgary Highlanders endured a two-hour inspection by Major-General E. C. Ashton. The War Diary reports, "he did not address the unit as a whole but interrogated both officers and some men individually about age, previous experience and training; civilian occupation and present training. An exemplary report resulted." WD *CH*, 29 April 1940.

22. Farran, p. 51.

23. On 4 July 1940 Major-General Odlum, the General Officer Commanding (GOC) 2nd Division reported that his infantry battalions were "no further advanced than they should have been in two months of effective training," C. P. Stacey, *Six Years of War* (Ottawa, 1955), 75.

24. Ibid., 85. Under the Iceland plan 6th Brigade was to be kept at Shilo to deal with emergencies on the Pacific Coast. This task would now be performed by the western units of 3rd Division which had been mobilized in May in response to the crisis in France.

25. Ibid., 292.

26. WD *CH*, Sept. 1940.

27. Stacey, 23.

28. *Montreal Star*, Nov. 1938 passim.

29. Colonel P.P. Hutchinson, *Wartime Achievements of the Black Watch (RHR) of Canada during the Second World War.* mimeographed N.D. 35 pages, DHH.

30. Ibid., 2.

31. Ibid.

32. *Montreal Star*, 13 Sept. 1939

33. Personnel files. Black Watch Archives, K.G. Blackader.

34. Ibid., I. L. Ibbotson.

35. Ibid., F.M. Mitchell, B.R. Ritchie. A.G. Stevenson.

36. Ibid.

37. Hutchinson, 2.

38. War Diary, Black Watch (WD *BW*) 21 Sept. 1939.

39. Ibid.

40. Ibid., 28 Dec. 1939, 31 Dec. 1939.

41. Ibid., 27 Jan. 1940.

42. The Black Watch had left Montreal with fifty Lewis guns which had been carefully reconditioned but they were required to give half of their supply to the Infantry Training Centre, WD *BW*, 4 March 1940.

43. Ibid., 11 April 1940.

44. Ibid., 4 June 1940.

45. Ibid., 6 June 1940.

46. Ibid., 12 June 1940.

47. Jacques Gouin fed), *Bon Coeur et Bon Bras* (Montreal 1980), 52.

48. "Histoire du Régiment de Maisonneuve," 22 Dec. 1939, Ostiguy Papers.

49. Gouin, 225–97.

50. Gabrielle Roy, *The Tin Flute* (Toronto 1947).

51. The best account of these matters is J. L. Granatstein and M. Histman, *Broken Promises* (Toronto 1977).

52. WD *BW*, Aug. 1939.

53. Ibid., 26 Aug. 1939.

54. Gouin, 271.

55. Clippings from *La Presse, Le Canada*, Ostiguy Scrapbook.

56. *Le Devoir.* 12 Jan. 1940, reproduced in War Diary, Régiment de Maisonneuve (WD *R de M*), 12 Jan. 1940.
57. WD *R de M.* 15 Jan. 1940.
58. Ibid., 6 Sept. 1940

CHAPTER 2
1. Cited in Farran, 62.
2. "In the first few weeks of the war the Regimental Commandant personally interviewed some 200 applicants for commissions in RHC and 77 of those were put on probation into the first class of POTS. Twenty-five percent of this class were young relatives of former regimental officers. . . . Eventually . . . more than a thousand applicants, twenty-five percent of whom were passed into POTS for training . . . [were interviewed]. After two months trial twenty-five percent of each class was eliminated as not up to regimental standard and the remainder commissioned into 2 RHC to await their turn to go forward on active service. When fighting came 1 RHC was almost entirely officered from POTS." Hutchinson, 6.
3. The best discussion of the training of the Canadian Army overseas is in John A. English, *The Canadian Army and the Normandy Campaign: A Study of Failure in High Command* (New York, 1991). Chapters 3, 4, 5 and 6.
4. 'Training Progress Report" War Diary 5th Canadian Infantry Brigade (WD 5CIB;, 20 Oct. 1940, 25 Jan. 1941.
5. War Diary, 5th Field Regiment
6. WD *5CIB*, 27 Feb. 1941 and Farran, 76.
7. WD *R de M*, 29 April 1941.
8. WD *5CIB*, 29 April 1941. Stacey notes that these early exercises "showed that neither division [1st or 2nd] was as yet very efficient in acting as a formed body". *Six Years*, 238.
9. Stacey, *Six Years*, 239 and Historical Officers Report No 34, Exercise Waterloo. Directorate of History and Heritage, Department of National Defence, Canada (DHH)
10. Quoted in Farran, 84.
11. Stacey, *Six Years*, 239.
12. "Exercise Bumper, Printed Narrative of Events." WD *5CIB*, Oct. 1941.
13. The first two-pounder anti-tank guns were issued in June of 1942. Farran, 118.
14. CMHQ Historical Officers Report No 49, DHH. See also Nigel Hamilton, *Monty: The Making of a General* (New York 1981), 494. The criticism of the "laborious" move of 2nd Division is linked to Monty's critique of Gen. Alexander, the Corps Commander.
15. Letter Odlum to all Unit Commanders, 6 October 1941. WD *R deM* Oct. 1941.
16. The Maisonneuve War Diary notes that when "Good Conduct" badges were issued in Jan. 1942, only sixty Maisonneuves who had no entries on their conduct sheets were eligible. WD *R de M*, 12 Jan. 1942, Farran, 98. But most "crimes" were absence without leave or minor disciplinary infractions. See T. Copp, "The Fifth Canadian Infantry Brigade: A Profile Based on Personnel Records," Paper presented to the Society of Military Historians, Durham N.C. 1991.
17. Stacey, *Six Years*, 425–26.

18. Gen. Sir William Morgan. "The Revival of Battle Drill in World War 2," *Army Quarterly and Defence Journal* Oct. 1973. This article was drawn to my attention through a footnote in John A. English's book *The Canadian Army and the Normandy Campaign*, 119. Dr. English's discussion of battle drill takes a somewhat different approach to the subject and should be read for an alternate view of its significance to the Canadian army. See also Bercuson, 34–39.

19. Canadian Battle Drill School, *Battle Drill*, DHH.

20. Stacey, *Six Years*, 240, makes the important distinction between Battle Drill which could be taught on a parade square and "Battle Drill Training."

21. Farran. 97–99. See also WD *CH*, Oct.–Dec. 1941.

22. Ibid.

23. Ibid., 100.

24. The Calgary history notes that 1st Division battalions were forbidden to attend. Farran, 98.

25. WD *R de M*, 30 Dec. 1941. Three Maisonneuve officers, including Lieutenant Jacques Ostiguy, attended this demonstration and battle drill techniques were introduced to the battalion during 1942. The Black Watch War Diary does not record attendance but battle drill training began in 1942.

26. Letter Crerar to Scott, 21 Jan. 1942. Farran, 106.

27. Crerar was appointed to command both 2 Div and 1 Cdn Corps on the same day. Roberts was Acting GOC 2 Div from 7 Nov. 1941 to 6 April 1942 and GOC 6 April 1942 to April 1943. Stacey, *Six Years*, 542.

28. CMHQ Report No 123, Battle Drill Training, 6–7.

29. Letter Crerar to Scott 5 Feb. 1942, Farran 109. The decision to return Scott to Canada "charged with the conduct of a course for senior officers" sounds suspiciously like a way of getting rid of this charismatic battalion commander, but there is no evidence to indicate this.

30. Report No 123.

31. Ibid.

32. See Nigel Hamilton, *Monty: The Making of a General 1887–1942* (New York 1981) for the most uncritical description of Montgomery's "genius" as a trainer.

33. G. W. L. Nicholson, *The Gunners of Canada, Vol. II* (Toronto 1972), 497.

34. Ibid., 502.

35. Ibid., 503.

36. B. L. M. Montgomery, "Notes on Infantry Brigades," Crerar Papers, Vol 2. The quotations in the following paragraphs are from the typed reports Montgomery sent to Crerar. John A. English, *The Canadian Army and the Normandy Campaign* has used this material in a chapter entitled "The Montgomery Measurement." The reader will find there a fuller discussion of this material and a somewhat different interpretation.

37. Ibid., 226–27.

38. According to the Regimental History, Montgomery propounded a new tactical doctrine during his brief visit to the Maisonneuves. He suggested that a battery of 25-pounder guns be placed in the vanguard of the battalion as an anti-tank force. Gouin, 77. This sounds remarkably like the kind of tactics which Montgomery would later criticize so severely.

39. Stacey, *Six Years*, Chapter 11.

40. Crerar Papers, vol 3 (D178).

41. Stacey, *Six Years*, Chapter xi and Montgomery "Notes."

42. B. L. M. Montgomery, "Beaver III Notes on Commanders," Crerar Papers vol 2.
43. At the last moment a company of the Black Watch and the mortar platoons of the Black Watch and the Calgaries were added to the order of battle so 5th Brigade was not entirely spared.
44. I have relied on Stacey's account of the raid for this brief summary. Stacey, *Six Years*, Chapter 11.
45. Stacey, *Six Years*, 402.
46. See S. Bidwell, *The Gunners at War* (London 1970).
47. This applies to both the "Beaver" exercises and "Tiger," Montgomery's last major scheme before taking up command of the 8th Army. For a very different view of 'Tiger" see Hamilton, chapter 15. But read Montgomery's words, not Hamilton's, and the actual nature of 'Tiger" as a scheme for developing armoured blitzkrieg tactics is clear.
48. Stacey, *Six Years*, 245.
49. Hamilton, 554, 555.
50. The Black Watch rifle company and mortar platoon lost 73 of the 104 men who embarked for France and the Calgary mortar platoon also took casualties, but 5th Brigade was largely intact.
51. Stacey, *Six Years*, 249.
52. English, 146. My own interviews with staff officers confirm this view.
53. Ibid., 147.
54. Farran, 126.
55. When Major-General E. L. M. Burns took command of the division the "Plans to Defeat Invasion" were still being updated. WD *5CIB*, 8 May 1943. 5 Field Reg't maintained batteries in position for coastal defence throughout 1942 and 1943. "History of 5th Field Reg't RCA," DHH.
56. WD *5CIB*, 28 June 1942 and battalion War Diaries.
57. WD *5CIB*, July 1943.
58. Ibid.
59. J.M. Hitsman, *Manpower Problems of the Canadian Army*, NDHQ Report # 63, Appendix L, DHH.
60. Stacey, *Six Years*, 252.
61. Farran, 132.
62. WD *5CIB* and WD *CH*, 10 Dec. 1943.
63. When Simonds took command of 1st Division he learned that 3rd Brigade, which Foulkes had commanded for some time, was judged to be insufficiently trained to participate in "Husky," the invasion of Sicily. For various reasons the brigade under its new commanding officer did take part in Husky, but Simonds never forgot Foulkes' record as a brigade commander. Interview T. Copp with George Pangman.
64. See the Crerar Papers, Vol. 3 for correspondence on this matter.
65. Brigadier Sherwood Lett returned to command 4th Brigade and Brigadier Hugh Young took command of 6th Brigade.
66. Information from 'Personnel File Major-General W.J. Megill" Library and Archives Canada (LAC).
67. G.L. Cassidy, *Warpath: The Story of the Algonquin Regiment, 1939–45* (Toronto 1948), p. 37.
68. Interviews. T. Copp with Maj. Gen. W.J. Megill, Kingston, Ontario.
69. WD *5CIB*, March, April 1944.

70. "History of the Fifth Field Reg't." DHH.
71. Personnel File Lieut.-Colonel E.D. Nighswander, LAC.
72. Megill Interview.
73. Terry Copp and Bill McAndrew, *Battle Exhaustion: Soldiers and Psychiatrists in the Canadian Army, 1939-45* (Montreal 1990), 40–41.
74. WD *5CIB*, Oct., Dec. 1943.
75. War Diary 2nd Canadian Infantry Division (WD *2CID*), 28 Dec. 1943.
76. Stuart Cantlie had served as a staff officer of 3rd Division while Megill was GSO I and Megill had developed a high opinion of him at that time. Megill Interview.
77. Personnel File S.S.T. Cantlie, LAC
78. Megill Interview and interviews with former officers of the battalions. Lieut.-Colonel MacLaughlan received the OBE in May of 1944. The citation read that he was, "thorough, dependable, capable and extremely hard working . . . he has set and maintained a very high standard of discipline and training in the battalion." WD *5CIB*, Appendix May 1944. Most Calgary officers interviewed would agree with this description, but would add that he was not as effective under battle conditions.
79. WD *2CID*. 14 Feb. 1944.
80. WD *5CIB*, 14 Feb. 1944.
81. Ibid., 13 March 1944. For a full account of the use of tactical air power in Normandy, see Christopher Evans, "The Fighter Bomber in the Normandy Campaign: The Role of 83 Group," *Canadian Military History* 8, no 1 (1999): 21–36, and Christopher Evans, *Tactical Air Power in the Normandy Campaign: The Role of 83 Group*. Unpublished MA Thesis, Wilfrid Laurier University, 1998.
82. WD *2C1D*, May 1944.

CHAPTER 3

1. Casualty statistics are from L. F. Ellis, *Victory in the West, Vol I* (London 1962). For a discussion of the Canadian experience in June 1944 see Terry Copp, *Fields of Fire: The Canadians in Normandy* (Toronto: 2003).
2. Military historians now distinguish between operations and tactics. Operations refers to an overall battle involving a number of units and arms, tactics to the techniques used by small units.
3. J. L. Granatstein, *The Generals: The Canadian Army's Senior Commanders in the Second World War* (Toronto, 1993)
4. Stacey, *Six Years of War*, 249.
5. N. E. Roger, *Diary*. LAC RG 24, Vol. 10,797.
6. Lieut.-General Guy Simonds, Directive Feb. 1944. For this and other directives issued by Simonds see Terry Copp, *Guy Simonds and the Art of Command* (Kingson, 2007).
7. See Evans. See also W. A. Jacobs, "The Battle for France" in B.F. Cooling (ed), *Case Studies in the Development of Close Air Support*, Washington 1990.
8. WD *BW*, 6 July 1944.
9. WD *CH*, 6 July 1944. MacLaughlan had a reputation as a strict disciplinarian.
10. Letter of Julien Bibeau, 9 July 1944, quoted in *Extrait de lettres écrit a sa famille*. Archives, *R de M*.

11. Relative safety but in eleven days before entering the battle the Calgaries had three men killed and one officer severely wounded. The Black Watch suffered a half dozen casualties.

12. WD *CH*, 8 July 1944.

13. Megill Interviews.

14. WD *R de M*, 14 July 1944

15. Terry Copp and Robert Vogel, *Maple Leaf Route: Falaise* (Alma 1983), 18. The most detailed account of Goodwood is in British Army of the Rhine, (BAOR) *Battlefield Tour (Operation Goodwood)*, June 1947.

16. "Dempsey's Notes on Operation Goodwood 21-253", copy in LAC RG 24, Vol 10, 559.

17. War Diary Royal Regiment of Canada, 18 July 1944.

18. Stacey, *Victory Campaign*, 173.

19. WD *BW*, 18 July 1944.

20. Ibid.; letter Major Alan Stevenson to Colonel P.P. Hutchinson Oct. 1944, Black Watch Archives.

21. Honours and Awards 5 BDE, RG 24, vol. 10,973.

22. WD *R de M*, 19 July 1944.

23. Statistics from Marchand, 259. See Terry Copp and Bill McAndrew, *Battle Exhaustion: Soldiers and Psychiatrists in the Canadian Army, 1939–45* (Kingston: 1990,123.

24. WD *CH*, July 1944.

25. War Diary Sherbrooke Fusiliers (WD *SF*), 19 July 1944.

26. 2 Canadian Division Intelligence Summary, 18 July 1944.

27. *Goodwood Battlefield Tour, 6.*

28. WD *CH*, 21 July 1944. Major Stuart Moore recalls that it did not prove possible to verify the report of the destruction of tanks. Letter Moore to Copp Jan. 1988.

29. The War Diary, 29 July states that "there have been comparatively few suffering from shell shock" but First Canadian Army exhaustion statistics suggest otherwise.

30. Hutchinson, 16.

31. WD *CH*, 19 July 1944. Major Stuart Moore drew my attention to this occurrence and stressed the difficulties the battalion experienced during the four days it was to remain in exposed positions at the top of the ridge. Moore interview and Moore "Notes on War Diary."

32. *Goodwood Battlefield Tour*, 58.

33. WD *SF*, Appendix B, 12–13.

34. Hutchinson, 16; WD *BW*, 20 July 1944.

35. Stacey, *The Victory Campaign* (Ottawa, 1960), 176.

36. WD *BW*, 19–21 July and Canadian Military Records Office, Unit Casualties, Black Watch, LAC. WD *BW*, June 1945.

37. *Goodwood Battlefield Tour*, 66–67.

38. Stacey, *The Victory Campaign*, 176.

39. *Goodwood Battlefield Tour*, 9.

40. WD 5 BDE Message Log July 1944, p 13.

41. WD *CH* 21 July 1944

42. 5 BDE Message Log 22, July 1944.

43. WD *SF*, July 1944.

44. WD *R de M.* 22 July 1944.

45. Honours and Awards, *R de M.*

46. Ibid. Major Ostiguy won the D.S.O. for this action.

47. WD *R de M*, 23 July 1944.

48. Marchand, Appendix 1.

CHAPTER 4

1. The directive and the letter to Eisenhower are in C. P. Stacey, *The Victory Campaign*, 181–83. The letter to Eisenhower is dated 23 July but Lt. Gen. Miles Dempsey discussed the operation with Simonds on the morning of the 22nd. Dempsey Papers PRO WO 285.

2. 2 CID Intelligence Summary #8, 23 July 1944, WD *2CID*, 19 July 1944.

3. II Canadian Corps Operational Instruction #3 Op. "Spring" 24 July 1944 and Gds. Armoured Division OO Nov. 2 Operation "Spring", 24 July 1944. WD *2CID*.

4. 2CID Intelligence Summary #8.

5. I am indebted to Roman Jarymowycz, who has provided the details of the dispositions of the 272nd Division from Canadian and German sources.

6. G. G. Simonds, *Attack by RHC—Operation "Spring"*, 21 Jan. 1946, 8 pages, CMHQ Report No. 150. Printed in *Canadian Military History* Vol 1, Nos 1, 2, Sept. 1992.

7. WD *2CID*, July 1943.

8. This and other work of the Army Operational Research group is discussed in Terry Copp (ed), *Montgomery's Scientists: Operational Research in 21 Army Group* (Waterloo, 2000).

9. The South Saskatchewan Regiment and the Essex Scottish could play no part in "Spring". The Fusiliers Mont Royal were greatly understrength but were assigned to clear the start line for the Royal Hamilton Light Infantry.

10. Queen's Own Cameron Highlanders, "The Battle of St. André-sur-Orne." Appendix to WD July 1944.

11. Megill Interview. The Camerons came under 5 BDE as of midnight.

12. 5 BDE Message Log, 24 July 1944.

13. Lieut.-Colonel D.G. MacLaughlan, "Account . . ." 6 pages 18 July 1944. DHH.

14. Capt. D. Harrison, "Account . . ." 1 page, 29 July 1944. DHH.

15. MacLaughlan, 1.

16. Quotations in this paragraph from Lieutenant Morgandeen, "A" Coy, "Account . . ." 2 pages 29 July 1944, DHH.

17. MacLaughlan. No exact timing of this report is available, but 5:30 A.M. seems probable.

18. Morgandeen, 1.

19. Ibid.

20. Lieutenant John Moffat and Sgt. Wynder, "Account . . ." 2 pages, 29 July 1944, DHH.

21. Ibid., 2.

22. Farran, 153.

23. Lieutenant Mageli, "C" Coy, "Account . . ." 2 pages, 29 July 1944. DHH.

24. Ibid.

25. Sgt. Palfencier, "Account . . ." 29 July 1944, 4 pages DHH.

26. Mageli, 2.

27. Lieutenant E.A. Michon, "D" Coy, "Account . . ." 29 July 1944, 2 pages DHH.

28. Ibid.; timing from "Message Log" WD *5CIB*, July 1944.
29. MacLaughlan, 3.
30. War Diary, 25 July 1944, Major E. Bennett, "Account . . ." 1 Aug. 1944, 7 pages, DHH.
31. Bennett, 1.
32. Ibid.
33. Personnel File, Major Phillip Griffin LAC.
34. Bennett, 1.
35. A Memorandum of an Interview with Major W.E. Harris, M.P., 24 Jan. 1946, 4 pages, DHH.
36. Michon, 2.
37. Ibid.
38. Sgt. Benson, Scout Platoon, RHC "Account . . ." 1 Aug. 1944, DHH.
39. Ibid.
40. Harris, 2.
41. Megill Interview.
42. Memorandum of Interview with Lieutenant Col. J.W. Powell, 9 Jan. 1946, DHH.
43. Ibid.
44. Interview, W.M. Wood with Terry Copp, July 1992.
45. Letter, Capt. J.D. Taylor to Lieut.-Colonel. D.H. Taylor, 15 Aug. 1944. Personnel File, Black Watch Archives, Montreal.
46. Pvt. M. Montreuil RHC "Account . . ." 1 Aug. 1944. DHH.
47. CMHQ Report No. 105, 10.
48. Ibid., 11.
49. Stacey, *Victory Campaign*, 192.
50. Honours and Awards, *R de M*, Author's collection.
51. CMHQ Report No. 105, 61.
52. Simonds, 4.
53. Stacey, *Victory Campaign*, 192-93.
54. Ibid., 193
55. Captain C. Cuddihy, "Account . . ." 2 Aug. 1944, DHH.
56. 5 BDE Message Log 25 July 1944
57. WD *CH* 25 July 1944.
58. Ibid.
59. Ibid.; Farran, 154.
60. War Diary, II Canadian Corps.
61. Dempsey's War Diary states that he met with Simonds at 9:30 P.M. on the twenty-fifth. "I told him to halt where he is, to hold all ground gained, no further attacks without reference from me." Dempsey Papers, PRO WO/15.
62. Simonds' "Attack . . ."
63. "Interview Terry Copp with Brig. D. G. Cunningham," 1983.
64. Letter Dempsey to Montgomery, 6 July 1944, Crerar Papers, vol. 3.
65. At 6:45 A.M. Foulkes called Megill "to say that D Coy. Calg not to dig in but to go wide and keep going." This was not terribly helpful to anyone, at this time Foulkes also placed the Maisonneuves on "one hour notice to move" and return to 5BDE command but he did not release them from divisional reserve until the afternoon.
66. Megill Interview.

67. Ibid.
68. "Message log" 5BDE, 25 July 1944.
69. Ibid., Megill Interview.
70. Ibid.
71. *History 5th Field*, DHH.

CHAPTER 5
1. Based on Weekly Field Returns, July 44 WD *BW*.
2. Letter, F. M. Mitchell to Lieut.-Colonel. W. E. MacFarlane, 20 Jan. 1945, Black Watch Archives. There are references to John Duchastel's role in this letter and in other sources.
3. Interview, T. Copp with Joe Nixon, 1989.
4. Megill Interview.
5. Letter: F. M. Mitchell to W. E. McFarland, 5 Jan. 1945, Black Watch Archives.
6. Nixon Interview.
7. F. M. Mitchell to Col. P. Hutchinson 22 Sept. 1944, Black Watch Archives.
8. Megill Interview, Moore Interview. Megill intended to recommend Major Vern Stott to replace MacLaughlan who had "frozen" during the later stages of the battle. David Bercuson offers a more sympathetic picture of MacLauchlan in *Battalion of Heroes*, 79–80.
9. Weekly Field Returns, 29 July 1944.
10. Lieut.-Colonel Charles Forbes, taped Memoir, 1989. The Weekly Field Returns confirm this view. WD *R de M*.
11. Weekly Field Returns, 24 July to 25 Nov. 1944. WD *R de M*.
12. CMHQ Report No. 169, 2.
13. G. Hayes, *The Lincs: The Lincoln and Welland Regiment at War* (Alma 1988), 27.
14. WD *CH*, 1 Aug.
15. Ibid.
16. Ibid.
17. Ibid.
18. Based on the message logs of the brigade and division.
19. Hayes, 28.
20. WD *CH*. 31 July 1944.
21. WD *CH*, August 1944.
22. Simonds was preoccupied with the planning of Totalize.
23. WD *5BDE*. 5 Aug. 1944.
24. WD *BW*. 5 Aug. 1944.
25. Letter, F. M. Mitchell to Col. P. Hutchins, 22 Sept. 1944.
26. WD *BW*. 5 Aug. 1944.
27. Weekly Field Returns, WD *BW*, August 1944. Prisoner of War figure is an estimate from descriptive evidence.
28. Personnel File Edwin Bennett, Black Watch Archives.
29. WD *5CIB*. 5 Aug. 1944 and WD *R de M*, 5 Aug. 1944.
30. Marchand. 8.
31. Lt. Gen. Richard O'Connor in his post-battle appreciation of Operation "Goodwood" maintained that getting the infantry forward in some kind of armoured vehicle was crucial to armour operations but he had no specific suggestions. He was greatly impressed with Simonds' solution which he described as a revolution in the use of armour. See Copp, *Fields of Fire*, 262.

32. Stacey, *The Victory Campaign*, 209.
33. BAOR Battlefield Tour *Operation Totalize*. DHH.
34. Ibid.; II Canadian Corps Intelligence Reports, Aug. 1944.
35. War Diary Royal Regiment of Canada (WD *RRC*), 8 Aug. 1944.
36. War Diary South Saskatchewan Regiment (WD *SSR*), 8 Aug. 1944.
37. Copp, *Fields of Fire*, 202–3.
38. Ibid., 204.
39. WD *CH*, 8 Aug. 1944.
40. Honours and Awards, DHH.
41. H. L. Bisiallon, "Account of the attack on Quilly . . ." 11 Aug. 1944. DHH.
42. Honours and Awards, Calgary Highlanders. DHH.
43. "The Cow" for the mooing sound of the rockets..
44. Farran, 158.
45. WD *CH*, 8 Aug. 1944
46. Ibid., 9 Aug. 1944.
47. Interview, Terry Copp with E. P. Ford.
48. Farran, 189.
49. WD *CH*, 9 Aug. 1944.
50. Kurt Meyer, "Notes on Operation Totalize." DHH.
51. Major-General George Kitching, "Notes on Operation Totalize." DHH.
52. WD 5CIB, 11 Aug. 1944.
53. WD *CH*, 12 Aug. 1944.
54. MacLaughlan "Account . . ." 15 Aug. 1944. DHH.
55. WD *CH*, 13 Aug. 1944.
56. Ibid.; W. D. Heyland, "Clair Tizon." DHH.
57. Honours and Awards, DHH.
58. "Account of S. Sask Regt in the attack on la Chesnaie from Clair Tizon and on Falaise." DHH.
59. Weekly Field Returns, WD *R de M*, Aug. 1944.
60. WD *R de M*, 13 Aug. 1944.
61. WD *R de M*, 13 Aug. 1944.
62. Personnel Record, Alexander Dugas. LAC.
63. Account of Pvt. Germain Desroches cited in Marchand, 102-3.
64. Honours and Awards, *R de M*, DHH.
65. Marchand, Appendix, 1.
66. CMHQ Report #181, 54.
67. Ibid., p. 55.

CHAPTER 6

1. General Montgomery's Directive M519, 20 Aug. 1944. Cited in Stacey, *Victory Campaign*.
2. Copp, *Fields of Fire*, App. C
3. Copp and McAndrew, 124-26
4. B. McNeel. "Cases of Exhaustion 2 Cdn Div." RG 24 vol. 12358. LAC.
5. Interview, Terry Copp with Burdett McNeel, 1988.
6. Ibid.
7. Copp, *Cinderella Army*.
8. WD *CH*. 23 Aug. 1944.
9. Ibid.

10. Ibid., 24 Aug. 1944.
11. Letter of Julien Bibeau, 24 Aug. 1944 *Extrait* . . .
12. WD *CH*, 25 Aug. 1944 and Casualty Returns.
13. WD *R de M* and Marchand, 119-20.
14. Lieut-Colonel F.M. Mitchell, "Account . . ." 27 Aug. 1944. DHH.
15. RCASC, "The Battle of Bourgtheroulde." DHH.
16. Mitchell, "Account . . ."
17. Lt. William Shea, "Account . . ." 5 Sept. 1944. DHH.
18. Ibid.
19. Mitchell, "Account . . ."
20. WD *BW*, 26 Aug. 1944.
21. WD *R de M*, 26 Aug. 1944.
22. GOC in C. Directive to Corps Commanders, 26 Aug. 1944. Cited in CMHQ Report No. 181.
23. 2 Div Intelligence Reports, 26/27 Aug. 1944.
24. War Diary 6th Canadian Infantry Brigade (WD *6CIB*). 27 Aug. 1944.
25. WD *CH*. 29 Aug. 1944.
26. WD 5BDE, 31 Aug. 1944.
27. WH *CH*. 31 Aug. 1944.
28. CMHQ Report No. 181.60.
29. Letter, Ed Ford to Terry Copp, 6 May 1991.
30. Letter, F. M. Mitchell to the Col. P. Hutchinson, 2 Sept. 1944, Black Watch Archives.
31. WD *CH*, August 1944, Field Returns.
32. WD *R de M*, August 1944, Field Returns.
33. Biographical information on Bibeau from document titled "Brigadier Julien Bibeau, DSO, ED, ADC." 6 pages Archives Régiment de Maisonneuve. Maisonneuve officers interviewed for this project described Bibeau as an outstanding, inspirational leader. Brigadier Megill offered a similar estimate.
34. B. H. McNeel, Re Cases of Exhaustion 2 Cdn Inf Div. McNeel reports his conversation with Brig. Megill without naming the battalion but McNeel (Interview with T. Copp, 1983) recalled that Megill was referring to the Maisonneuves.
35. For a discussion of Montgomery's strategy and the Canadian part in his plans see Terry Copp and Robert Vogel, "No Lack of Rational Speed: First Canadian Army Sept 1944," *Journal of Canadian Studies*, 1983.
36. P. Fafard, "Account . . ." 6 Oct. 1944. DHH.
37. Ibid.
38. Marchand, 131.
39. WD *CH*, 8 Sept. 1944.
40. Gouin, 125.
41. A. Pinkham, "Account . . ." 17 Sept. 1944. DHH.
42. Hutchison, 20.
43. Charles Forbes, *Fantassin* (Montreal 1984).
44. Fafard, 2.
45. WD *CH*, 10 Sept. 1944.
46. Ibid., 12 Sept. 1944.
47. J. L . Moulton, *The Battle for Antwerp*, is the best account of these events.
48. War Diary 4th Canadian Infantry Brigade (WD *4CIB*), 20 Sept. 1944.
49. War Diary Royal Hamilton Light Infantry (WD *RHLI*), 22 Sept. 1944.

50. WD *CH*, 18 Sept. 1944.
51. WD *5CIB*, 20 Sept. 1944.
52. Ibid., 21 Sept. 1944.
53. Megill Interview.
54. Mitchell to Hutchinson, 25 Oct. 1944, Black Watch Archives. In a letter to Hutchinson dated 26 Sept. 1944 Mitchell stated, "I provoked my removal."
55. Ritchie had in fact just been transferred to command the South Sasks. Lieut.-Colonel Denis Whitaker, a veteran RHLI officer wounded in Normandy, took over the Rileys. Ritchie came to the Black Watch and Stott replaced Ritchie as CO of the South Saskatchewan Regiment.
56. Megill Interview.
57. Calgary Highlanders. Honours and Awards.

CHAPTER 7
1. The terms "Scheldt Fortress North" and "South" were used by Hitler in his orders of 5 September 1944 designating areas which were to be defended to the last man.
2. Directive quoted in Stacey, *The Victory Campaign*, 380.
3. Ibid., 366–67. The War Diaries of 6th Brigade battalions provide a graphic picture of the fierce German resistance which forced the Fusiliers Mont Royal and South Sasks to abandon the small bridgehead they had won.
4. Riley won the Military Cross for this action. W. J. Riley to Terry Copp, 25 May 1987.
5. WD *BW*, 28 Sept 1944.
6. Interview with Charles Gordon Bourne, *St Lambert Hometown News*, March 1945. Personnel File, C. G. Bourne, Black Watch Archives.
7. Maisonneuve casualties for the week 28 Sept. to 4 Oct. were nine killed, thirty-seven wounded.
8. WD *CH*, 1 Oct. 1944.
9. WD *BW*, 1 Oct. 1944.
10. Ibid., 2 Oct. 1944.
11. Ritchie to Hutchinson 18 Oct. 1944, Black Watch Archives.
12. 2 Div Intelligence Reports, 6 October 1944.
13. 2 Cdn Corps Intelligence Summary 7 Oct. 1944.
14. Document captured by Toronto Scottish Reg't reproduced in Copp and Vogel, *Maple Leaf Route: Scheldt*, 27.
15. The best discussion of Montgomery's overall strategy and its impact on First Canadian Army in this period is Stacey, *The Victory Campaign*. See also Copp, *Cinderella Army*.
16. Interrogation Report Lt. Gen. Erich Diestel, Copp and Vogel, *Scheldt*, 28.
17. War Diary Fort Garry Horse (WD *FGH*), Oct 1944.
18. Honours and Awards, Calgary Highlanders.
19. WD *FGH*, 7 Oct 1944.
20. WD *CH*, 8 Oct 1944.
21. Honours and Awards, *R de M*.
22. WD *BW*, 8 Oct. 1944.
23. Ibid.
24. WD *FGH*, 8 Oct. 1944
25. WD *BW*, 8 Oct. 1944

26. First Canadian army Intelligence Summary, 7 Oct. 1944, WD *1CA*.

27. German parachute regiments in 1944 were made up of Luftwaffe ground personnel re-trained in infantry combat. They were not trained as parachute or air landing troops.

28. Porter was wounded and evacuated on the tenth. The Calgaries also lost two artillery FOOs, Majors Macmallan and Campbell. Lieutenant Jim Ireland, who commanded the troop of 2nd Anti-Tank Regiment 17-pounders attached to the Calgaries, was also wounded. WD *CH*, 8 Oct. 1944.

29. WD *CH*, 11 Oct. 1944.

30. F. A. v.d. Heydte, *Muss ich sterben, will ich fallen* (Vowinckel 1987), 189. (Trans. R. Vogel)

31. WD *BW*, 9 Oct. 1944.

32. WD *5CIB*, 10 Oct. 1944.

33. Ibid., 11 Oct. 1944

34. WD *SSR*, 11 Oct. 44

35. WD *5CIB*. 11 Oct. 44

36. Megill Interview.

37. The limitation on ammunition expenditure may have been officially removed but 2 Division's message log reveals that considerable effort was required to actually obtain the amounts required and it was not until 8:00 P.M. on the twelfth that "requests for both mortar and artillery ammo" were approved. Message log 2CID 12 Oct. 1944.

38. Stacey, *The Victory Campaign*, 387.

39. Ibid., 388. See also Copp and Vogel, *Scheldt*, 42–43.

40. Message log 2 CID 9 Oct. 1944.

41. The four company commanders were Captain N. G. Buch, who had served with the battalion since 1943, Major D. H. Chapman (26 July 1944), Major E. V. Pinkham (31 May 1944), and Major Ewing (30 Aug. 1944). All were Black Watch officers. WD *BW* Field Returns.

42. WD *BW*, 13 Oct. 1944; WD *5C/B*, 13 Oct. 1944.

43. Message log 2CID, 13 Oct. 1944.

44. WD *FGH*, 13 Oct. 1944.

45. Stacey, *The Victory Campaign*, 384.

46. 2 Div Message log, 13 Oct. 1944.

47. WD *BW*, 13 Oct. 1944.

48. Ibid.

49. 2 Div Message log. 0945 hours, 13 Oct. 1944.

50. Ibid.

51. WD *BW*, 13 Oct. 1944.

52. Lieut. A.V. Mills to Col. A.L.S. Mills, 22 Oct. 1944, Black Watch Archives.

53. Lieut. W.S. Shea, IO RHC, "Account . . .", 15 Oct. 1944. DHH.

54. Lieutenant Allan Mills also insisted that RHC replacements were poorly trained. On 19 October, after the RHC had received more than a hundred new replacements, the adjutant examined the personnel records of the entire battalion and reported that 269 of the 600 were from arms other than infantry. Two-thirds of these men had "four weeks or less infantry training." Appendix A, WD *BW*, Oct. 1944. This group did not see combat until February 1945. Lieut-Colonel Ritchie's views may also be quoted: "Our last batch of officers are all reallocation officers from RCA, RCASC, and RCE. They are honestly keen and very

good chaps and if we get sufficient time before we are heavily committed, all should go well." Ritchie to Hutchinson, 22 Nov. 1944, Black Watch Archives.

55. WD *BW*, Oct. 1944.

56. The records of the fifty-one Black Watch ORs killed in action on 13 Oct. 1944 show that the average length of service in the army was two years. Four had joined the army in 1944 and 14 had been transferred to the infantry during 1944. All of the fourteen had been through an intensive conversion course. Personnel Files, LAC .

57. WD *BW*. 16 Oct. 1944.

58. This controversy is described in Stacey, *The Victory Campaign*, 386-91. The letters may be found in *The Eisenhower Papers*, vol. 4. The version here is taken from Copp and Vogel, *Scheldt*, 42–43.

59. Stacey, 390.

60. Copp and Vogel, *Scheldt*, 130–34.

61. Information from interviews and questionnaire responses. See also "Ross Ellis Papers," Glenbow Museum Archives, Calgary Alberta for biographical information.

62. WD *4CIB*, 22 Oct. 1944. Foulkes prefaced his remarks with the statement that he was acting under the express orders of General Montgomery.

63. Sixth Brigade, attacking north on the right flank, also met "stiff opposition". WD *6BDE*, 23 Oct. 1944.

64. War Diary Essex Scottish Regiment, 24 Oct. 1944.

65. The 52nd Division was equally uncertain about the Canadians. The author has long had a particular interest in the 52nd (Lowland) Division. My uncle, CSM Douglas "Paddy" Copp, was a professional soldier who served as senior NCO in divisional signals. He viewed the Canadians as tough soldiers who, by the standards of the 52nd, were ill-disciplined. In 1986 I had the opportunity to meet a number of officers of the division at the Canadian Studies Centre of the University of Edinburgh. I wish to thank the director, Ged Martin, for the opportunity. It was clear that my uncle's view of the Canadians was widely shared.

66. D. G. Godspeed, *Battle Royal* (Toronto 1962), 509.

67. Marchand, 161.

68. WD *BW*, 29 Oct. 1944.

69. WD *4CIB*, 30 Oct. 1944.

70. WD *RRC*, 30 Oct. 1944.

71. "Message Log" WD 2C7D, 31 Oct. 1944.

72. Although 157th Brigade was supposed to relieve 4th Brigade early on the 31st, it was not until mid-day on the first of November that this was accomplished. Ibid.

73. WD *5CIB*, 31 Oct. 1944

74. Megill Interviews.

75. Megill. "The Capture of Zuid Beveland" 8 Nov. 1944. p. 2. DHH.

76. Casualty Returns, Black Watch.

77. Megill, "Zuid Beveland . . .", 2.

78. WD *CH*, 21 Oct. 1944.

79. Ibid., and Megill, "Zuid Beveland."

80. Ibid.

81. Interview, Gordon Sellar; letter, Sellar to Copp, 9 Dec. 1991.

82. WD *CH*, 1 Nov. 1944.

83. Ibid.
84. "Message Log" WD 2CID. 1 Nov, 1944.
85. Megill, "Zuid Beveland," 3.
86. WD *5CIB*, 1 Nov. 1944
87. WD *CH*, 1 Nov. 1941.
88. Megill. "Zuid Beveland."
89. Guy de Merlis, "Notes in Response to Questionnaire for Maisonneuve Veterans", Nov. 1989, 8. Charles Forbes, 'Transcript of Taped Memoire," Sept. 1989. Author's collection.
90. Capt. J. L. Field, "Account . . .", 5 Sept. 1945. DHH.
91. Honours and Awards, *R de M*, DHH.
92. Ibid., 214.
93. Honours and Awards, *R de M*, DHH.
94. Field, 2.
95. Gordon Blake, *Mountain and Flood: The History of 52nd Lowland Division*, 96–98.
96. Stacey, *The Victory Campaign*, 425.

CHAPTER 8

1. CMHQ Report No 173, *The Watch on the Maas*, 12.
2. G. G. Simonds, "Absorption of Reinforcement Personnel," 28 Oct. 1944. Printed in Copp, *Guy Simonds and the Art of Command.*
3. Burns to Crerar, 6 Aug. 1944, Crerar Papers, vol 3.
4. Interview, Maj. Gen. B. Matthews, 10 June 1987.
5. Ibid.
6. Megill Interviews.
7. *CMHQ Report 173*, 13.
8. 2 CID, Special Report No 1, 9 Dec. 1944. WD *2CID*.
9. Ibid., 3.
10. Brig F. D. Lace, "The Role of 2 Canadian Infantry Division Artillery in "Veritable," 13 Feb. 1945. DHH.
11. CMHQ Report No. 173, 30.
12. CMHQ Report No. 185, 31–32.
13. Megill, "Role of 5 Canadian Infantry Brigade in Veritable." DHH.
14. John J. Shaw, *Calgary Highlanders at "Veritable"*. Unpublished memoir, 10 pages. Author's Papers.
15. Letter, Major D. O. Kearns (Calgary Highlanders) to Lt. Col J. Bibeau, 12 Feb. 1945, WD *R de M*.
16. WD *R de M*, 8 Feb. 1944. Maisonneuve casualties were 2 killed and 21 wounded.
17. Appendix WD *CH*, Feb. 1945.
18. CMHQ Report #185, 133.
19. Gouin, 201.
20. W. J. Megill, "The Role of 5th Brigade in Operation Blockbuster." DHH.
21. Appendix War Diary First Hussars, Feb. 1944.
22. Honours and Awards, Black Watch.
23. Megill, "Blockbuster", 2.
24. De Merlis, 5.
25. Honours and Awards, *R de M*, DHH.
26. Ibid.
27. Copp and McAndrew, 148.

28. WD *CH*, 27 Feb. 1945
29. Statement by Cpl. N. J. Parisien, Honours and Awards, Black Watch.
30. Honours and Awards, Black Watch.
31. Megill, "Blockbuster," 2.
32. Hutchinson, 27.
33. Megill Blockbuster, 3 and Message Log 2 Division, 5 March 1944.
34. WD *R de M*, 5 March 1945.
35. Journal, 9th U.S. Army, 4–7 March 1945. General William Simpson Papers, USAMHI.
36. Montgomery to Alan Brooke, 6 March 1945 Alan Brooke Papers.
37. Megill, "Blockbuster," 4.
38. Bibeau letter of 19 March 1945, quoted in *Extrait de Lettres* and Citation for Military cross, LeAndré Lacroix. Lacroix also received the Bronze Lion from the Dutch government for his actions in leading the capture of the sugar refinery in Groningen. Collection of Author.
39. CMHQ Report No. 186, 57.
40. Honours and Awards, *R de M.*
41. Farran, 205.
42. WD *5CIB*, 10 March 1945.
43. Simonds stated he had "no knowledge of the plan," CMHQ Report No 186, 57n. Megill recalls it as a "pep talk." Megill Interview.
44. Fifth Brigade's share was 101 dead and 333 wounded.
45. CMHQ Report No. 186, 63.
46. Copp and McAndrew, 148.
47. Crerar Directive 2 April 1945. Stacey, *The Victory Campaign*, 546.
48. WD *CH*, April 1944.
49. Heyland Interview. Bercuson, 229.
50. Letter, V. E. Traversy to Col. P. P. Hutchinson, 29 April 1945. Black Watch Archives.
51. Letter, S. W. Thomson to T. Copp, April 1992.
52. Brigadier J. M. Calvert, "Operation Amherst," April 1945. DHH.
53. Great Britain, Naval Intelligence, *Netherlands* (London: HMSO, 1943), 220.
54. Dan Byers, "Operation Canada" *CMH*, Vol. and No. 3, 1998, 35–45.
55. WD *6CIB*, 14 April 1945.
56. WD *CH*, 14 April 1945.
57. WD *BW*, 15 April 1945
58. Citation, Jean Marie Beaulieu for the DCM, May 1945. Honours and Awards, DHH.
59. W. J. Megill to T. Copp, 27 Jan. 1992; Guy de Merlis to T. Copp, 7 Feb. 1992.

Bibliography

I. PRIMARY SOURCES

Archival
Library and Archives Canada (LAC) Record Group RG 24, MG 30 E157 Crerar
    Papers
National Personnel Record Centre Files
The Black Watch (RHC) of Canada Archives (Montreal) Personnel Files
Archives, Le Régiment de Maisonneuve (Montreal) Miscellaneous Documents
The Glenbow Museum Archives (Calgary) Ross Ellis Papers Clarence Crockett Papers
Directorate of History and Heritage, Department of National Defence (Ottawa)
Canadian Military Headquarters, (CMHQ) Historical Officer Reports,
    http://www.mdn.ca/DHH/history_archives/engraph/cmhq_e.asp?cat=1
Laurier Centre for Military Strategic and Disarmament Studies Air Photo Collection
Fifth Brigade Research Project: Correspondence, Memoirs and Interview Tran-
    scripts. C. Cuddihy, G. de Merlis, C. Forbes, E. P. Ford, A. Gurneau, W. D. Hey-
    land, W. Lyster, D. G. MacLaughlan, B. Matthews, W. J. Megill, S. Moore, J.
    Nixon, J. Ostiguy, W. J. Riley, G. Sellar, J. J. Shaw, M. Tennant, S. W. Thomson, W.
    B. Wood. LCMSDS Archives
Public Record Office (London, U.K.) War Office Records (PRO WO)
Archives, United States Army Military History Institute (Carlisle, PA)

Newspapers
The Calgary Herald
The Montreal Star
La Presse
The Glen (Regimental Newspaper, The Calgary Highlanders)
Clippings Scrapbook, LCol Jacques Ostiguy

II. SECONDARY SOURCES

Bercuson, David. *Battalion of Heroes: The Calgary Highlanders in World War II.* Toronto:
    Penguin, 1994.
Blake, George. *Mountain and Flood: The History of the 52nd (Lowland) Division 1939–46.*
    Glasgow: Jackson, 1950.
Copp, T. *Fields of Fire: the Canadians in Normandy.* Toronto: University of Toronto
    Press, 2004.
———. *Cinderella Army: The Canadians in Northwest Europe, 1944–1945.* Toronto: Uni-
    versity of Toronto Press, 2006.

————. *Guy Simonds and the Art of Command.* Kingston: Canadian Defence Academy Press, 2007.

Copp, T., and R. Vogel. *Maple Leaf Route.* 5 vols. Alma: MLR, 1982–88.

Copp, T., and Bill McAndrew. *Battle Exhaustion: Soldiers and Psychiatrists in the Canadian Army, 1939–45.* Montreal: McGill-Queens, 1990.

Ellis, L. F. *Victory in the West.* 2 vols. London: HMSO, 1962.

Evans, Chris. "The Fighter-Bomber in the Normandy Campaign: The Role of 83 Group." *Canadian Military History* 8, no. 1 (1999): 21–36.

English, John A. *The Canadian Army and the Normandy Campaign.* New York: Praeger, 1991.

Farran, Roy. *The History of the Calgary Highlanders, 1921–1954.* Calgary: 1954.

Goodspeed, D. J. *Battle Royal: A History of the Royal Regiment of Canada.* Toronto: 1962.

Gouin, J. *Bon Couer et Bon Bras.* Montreal: 1980.

Granatstein, J. L., and J. Hitsman. *Broken Promises.* Toronto: Oxford, 1977.

Hamilton, Nigel. *Monty: The Making of a General, 1887–1942.* London: Hamish Hamilton, 1981.

Hayes, G. *The Lincs: A History of the Lincoln and Welland Regiment at War.* Alma: MLR, 1986.

Marchand, G. *Le Régiment de Maisonneuve Vers La Victoire.* Montreal: Les Presses Libres, 1980.

Moulton, J. L. *Battle for Antwerp.* New York: Hippocrene, 1978.

Nicholson, G. W. L. *The Gunners of Canada.* Vol. 2. Toronto: McClelland and Stewart, 1972.

Roy, R. H. *1944: The Canadians in Normandy.* Toronto: Macmillan, 1984.

Stacey, C. P. *Six Years of War.* Ottawa: Queen's Printer, 1957.

————. *The Victory Campaign.* Ottawa: Queen's Printer, 1960.

Whitaker, E. Denis, and Shelagh Whitaker. *Tug of War.* Toronto: Stoddart, 1989.

Acknowledgments

The author wishes to thank Wilfrid Laurier University for research grants which permitted travel to Calgary, Montreal, and Ottawa and for a grant which allowed Dr. Christine Hamelin to examine personnel records at the National Personnel Records Centre, Library and Archives Canada. The author also gratefully acknowledges the assistance provided by a National Defence Post-Doctoral Fellowship administered by the Canada Council.

The veterans from the 5th Brigade who have assisted with this project are listed in the bibliography. To all of them and the scores of other veterans I have met and talked with over the past decade, I offer my sincere thanks.

A number of professional colleagues have provided advice and encouragement, including Carl Christie, John A. English, Jack Granatstein, Steve Harris, Jack Hyatt, Roman Jarymowycz, Bill McAndrew, and Des Morton. Robert Vogel has helped me to think critically and carefully about this topic and much else in military history.

Mike Bechthold and Evelyn Jones have proofread the manuscript with me. They have tried to correct the flaws in my spelling, grammar, and prose style. They are not, however, responsible for the final result. Evelyn has word processed each draft of the manuscript and has provided the camera-ready copy for publication. Mike has created the layout for the photographs and drawn the maps.

Index

Page numbers in italics indicate illustrations

Stackpole Military History Series

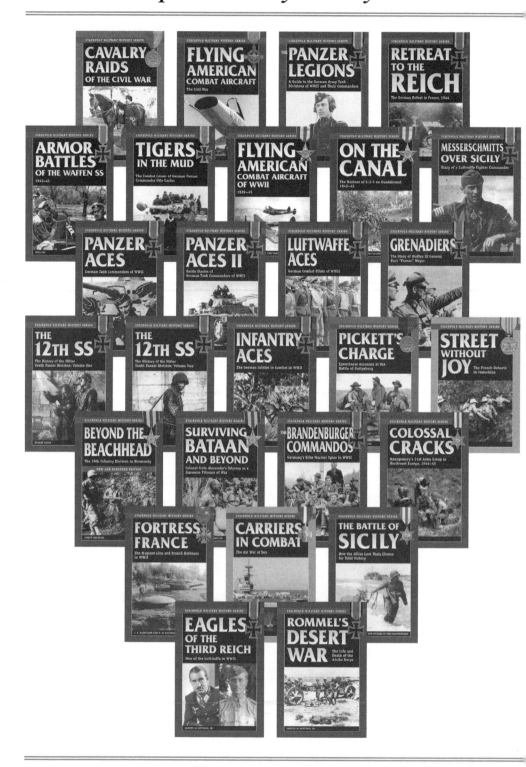

Real battles. Real soldiers. Real stories.

Stackpole Military History Series

D-DAY TO BERLIN
THE NORTHWEST EUROPE CAMPAIGN, 1944–45
Alan J. Levine

The liberation of Western Europe in World War II required eleven months of hard fighting, from the beaches of Normandy to Berlin and the Baltic Sea. In this crisp, comprehensive account, Alan J. Levine describes the Allied campaign to defeat Nazi Germany in the West: D-Day, the hedgerow battles in France during the summer of 1944, the combined airborne-ground assault of Operation Market-Garden in September, Hitler's winter offensive at the Battle of the Bulge, and the final drive across the Rhine that culminated in Germany's surrender in May 1945.

$16.95 • Paperback • 6 x 9 • 240 pages

Stackpole Military History Series

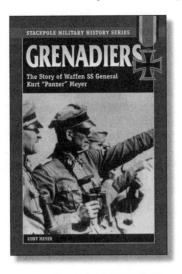

GRENADIERS

THE STORY OF WAFFEN SS GENERAL
KURT "PANZER" MEYER

Kurt Meyer

Known for his bold and aggressive leadership, Kurt
Meyer was one of the most highly decorated German
soldiers of World War II. As commander of various
units, from a motorcycle company to the Hitler Youth
Panzer Division, he saw intense combat across Europe,
from the invasion of Poland in 1939 to the 1944
campaign for Normandy, where he fell into Allied
hands and was charged with war crimes.

$19.95 • Paperback • 6 x 9 • 448 pages • 93 b/w photos

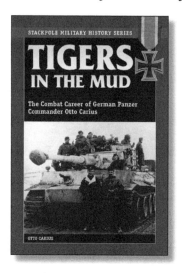

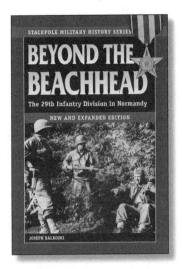